"WHY DOESN'T
ANYBODY LIKE ME?"

"Why Doesn't Anybody Like Me?"

A GUIDE TO RAISING SOCIALLY CONFIDENT KIDS

Hara Estroff Marano

QUILL

WILLIAM MORROW

NEW YORK

It is the policy of William Morrow and Company, Inc., and its imprints and affiliates,
recognizing the importance of preserving what has been written, to print the
books we publish on acid-free paper, and we exert our best efforts to that end.

Library of Congress Cataloging-in-Publication Data

Marano, Hara Estroff
"Why doesn't anybody like me?" : a guide to raising socially
confident kids / by Hara Estroff Marano.
p.   cm.
ISBN 0-688-14960-X
1. Social interaction in children.   2. Social desirability in
children.   3. Interpersonal relations in children.   4. Popularity.
5. Self-confidence.   6. Child rearing.   I. Title.
HQ784.S56M37   1998
649'.1—dc21   98-4037
                                                                   CIP

Printed in the United States of America

First Edition

1   2   3   4   5   6   7   8   9   10

BOOK DESIGN BY ANN GOLD

www.williammorrow.com

For Jere

ACKNOWLEDGMENTS

Writing a book is a solitary enterprise that requires a thoroughly supportive immediate environment. A family has to rearrange its workings, stand on its head, and often wait for dinner. My husband, Jere Daniel, never once questioned my priorities when the book took precedence over everything else. He made me many cups of tea, and he kept the bed warm for me on those nights when words were flowing too well for me to up and quit just because it was midnight.

Jere shared my exhilaration when the manuscript for this book was finished. But sadly, he died before the book appeared in print. I will never be able to repay his encouragement and belief in me.

CONTENTS

INTRODUCTION

"What were you thinking when you held him for the first time?" I asked my good friend Dana, a smart and sensitive woman, a day after she gave birth to Liam, her first child, knowing that this is a time for secret dreams to reveal themselves. "You know," she said, seeming surprised at her own answer, "I just kept looking at him hoping he'll have friends and be well liked."

Honest as her answer is, it falls into a cultural chasm. Judging from the shelves on parenting in our bookstores—clearly an index of our anxieties—we admit to wanting smarter kids, kids who know how to think, more confident kids, kids with more self-esteem, kids who are happy, who are proud, who are responsible, and even kids who can kick Type A personality traits.

But we have not yet begun to talk openly about wanting kids who are popular. It's as if there's a taboo against saying it out loud. This is undoubtedly due to a misconception about what popularity is. Social life is typically regarded as trivial.

Among children, however, popularity is not about being asked to the prom. It's about being well liked by peers. It's about furnishing a context for all mental growth, and about developing the social skills that underlie relationships that endure for life. It also turns out that the same qualities that make children well liked by peers foster a more humane and moral world.

Here's the kicker: Popularity often is the single greatest determinant in a child's happiness and success *at school*. Social development is the cradle of intellectual development. What's more, children who have no friends at school typically hate going to school. Eventually they drop out.

Americans have spent the past two decades hurrying their children to grow up. In fact, for a certain group of middle-class children, all "leisure" time has been sacrificed to the competitive fast track crammed with all kinds of lessons and activities. This is not the natural way childhood wends its way to adulthood. In this hothouse environment, even early education has been intellectualized—peer play has been taken almost totally out of it.

The Measure of Success

Yet talking with parents and teachers reveals that every parent truly wants to raise children who are well liked by their peers. Not only is popularity one of the few early signs of our success at the long-term enterprise of parenting, it is one of the few early indicators, perhaps the only one, that our children have a good shot at attaining satisfaction in the life they must eventually build for themselves. Honestly recollect your own school years. The social life of children colors the entire experience of childhood. It shapes personality for life.

This, increasingly, is what most people regard as the true measure of success—not material wealth, not a career at all costs, but a balance of pursuits that includes meaningful relationships. There is a growing awareness that Western culture operates on a narrow bandwidth of human intelligence. With overemphasis on linear, deductive, analytical thinking, we diminish respect for social intelligence—and don't explicitly educate for it. Yet we sense in our bones that people are innately social creatures and that the ability to be at ease among others, to be well enough liked by them, and to give and receive emotional support, counts. It is the tenor of our success in forming and maintaining relationships that affects us most deeply in our real lives and most heavily influences our day-to-day happiness—and even our health.

Oops—We Contradict Ourselves

For over a decade, I have been closely following research on social relationships and people's success (or failure) at them. I have been struck by the findings. The social learning that takes place among peers plays a huge role in that ultimate peer relationship, marriage. Whether it's marriage or friendship—and there are great parallels between them—relationships aren't a luxury; they are absolutely vital to human functioning. They are especially crucial for the full development of children. Social competence, the evidence indicates, is embedded deep in human culture and in the individual human psyche. Being liked by others matters.

Still we steadfastly dismiss it. Popularity is a lot like beauty. We hold strong, morally tinged public beliefs about it, and separately we maintain a set of private beliefs about it. Some people pursue popularity openly, although the more they lunge at it, the more likely it is to elude them. Others pursue it furtively, offhandedly.

Publicly we hold that popularity doesn't matter. It's superficial. An accessory to life. Privately, we sense that it does matter; in fact, on some level we know that it does. And if we fail to acknowledge that about ourselves, we certainly—desperately—know it about our children. Are there words that can stop a parent's heart faster than "Mommy, nobody wants to play with me"? To adults it is the ultimate triple blow. We feel the child's pain and feel in those words that we, too, have been rejected. And we sense that we have somehow failed in the job of parent.

This contradiction, the public/private split about the value of being liked by others, is the cultural fault line from which this book springs. Enough is known about the workings of the mind to indicate that splitting things up like this is a basic defense maneuver. It tells us a great deal about the psyche's need to protect itself, or at least play hide-and-seek with the truth. And that is a big clue that we are dealing with something powerful and important, as indeed being liked is.

I have come to see that our public beliefs about popularity are myths we invoke to protect us from the painful possibility that we may not have been invited to the party.

Dumb and Undemocratic

How have we come to such a troubled view of popularity and publicly to treat it so dismissively? The research on children's social development is vast—but this is one issue it does not tackle. What information I have gathered suggests the answers have a particularly American twist.

Popularity is felt to be alien to our democratic ideals; we see that it is distributed randomly, unpredictably, unfairly. There are those who console themselves by dismissing popularity as an insufficiently weighty topic. Or disparage the intelligence of those who are popular.

A more sophisticated variation on that theme takes into account the evidence that in general women openly value social relationships more than men do—and trivializes social competence as a strictly "female" skill, as if men have more important things to do with their time. (It is important to note that men suffer from the lack of social relationships more than women do, and they suffer internally, with higher rates of death after the loss of a close relationship.) Yet another variation on the theme is the belief that those who are popular are false, and that to become well liked they cannot be their true selves. The social is so suspect that we imagine that the popular have to be contorting their true selves in order to conform to the standards of others.

John Wayne Never Died

As Americans we subscribe to a powerful set of beliefs that help us define ourselves, and right at the top is a mythology about individualism. We are wholly autonomous beings, Rugged Individualists, all spiritual heirs, if not political ones, of John Wayne, second cousins to the Marlboro Man. We habitually ascribe any success to our own individual powers. We fail to see that emotional support from friendships or other relationships is the true pillar of self-reliance. We cannot embrace popularity because our mythology of self-sufficient individualism obscures the reality of our fundamental social nature.

In fact, our mythology is so blinding we can't even see that we have self-esteem exactly backward, which is why we often lack it.

Mark B. Leary, a professor of psychology at Wake Forest University in Winston Salem, North Carolina, contends that self-esteem has no intrinsic value. Instead, it is really a kind of meter built in to us to detect—and prompt us to avert—the threat of social rejection. Low self-esteem, then, is a wake-up signal. When self-esteem is low, the appropriate response is not to turn our attention to our inner selves but to repair our standing in the eyes of others, to behave in ways that maintain connections with other people. It is a time to check one's own behavior for things that could be turning people off (like being self-focused). But instead of filling the tank, we just keep trying to fix the meter.

The "sociometer" is built in to us not just because we are happiest basking in the acceptance and praise of others, but because without them we would not have survived in the first place. "Early humans who struck out on their own, who had no 'need to belong,' were less likely to pass on their genes to successive generations," says Leary. So the self-esteem system evolved to monitor the degree to which we are being accepted and included—versus rejected and excluded.

Although the self-esteem system is strongly tied to maintenance of supportive social relationships, you could be forgiven for noticing that a negative readout has not sent everyone flying into the arms of another. "Western culture has taught us to march to our own drummer—in effect, to override the sociometer," Leary maintains. "Our ideology of individualism forces us to buck this internal monitor. So when we are feeling low, we don't attempt to do what we need to do to fit in."

Leary's cleverly done studies show that just imagining social rejection lowers people's self-esteem. So do actions that pose a possibility of rejection. Interestingly, he found, those who were rejected went on to engage in outsize attempts to repair their standing with others. Even though deep down they felt less positive about themselves, they described themselves to newcomers in even more positive terms than did those who had not been rejected. The reason is that loss of self-esteem increases the motivation to be liked by all others, not just by those who rejected you. One conclusion: The impetus for so much success in life comes from the desire to be liked by others.

A Matter of Magic?

But perhaps the primary reason we downplay popularity is that we lack complete information about what it really is and how one achieves it. Not knowing how popularity works, we mistakenly think that it just magically happens, that it is beyond anyone's control. But all available studies show that popularity is scarcely a mysterious entity. It is actually contingent on respectable—admirable—attitudes and skills that start building very early in life.

This much the research shows for sure: Some children live in wonderfully warm and attentive environments where these skills are modeled, and children absorb them in the air they breathe, without consciously learning them. But they are skills nevertheless. And they can be consciously learned by everyone.

Supportive Surroundings

A seismic shift in the sciences is forcing a changing perspective on human nature. There is a new awareness that all behavior unfolds in a specific context, and to understand a behavior, it is necessary to understand the context. Development proceeds only in the presence of a *supportive environment*.

This is true of our genes as well. To become human we do not just unfold some genetic destiny, although scarcely a week goes by without some "news" that a gene has been found that delivers social skills. PARENTAL ORIGIN OF CHROMOSOME MAY DETERMINE SOCIAL GRACES, SCIENTISTS SAY, blared *The New York Times* in 1996. But even at this basic level, life is interactive. Genes contain only the blueprints for all the biochemicals it takes to run us. A *supportive environment* is still required for development to unfurl according to plan.

The environments children grow in are crucial. The relationships children are exposed to when young structure their developing brains and influence their behavior enduringly, if not indelibly. Their language, their communication skills, their very thinking develop only in interactions with others. It may be that the current vogue of overstating the genetic role in behavior leads people to misunderstand the importance of social skills and underestimate their complexity.

Children, it's clear, develop first in a family context. The next great force children encounter, and the most enduring, is their peers. Starting at a very early age—when they first set foot in preschool, certainly by the time they enter kindergarten—children inhabit the context of friendships and peer relationships for good, and these assume increasing importance for the way kids develop, although little of this information has so far seeped out of academic circles.

Beyond Parents

When Lilly or Luke walks in the door and moans "Why doesn't anybody like me?" the common response is "Well, Mommy and Daddy love you." Or "Forget about them. There are lots of other kids out there." But neither of those responses gets to the heart of the matter. In fact, they just confirm a child's worst fear—that nobody *but* Mommy or Daddy *could* love them.

Mommy and Daddy's love is absolutely essential, but there comes a point when it alone is not sufficient, when the epicenter of acceptance shifts from home to school. And it is *not* possible to forget about those who are rejecting a child, because they *are* needed. *They* create the climate a child lives in most of the day. If a child even imagines that he or she cannot fit in, that will forever color the experience of school. And of life.

Social skills, however, are not merely self-serving, a ticket to individual happiness. The social development of children has an impact on the whole society. Studies show that a downward spiral of behavior starting with the subtleties of peer rejection puts children at risk not only for dropping out of school but for becoming pregnant as teens, turning to drugs and alcohol, even criminality, and needing mental-health services later on. In short, the socially unskilled are a high cost to all of society.

More Important Than Ever . . .

The ability to get along with peers is more important today than it has ever been. More children are spending more of their time with age-mates, in day-care centers and preschools. Children are more in contact with peers, exposed to them earlier. Peer relations matter more, and they matter earlier.

They also subserve human interconnectedness, an awareness of which is now growing. The social development of children determines the willingness of the next generation to cooperate in achieving important goals—a feat that increasingly determines the fate not just of families but of businesses, cities, nations, and entire ethnic populations.

Our keenest experts inform us that the survival of us all now depends on social cooperation among individuals. According to the eminent psychologist Mihaly Csikszentmihalyi, "the interconnectedness of human activities and interests is going to increase even faster than we are accustomed to in the third millennium. Our actions will affect everyone living on the planet, and we will be affected by theirs." In other words, cooperation, a basic social skill, can be thought of as a basic survival skill.

The exercise of democracy actually rests on social skills. Democracy demands that its constituents be assertive—the first defense against exploitation. Our opinions and voices matter; they influence the nature and agenda of government. But so do the opinions and voices of our neighbors matter. To the degree that we take turns when speaking up, listening to the opinions of others without bullying them, we preserve the democratic process. And to the degree that we can cooperate, with both those with whom we agree and those with whom we disagree, we maintain a democratic society.

. . . but Under Siege

The social development of all children—who create the fabric of society in the next generation—is under assault from several developments. These range from fear of crime to the computerization of basic transactions to the marital conflict that marks many families. In addition, there is a tendency for today's children to be given *things* rather than time with important adults of the household. Yet we become social beings only through interactions with others. As a result, today's children are having more difficulties relating to people; more children are growing up socially disadvantaged.

. And social rejection has taken on an ominous new power. Across the country, the 1997–1998 school year was most remarkable for a series of deadly school shootings. Pearl, Mississippi; West Paducah, Kentucky; Jonesboro, Arkansas; Springfield, Oregon—these were the instructive lessons in the geography of rejection rage.

In each case, a child who was picked on and ridiculed by peers exploded in rage. Social rejection has always been a powerfully negative experience. What gives it lethal new force is the combination of easy availability of deadly weapons and the glorification of and incitement to violence that marks a strain of popular culture. The point cannot be stressed enough: Children who are rejected by their peers are far more susceptible than other children to the darkest messages in the media—whether in pop lyrics or in violent films and videos. And because they spend less time in positive pursuits with peers, they are more exposed to those messages. The effect is circular. As rejected children become more preoccupied with violence, they become even less liked by their peers—and spend more time alone with the media imagery that both validates and empowers their discontent. These are the children for whom the countless depictions of violence in the media are more than a source of entertainment and desensitization; they are instruction manuals.

Independence Is Overrated

The dark side of our all-powerful belief in individualism is loneliness. Americans are lonely people. More and more, we live alone. And we die alone. Even if we have dethroned the myth of the *tough* guy and the American frontier, we still subscribe to the myth of the *lone* guy.

At a recent commencement ceremony I attended, a highly successful graduate receiving an alumni award delivered ten hard-won rules for a successful life. Number ten was "Independence is overrated." Perhaps it was significant that she was African-American, embedded in a culture that still maintains the kind of web of human connectedness that is often disparaged by the larger culture. Nevertheless, every adult in the audience had had enough life experience to know exactly what she meant. They applauded loudly.

■

In the chapters ahead, *"Why Doesn't Anybody Like Me?": A Guide to Raising Socially Confident Kids* explores the social development of children and its importance. Every chapter provides explicit help to parents so that they can actively, positively foster the often-overlooked social domain of children's lives. The goal is not to make every child popular. It is to see that every child is at least socially competent, so that every child can choose his or her own course through life, and so that no shot at success in life is foreclosed to him or her.

"WHY DOESN'T
ANYBODY LIKE ME?"

CHAPTER ONE

What Is Popularity?

O n a late-spring day, when the early-morning air is still soft and encouraging, I saunter down a few blocks to the playground that, for as long as I have lived here, has served as a kind of nerve center of my neighborhood. My sons are grown and no longer inhabit the swings and slides and seesaws and spaces for chases, although they still have close friends, now scattered around the country, they first made there. And the parents with whom I struck up conversations while my sons cavorted have long since turned their attention elsewhere, although some are still in my circle of associates. Yet I go, freely, even eagerly. I am drawn to the sound of children talking to each other. The starts, the stops, the trills, the laughter, the cajolings, the running, the groupings, ungroupings, and regroupings, the sheer thrum of activity—they are, to me, a kind of music. And if in the sweet cacophony of voices I hear all the playfulness of a Mozart sonata, I also hear astonishing intimations of their whole lives.

"C'mon, guys, we gotta get on our equipment," says six-year-old Katy to a gaggle of kids who have gathered around her. She leads them a few yards over to the stroller that carried her younger brother to the playground and plucks out an assortment of old scarves she has brought so that others can join in imaginative play. She hands them out, and luckily there are enough to go around, as everyone ties one more or less across their shoulders. For herself, Katy has brought a once-spiffy satiny cape emblazoned with stars and stripes. "I'm Captain America," she says. No sooner do they start running about when a large group of smaller kids arrives in the playground. Before long, Katy, followed by her caped cronies, is leading about a ragtag band of kids of various ages. "Hup, two, three, four," Katy sets the pace as they march. And as others in the playground drop what they are doing to watch this impromptu parade, Katy invites them into the line and assigns them a marching partner. Soon enough half the playground has joined in the fun. Eventually they circle around the coiling slide, changing their chant to a cheer whenever a child slides down. Most of the kids coming down the slide are utterly dazzled to be landing into such a receiving line. This goes on for several minutes. In the meantime, Katy's older sister has arrived at the playground toting a camera. Finally Katy runs out of steam and runs off to tinker with the camera. Soon her whole group disbands, drifting off to other pursuits.

"Daa-dee, daa-dee," sings eight-year-old Gabrielle with mock irritation at her father for not anticipating her latest move. Then she takes off again on their game of tag, erupting with laughter every few seconds as she evades his grandly futile attempts to snare her, then taunts him with a round of "daa-dee, daa-dee." While her father conveys to her his great pleasure in playing on her terms, he probably also knows she gets more than laughs out of the game. With every whoop and surprise, the rhythm of give-and-take—the fundamental cadence of all social life—is imprinting itself deeply into her soul. Gabrielle's father cuts a very compelling figure darting around the child-size structures like a large dancing bear, and these improbable playmates have attracted the attention of Sarah, stationed on the sidelines, where she is polishing off an apple. No sooner does she take her last bite when she asks to join in. After a few rounds, Papa Bear bows out, and Gabrielle and Sarah seamlessly spin their own merry game.

"I'm gonna get even, I'm gonna get even with that creep," Alex is suddenly sputtering, his face filled with fury and frustration, as three of his playmates restrain him. A sturdy ten-year-old who owns the soccerball cum basketball, he was just a second ago hoping to sink the winning "basket" into the makeshift hoop, in another corner of the playground, when Kyle backed into him, sending the ball wildly off course. "Get even." The words roll around in my head. These fighting words, I have come to understand, are the outer wrapping of an inner certainty that has probably already etched itself in Alex's brain—that Kyle's misstep was hardly accidental, and therefore it merits revenge. Attributing hostile intentions to others allows him to contemplate, even justify, aggressive behavior. Alex already has the distinctive thinking style of a bully.

Accidents, missteps, spillover from other games are part of the life of the playground. Yet Alex is unable to let things be. Even as the words "getting even" tell me something about Alex, they tell me more about friendship. There is in us all a yearning for reciprocity, for mutuality, to be entirely even and eye-to-eye with at least one other, and so we make emotional investments in friends. Somewhere at the heart of friendship is a mutuality of influence, a deep need for feeling equal. Yet Alex is quick to perceive asymmetry, inequality; and the cooperative venture of a moment ago is suddenly a memory, ruptured by self-centeredness and competition. Because it is a way of seeing that generalizes to other settings, he will probably carry this misperception of the way things really are, this need to right wrongs only he sees, this inclination to reactivity, into the rest of his life.

Although I am witness only to small scenes from a playground, and know nothing of the rest of these children's lives, I have learned to see what is really going on inside these seemingly trivial transactions. Look at Katy. She has found a way to recruit other children into play when the spirit moves her. She is so willing to share her possessions she has brought playthings for children she has not yet met. She seems to understand intuitively both the longing and the reluctance of those standing on the sidelines, and she assigns them active partners for marching around the playground. She openly encourages little ones as they tumble down the slide. Even as she acts on her own imagination, she helps others to join in the fun. Is it any surprise she is very well liked? And the more she can pull a group of kids together, the more sophisticated will be her future ability to be with others whenever she wants.

Gabrielle would undoubtedly swear it otherwise, but the hide-and-seek of tag is more than child's play; it is also rehearsal. With his own delightful capacity for silliness, her big bear of a father is merrily patterning for her the rhythm of being with others. In all likelihood, she will automatically, effortlessly repeat this pattern of turn-taking in all of her own conversations and contacts, without ever quite realizing just how she learned to do so.

As for Alex, I have seen him go up in flames with others over small or at least highly questionable "provocations" that even his playmates would ignore; he seems to be literally locked into this response style. He is lucky for now that this group of active boys not only wants to continue the game and play with him, but keeps him from going after Kyle. But a spate of studies suggests that his hotheadedness will gradually circumscribe whom he gets to hang out with, and that will only reinforce his hostile tendencies.

The Power of Popularity

Would you rather have a child who is popular or one who is brilliant?

The question itself is a reflection of widespread misunderstanding about popularity and, more broadly, peer relationships in children. Most people think that popularity is like manna—something that falls out of the heavens anointing a favored few. And further, that for those whom it anoints, social life is all-consuming. But psychologists have begun to pay close attention to the social development of children— the ability of people to accept each other and cooperate seems increasingly to hold the fate of everything from countries, now more commonly made up of diverse populations, to corporations, where teams are becoming the modus operandi, to families, where we are first civilized.

What's more, the relationships children form with their peers become a powerful medium in which individual development takes place. They shape people's character, emotional intelligence, cognitive abilities, general mental health and resilience. Peer relationships in childhood are sensitive gauges of children's psychological functioning. And they are the best available indicators of how children will eventually turn out in life.

The ability to gain acceptance by others ensures that individuals can create a place for themselves inside the web of human connectedness. The ability to form close friendships and maintain contact with others is a natural countercheck against most of the ways the mind can go off track. It is the closest thing to insurance against loneliness, one of the most physically and emotionally destructive of human conditions and one of the greatest sources of stress. Even among children who are generally not accepted by their age-mates, having a single mutual friend may shield them from feelings of loneliness. It also shores up their feelings of self-worth. And, of course, the ability to form close friendships presages the ability to negotiate that ultimate peer relationship, marriage.

The Parsing of Popularity

As they parse popularity, getting a holistic fix on the forces that shape children's development, psychologists have made a number of startling discoveries. They all add up to one thing: Most of our preconceptions about popularity are all wrong.

- Popularity and peer acceptance require a sophisticated intelligence. The eminent psychologist Howard Gardner cites interpersonal intelligence as one of seven major mental domains. In fact, given what psychologists have recently been discovering about the way children develop, social understanding is vastly underrated and may be the cradle of the entire intellect. It can be seen at work in children younger than one year.
- Competence with peers hinges on a kind of advanced emotional understanding.
- Children who are popular devote *less* time to socializing than do many other children.
- What children like in other children is their kindness, and if there were more popular kids, everyone, and the planet itself, would be better off.

Let's get something straight. Popularity is not only about how to make sure your child gets invited to the birthday party. Nor is it about social conformity. Two decades of research have proven that popularity is hardly something mystical and magical. It is not a gift bestowed on just a favored few. It hinges on qualities that are integral attributes of who people are. It is the result of measurable attitudes and behavioral skills that can be deliberately, successfully cultivated and that, as much as any other, will ensure happiness and success throughout life. Most parents wouldn't think twice about making sure that their children have physical and intellectual skills that will serve them for life. Yet social skills are generally considered an accessory, a luxury. The truth is, they are an important component and facilitator of cognitive abilities, probably even the crucible for their development, and stand in their own right as one of the most important ways to put meaning into life.

If there is a master balancing act in people's lives, one we all constantly struggle with, the one with the highest stakes, it is the regulation of distance and closeness to others in our lives. It is an enormously complex and challenging task with almost unquantifiable subtleties and contingencies. Our own ever-changing wishes and needs can be met only in the context of others' needs. Understanding the intricacies of human relationships is a task few of us master in our lifetime; in fact, one of the resonant themes of literature, from the great Greek tragedies to potboiler airport fiction, is the tension between our condition of isolation and the cords of human attachment. We have come to accept—even expect—as a convention the deathbed scene in which apologies, confessions, revelations, and reconciliations salvage the relationships we never got quite right before then. Whole theories of psychology have been built upon the conflict between our need for attachment and our drive for autonomy and individuality—known as individuation in psych talk.

Peer play in childhood is the "Look, Ma, no-hands" arena in which we first get to work out relationships on our own. Popular children are those who have absorbed or divined the skills—since nowhere are they codified and written for them—at an early age and have the great luxury of exercising some degree of control in meeting their need for companionship. They have friends they can call upon when they want or need to.

Over the past two decades, researchers have documented how babies arrive in the world with an amazing amount of social readiness. Their eyes already prefer human faces to other objects, and their ears are particularly attuned to the human voice. From the moment of birth onward, by way of the responsiveness of a parent to a child's needs, the smile of a caretaker, the rhythm of peekaboo, and much more, children are constantly expanding their repertoire of social skills. Children who are popular have gained a disposition toward people as figures they can trust. And they have mastered a particularly broad array of skills. Skills in communication and in negotiation. Skills in powers of observation and the ability to read correctly the emotional states of others. Skills in sophisticated cognitive functions like interpreting subtle environmental cues and figuring out other people's intentions. Skills in regulating their own emotional states. And skills in evaluating, selecting, and enacting appropriate responses.

The Two Sides of Social Competence

Social competence consists of two facets that do not entirely overlap. Think of them as two concentric circles with a solitary person at the core. The outer circle represents overall group acceptance, being liked by one's peers, feeling part of a group. The inner circle is friendship, the ability to form and maintain close personal relationships with individual members of the peer group. Both having a friend and acceptance by the peer group demand some social skills. In return, both compartments of social life contribute in distinct ways to a child's development, including sense of self-worth, school achievement, general life adjustment, and well-being. And both not only reveal but further foster social understanding and individual development.

Acceptance by the peer group makes the most demands on social skill. But winning acceptance also has an unusually high payoff. Of all the environments to which children are exposed, outside the family, the peer group exerts the greatest influence. It is the mechanism through which we make our psychological adjustment to the world; after all, each cohort defines the world anew. The peer group, then, interprets the culture anew and becomes the means by which it is transmitted to each child. Acceptance by the peer group fosters growth and learning, and provides motivation to do so. What's more, as we both seek out and construct our own place within the peer group, it shapes and modifies personality characteristics for life. Developmental psychologist Judith Rich Harris points up the importance of the peer group by taking an extreme view of it: Parental love, protection, and resources all are necessary, she says, but within any cultural or neighborhood group, you could switch all the parents around and it wouldn't make a difference to how the kids turn out.

What socializes children is, pure and simple, other children, essentially the sex-segregated groups of middle childhood and the cliques of adolescence. That's where children learn the rules, standards, and beliefs about appropriate conduct and attitudes—and especially the rules of social behavior. What children gain from peer groups is a frame of reference. Parental attitudes are still important at this age, but now they are first filtered through the peer group. "Parents are yesterday; peers are tomorrow," says Harris. Children find out what kind of people they are by comparing themselves with others in the peer group, and they try out what kind of people they want to be. Status in the peer group, and attempts to find one's niche within it, many researchers have found, leave skid marks on the personality and feelings of self-worth.

But even children who are widely ignored or disliked by the general peer group may find themselves a friend. And under the right circumstances the caring responses of a single friend can mitigate, if not counteract, the negative effects on self-worth of neglect or rejection by an entire peer group and, to a remarkable extent, even hostile family experiences.

Call it reciprocity, call it mutual regard, the most striking feature of friendship is the assumption of equality. There is, by definition, a two-way flow of affection. Oh, what psychological riches lie in the reciprocity of liking; friends provide acceptance, validation, caring, a source of trust. They provide help and guidance. Friendship, in other words, supports the psyche, that ineffable core of each of us we refer to as "the self."

Friendship is a warm and comfortable chamber in which children gain emotional security. Friends are a source of companionship, a vehicle for play and fun. A friend is someone to confide in, to reveal oneself to. Friendship provides a safe haven for exploring oneself, and the larger world. Over the course of middle childhood, from ages six to ten, friendship becomes the main stage on which the drama of development unfolds. Friendship makes children feel good about their very existence; it is a powerful source of self-esteem. And yet in choosing friends, kids are also learning in a nonthreatening way to expand their own vantage point in life, to gain more than the solitary perspective imposed on every human being. While it is probably the most powerful pillar of the self, friendship is also the most accessible and rewarding way that life provides for breaking out of the prison of self.

The Power of Rejection

There are many shades of social competence, but only one cast to its opposite. The hard underbelly of popularity is social rejection. Social rejection is a powerful negative experience—perhaps the most psychically painful of all experiences. Rejection affects people profoundly for decades to come.

Socially rejected children are subjected to a daily social climate that is resolutely negative. It is not a climate they can simply avoid; maltreatment at the hands of peers is the most significant part of the school experience for them, so much so that these children are at great risk for ultimately dropping out of school. Rejected kids drop out of school at more than twice the rate all students do. They develop academic problems at far greater rates and are suspended from school more. School is simply a very unpleasant place to be. Rejected kids experience high degrees of emotional loneliness and over time become more and more socially isolated. They feel left out. They feel unneeded and unsupported. They never feel they have anyone to turn to, no allies, no source of nurturance. These feelings set up a disabling downward cascade in which their own feelings and beliefs about social failure virtually guarantee the kind of behavior that begets more rejection. And continuing rejection keeps them excluded from a primary arena of successful functioning.

The emotional experience of rejection is a source of great personal distress and carries with it multiple forms of maladjustment in current and later life. Those who are rejected develop ''internalizing'' mental health problems such as anxiety and depression, and ''externalizing'' ones such as drug and alcohol abuse, delinquency, and criminality. Even when overt rejection ends, depression endures, carried into adulthood. Those who are rejected in middle childhood are at special risk for delinquency in adolescence, especially if they are also aggressive. Studies show that in both the long term and the short term, rejection also gives rise to anxiety about social situations and avoidance of them. Rejection breeds resentment, and often fosters a deep desire to get even with perceived victimizers. As a result of the isolation that rejection brings, it becomes a virtual incubator of distorted ways of thinking.

All people are subject to experience loneliness sometime in their life; it is especially common among people in new situations, such as those moving to a new school or going off to college. Typically, it is situational and not a lasting thing. But those children who are rejected are subject to prolonged, unremitting loneliness and unhappiness throughout life.

Sure, social status can change at the drop of a baseball cap, and sometimes kids who are neglected at six or seven are running with the regulars at age eleven. The status of a neglected child tends to change with circumstances. And indeed there are children who are quite happy to play alone; those who are alone because they want to be are not the same as kids who are alone because they don't know how or can't succeed at forming friendships or joining in group play. Solitude is one (good) thing, loneliness another.

The sad truth is, once a child is rejected, he is almost always rejected. For if one thing has become clear in current research it is that social status becomes a self-fulfilling prophecy. Rejected children tend to be painfully aware from a very early age—at least third grade—that their behavior is not desirable and that they are not socially competent. They know they have trouble getting others to play with them, in initiating and/or maintaining friendships, and especially in negotiating the conflict that is inherent in all relationships. Rejection has a progressively negative effect on such children. They feel socially inadequate and develop negative perceptions about themselves—laying the groundwork for a lifelong tendency to depression. Without playmates, they lack the opportunity to acquire the skills of social competence, further eroding their social standing and leading to increasingly greater levels of loneliness.

Unless actively intercepted, unpopular social status tends to worsen. Peer rejection proves to be one of the few aspects of early childhood that is consistently associated with emotional and behavioral problems in adolescence and adulthood.

Popularity, however, is not simply an attribute of the individual. It is the response of a group to a person. The trouble is, once a child is rejected by a group, the group tends to maintain its negative perception of that person. Individual behavior may ignite rejection by one's peers, but group dynamics play a big role in maintaining that status. Rejected children have less behavioral leeway; children regard negative behavior in a rejected peer differently than the same behavior in an accepted peer. Further, having negative expectations about that child, they behave more negatively toward him or her, which only triggers more negative behavior from the rejected child. Further, even if rejected kids eventually change their behavior, the reputation others have formed of them keeps them from being seen in a positive light; the same actions from another child could be perfectly acceptable. Rejected children, then, tend to get trapped in self-perpetuating cycles of behavior.

Who Are Popular Kids?

Popularity is a measure of a child's social standing with peers. Popular children are those who are consistently liked by their peers. Studies that include observation of kids in the classroom and in the playground show that popular kids have specific positive qualities that appeal to their peers (and to their teachers, too). They are people who value other people—and know their own value to other people. They are sought out as friends, and actively seek others out for friendship. They make friends easily. Whether the teachers are evaluating the children, or other children are evaluating their peers, both are equally adept at spotting kids who are well liked and those who are not. What behavior do children seek in other children? Children consistently seek out other children who are:

- helpful. Helpfulness correlates more strongly than any other attribute with measures of peer acceptance. Kids like other kids who give them help when they need it.
- kind. Children like children who are nice to their peers.

- sharing
- giving
- cooperative
- responsive to distress. These children are empathic. They seem to be able to recognize and understand another child's emotions. They spontaneously try to cheer up an unhappy child.

Children who behave this way—and girls, even at age three, are particularly good at this—have so-called prosocial skills. They can engage in behavior that benefits others. Prosocial behavior demonstrates the capacity for noticing others. For caring about others. For responding to others. It bespeaks a sensitivity to others, and particularly an alertness to signals of distress, an emotional understanding of others, a capacity to take the perspective of others, and, in ways that are still not entirely clear but are the object of much research activity, the ability to make and test inferences about other people—that is, a kind of extraordinary reasoning ability. Prosocial skills reflect the capacity for empathy.

Popular kids know how to approach others. They are not only friendly, they are *good* kids. When schoolkids rate their peers and rate the qualities that influence their choices, helpfulness comes out on top. Kids like kids who try to help someone who has been hurt. They want as their friend a child who shows sympathy for someone who has made a mistake. They are high on kids who help other children who are having trouble with a task.

Being socially competent, popular children do not bully, nor are they bullied. They grow up with a moral component to their behavior. They do not inflict pain on others, nor are they forced to construct a world view in which pain is justified or necessary. They learn, early on, how to handle the conflict that is inevitable in interpersonal relationships. For conflict among friends helps children realize that their own outlook has its limits and is only a partial window on the world.

Popularity does not mean that social activities will dominate a child's life. It means a child has a set of social skills that will help a person create the kinds of satisfying relationships he or she wants. Indeed, experiencing themselves as socially competent seems to obviate the need for children to devote most of their time cultivating relationships or seeking friends.

POINTERS FOR PARENTS

GET TO KNOW YOUR CHILD'S WORLD.

- Observe your child. Listen to your child: Does he ever talk about other kids? Does she complain about the way other kids treat her? Aggressive kids are always complaining that social problems are someone else's fault.
- Talk to your child. In the most matter-of-fact voice you can summon, ask your child what she is doing. With whom. Get a picture of your child's daily life. Some questions to ask:
- "How did things go today?" or "Tell me, what was your day like?"
- "Who do you like in your class?" "What do you like about————?"
- "Who is nice in your class?" "Who is mean?"
- "Who are your friends?"
- "What kinds of things do you like to do together with your friends?"
- "Who in your class really likes you?" "How do you know?"
- "Who do you think doesn't like you?" "How do you know?" "What kinds of things do you say to him?"
- "What do you do during breaks?"
- "Do you ever wish you had more friends?"
- Listen to your child. Smile at your child. Touch your child. Nod in response to your child's conversation. Not only are you modeling the social skills you want your child to develop, you are constructing a base from which your child can feel safe to explore the world. You will also learn when social problems may require more support.
- Be sure to demonstrate that you have all the time in the world to hear what your child has to say. Turn off the phone, or at least turn on the answering machine. Or go

for a walk in the woods. Only then will your child feel comfortable enough to reveal her world. Children often do not bother talking about their life if they pick up a signal their parents aren't paying full attention. And it's amazing what they will tell you if they feel you will not punish them or be angry or disappointed in them for what they have to say.

- Remember to have a conversation, not give a lecture.

ASK YOUR CHILDREN HOW PEERS TREAT THEM.

- Children are often ashamed or afraid to bring up the subject. Parents must.
- Ask your child to tell you something good that happened that day. Then ask her to tell you something bad that happened.
- One way to get children to talk about hurtful social experiences they may be having is to talk about past experiences of your own. "Did I ever tell you about the time my best friends threw rocks at me, how terrible it felt?" Let kids know it happens and how a child might feel, advises Dr. Jacquelyn Mize of Auburn University in Alabama.
- Also, read books about friendship—the Frog and Toad series, the George and Martha series—or watch videos such as *Harriet the Spy* together. As you go, ask your child to think about how the character was feeling, and ask, "Has anything like that ever happened to you?" You can do it only when children are open to it, and not in a teachy way.
- When you suspect something might be an issue and that your child's feelings were hurt but she isn't talking about it, describe a hypothetical situation. Explain the reasons for social behavior. And ask, "What do you think a person should do?"

WHAT TO DO WHEN A CHILD SAYS,
"NO ONE WANTS TO PLAY WITH ME."

- Take it seriously. And be thankful your child trusts you enough to confide this very distressing information.

- Don't try to persuade him that it couldn't possibly be true; that only convinces a child you can't be trusted with such sensitive information.
- Tread gently. Children who are being picked on feel ashamed, and blame themselves for their difficulties; they are reluctant to talk to parents in the first place for fear of being reprimanded. Your child's feelings on this matter are not trivial.
- Engage your child in a conversation about any recent changes in her social milieu. Is she being picked on; has a bully joined the class?
- Talk to the teacher to find out what is going on in school. Ask the teacher for advice. But don't stop there.
- Find out from your child what social tasks she has the most trouble with, and together explore and rehearse steps your child can take.

DON'T BLAME YOUR CHILD FOR PEER PROBLEMS.
Social relationships are highly complex; it takes most people a lifetime to master the skills they call on. Sometimes even that's not enough.

Sorting Themselves Out—and In

Socially speaking, children sort themselves into five basic groups: the popular, the socially average, the rejected, the neglected, and the controversial. They do this on their own, automatically and naturally, without any prompting at all, as every parent knows who has had a child skulk in the door and utter those gut-wrenching words, "Mommy, I have no friends." Or "Nobody wants to play with me." Children form their own social groupings so reliably and consistently, and especially at school, with consequences that echo for decades, that scientists can clearly observe these processes. Because it reflects basic deep-seated behavioral styles, the social grouping of children tends to be under way early, probably by age three, certainly by kindergarten, and it tends to be quite stable and enduring.

When psychologists study children, they deploy a surefire way to distinguish which kids are which: They ask the children themselves. In a typical study, researchers want to scrutinize exactly what distinguishes the behavior of kids in each group, or they want to see how the social status of each child tracks from year to year, to detect the consequences of having more or fewer friends. They will present pictures of every child in an entire class to each child, and then ask him or her to "name three children you like to play with" or "name three of your best friends" and "name three children you don't like to play with" or "don't like." By counting up the number of positive and negative peer nominations children receive, they can calculate how popular each child is, how much they like one another—formally called sociometric status.

Researchers also observe children directly, monitoring their play in natural settings, like the playground, and in specific types of situations they create in playroomlike laboratories. In order to avoid distorting kids' play by their presence, they make audio and video recordings of children at play, and carefully count and classify every sequence of behavior, going over the tapes again and again to extract every nuance of approach and rebuff. It can take four hours or more for an experienced viewer to go over every element of interaction that takes place in ten minutes of tape.

Usually, researchers cross-check their observations by asking teachers to rate the social performance of each child, from a long checklist of behaviors. Teachers and parents are generally reliable informants about children's social behavior, and are especially adept at detecting problems. However, teachers see only what goes on in the classroom, not in the corridors, schoolyards, or in the neighborhood, so they may not be privy to all the social connections a child may have. Moreover, kids often go to great lengths to carry out their misdeeds away from the watchful eyes of their teachers. In addition, teachers' observations can be subject to some bias.

Five Kinds of Kids

THE POPULAR—20 PERCENT

These children are well liked by many children (and adults), disliked by few, and they have emotionally close, long-lasting one-to-one friendships with peers. They make friends easily and well, and they keep them. Their friendships are intimate and satisfying. In one study of eight-to ten-year olds, 95 percent of popular kids had at least one mutual best-friendship in the classroom. And they have no trouble being accepted by and assimilated into the larger group of peers, many of whom are mutual friends. Most of their friends are also popular children. As a result, they are able to create a large, supportive social network. In the schoolyard, popular children can often be seen in cooperative play or engaged in social conversation. Like Katy, popular kids seem to walk a graceful line between noticing and accommodating the needs of others, on the one hand, and pursuing their own goals, on the other. They readily become leaders.

They are highly skilled at information-gathering. And they have mastered a very rich grammar of communication. They scan their surroundings for relevant social information and use it in their conversations and actions. They make good judgments about when to enter into the play of others, and can wait until there is room in an activity for another person. They "read" others' intentions well. They are sensitive to signals from peers that convey such information as what their interests are, or whether they want to be left alone. These children respond in a clear and highly connected way to others' offers to join in the play, a way that is congruent with and contingent to what is said to them. The connectedness of their communication is, in fact, one of its most outstanding features. What's more, popular kids communicate simply; they don't blurt out embarrassing things about their feelings but offer concrete information about the situation they're in. They make comments relevant to ongoing play and they are able to adapt discourse to the demands of whatever situation they are in. In addition, they accurately perceive the effects of their behavior on others.

About one in five children registers as popular among their peers.

And they do so with great consistency, because they possess qualities others always like. Popular children are surrounded by others; as a result they have a rich supply of opportunities to observe social skills and to practice them. Small wonder they develop social confidence and expect success. By virtue of their social power, popular children have high status in their peer group, further increasing their desirability as play partners and friends. In addition to engaging in prosocial behavior, they are also frequently the recipients of prosocial acts.

Psychologist Jacquelyn Mize studies the social behavior of preschool children and carefully observes them at play. Even at that early age, differences in social competence are distinct, she has found. She has noted in the behavior of four- and five-year-olds many of the markings of social competence at later ages—and *all* of the features that characterize social competence at any age. She describes a simple exchange that occurred in a classroom of four-year-olds.

> Wendy is busily setting a table in the housekeeping corner when Angela approaches. Looking up, Wendy says: "You can play; you be the baby. I have to go to work now."
>
> "I don't want to be a baby—I want to be the mommy," Angela responds petulantly.
>
> "I know; you can be the other mommy and we have coffee at work," Wendy counters affably.
>
> Angela appears to accept this suggestion and Wendy rummages through a pile of dress-up clothes to find a pair of high heels, which Angela puts on. Angela clomps to the toy typewriter and bangs on the keys.
>
> "Yeah," Wendy exclaims exuberantly, "we gotta get our work done fast."

For all its seeming triviality, this little interaction is really quite remarkable. It is not just about exercising imagination. It's not just about playing house or modern mommy. It's not just about little children rehearsing future roles. It's about very young children spontaneously solving exactly the same kind of sophisticated problems adults face at work, at love, at home, at play all the time—assimilating a new person into an ongoing activity, defusing defiance, finding common ground, turning a potential enemy into an ally, recruiting the support and cooperation of another, enlisting others in the pursuit of a goal. What's more, the four-year-olds solve them with enviable ease and directness, while keeping it all a game. It showcases a behavioral style that has all the earmarks of social competence and at an absurdly early age.

Wendy is *positive and agreeable,* even in the face of her play partner's negativity. She has transformed a potentially unpleasant episode into a positive one, by use of a "turnabout": rejecting one offer but simultaneously initiating a new offer, in keeping with the topic, to beget a new acceptance. Whether they are toddlers or adults, well-liked and socially competent people have a generally positive orientation and they offer positive suggestions or directions to peers.

Wendy is *tuned in* to the situation and the context. The offer to Angela of a pair of high heels is relevant to Angela's interest in being a mommy. Yet it's in Wendy's orbit of interest, too; creating another mommy-worker continues the previous line of play without interruption. In fact, it enlarges the pleasure of the play. It's appropriate in the specific context of play they were in. Whether boys or girls, socially competent children pay attention, yet are flexible and even creative; they can adapt what they are doing to accommodate others; they have the ability to consider others' ideas for play. They find a role for others.

And Wendy's behavior is *synchronous;* she positively meshes her actions with the behavior of her partner in this exchange. She immediately noticed and responded to Angela, and her response was contingent on Angela's; when Angela flatly rejected Wendy's first suggestion to "be the baby," Wendy immediately countered with an alternative, one that not only fit in with but amplified Angel's interests. There was a kind of rhythmic dance, a reciprocity of movement. Socially skilled children are responsive and sensitive to others.

Wendy is so accomplished that she has created Angela's success at what is probably the most daunting of social tasks for children (and scarcely a breeze for adults)—to enter into joint play with another child or a group, and to be assimilated into a group. Given the mobility of American families and the frequency with which children are relocated to new schools, this may be one of the most useful of abilities. It is definitely the most important task, because gaining entry into peer play is a prerequisite for all further social interaction.

Yet even for popular kids this is a difficult challenge. In one study of second- and third-graders, 26 percent of the efforts of *popular* students were rejected or ignored by their classmates. Among children in nursery school, even those who know each other well, more than 50 percent of all entry attempts are rejected; 54 percent of the time, the response to the question "Can I play?" is "No, you're not our friend." That leads to the obvious conclusion that one of the handiest social skills of all may be the knowledge that even the best attempts to enter into play with others may be met with rejection. Still, how children negotiate the entry situation is powerfully telling; it is the single sharpest diagnostic test of a child's general social skillfulness.

And when popular children make approaches to others that are in fact rejected, they don't attribute the rejection to internal causes—their own incompetence, unlikability, or inability to make friends. They assume rejection can result from many factors—incompatibility, someone else's bad mood, a misunderstanding. They develop an attitude of resilience, using the social feedback they get as information to shape another go at acceptance.

And should they reject others' efforts to join with them, they do it in a positive way; they invariably offer a reason or counter with an alternative idea: "You can bring the fire engine over here later." Or "When we need a mommy you can come and be her."

Popular children know how to decipher the emotional states of others and to make and test inferences about the intentions of others. They come to realize that other people have other perspectives based on their experience, and they acquire the ability to assume another's point of view—the basis for empathy. They are able to take the frame of reference of those kids they want to join. They understand the needs of others. And when conflicts arise, they can make accommodations. Popular children are skilled at resolving conflicts within their relationships.

Popularity among children fosters the capacity for empathy, reciprocity, mutuality. These turn out to be skills that are the foundation for all rewarding social relationships, whether in the bedroom or in the boardroom. They are the natural brakes against any kind of exploitation of others. Mutuality, after all, is the basis of morality, the golden rule—doing unto others as you would want done to you.

One reason popular children are popular is that, even in preschool, they can recognize the expression of specific emotions, and they do this even before they can verbally put a label on the feelings. They understand what gives rise to emotions in themselves and ultimately in others. They come to see that there is a relationship between emotions, situations, and events that stir them up, and how that translates into behavior. As a result, they can respond to the emotional needs of others.

If there's any doubt that accurately interpreting the expressive behavior of people is a cognitive high-wire act, involving complex reasoning, perhaps the results of studies of hundreds of children will be persuasive: Even discounting differences in I.Q., elementary-school children who score well on understanding of emotional expression also score well on tests of math and reading achievement. The same children are also rated as likable by their peers.

In addition, they have acquired one of the most fundamental abilities underlying performance in all human activity: They can modulate their own emotional states. Children who learn to regulate their level of emotional arousal, the bodily tension created by intense feelings—especially the negative emotions of sadness, fear, anger, and shame—are able to pay attention to other children, to say nothing of teachers and parents, and to the world at large. How this skill is acquired and what it consists of will be discussed in Chapter Seven. But unless children develop techniques for regulating their feelings, intense negative emotions divert mental energy to defensive coping, prompt kids to display anger and frustration, and limit the amount of information that children—or anyone—can take in.

THE SOCIALLY AVERAGE—25 TO 30 PERCENT

These are children who are liked by some children and actively disliked by a few. They are occasionally the targets of aggression by their peers. They have not been studied as well as other social groupings of kids, because their social status seems to be more a matter of default than the product of a specific behavioral style. As a result, the social status of children ranked as socially average may change over time. This much is known: Socially average children are not hugely different from popular children, except that they spend more time as onlookers, on the fringes of groups playing in the schoolyard. And they are less skilled at doping out the social intentions of others.

Girls of average social status tend to have as many friends as girls of popular social status, while boys of average status have as few friends as unpopular boys.

THE REJECTED—20 PERCENT

These are children who are actively disliked by their peers—widely disliked by the peer group and with few friends in class—and actively excluded from social activities. When classmates are asked to name children they like and those they don't, these children receive few if any positive nominations and many negative ones. Few social overtures are made toward them. When they try to join in a group of peers, their behavior tends to be disconnected, out of step with, and downright disruptive of ongoing activity. Rather than making comments relevant to ongoing activity, they typically draw attention to their own needs and interests—giving their own unsolicited opinions and talking about themselves. As a result, while they make as many overtures to others as popular children do, theirs are frequently ignored or frankly rebuffed. They not only have difficulty interacting with peers at the group level, they have trouble establishing reciprocal friendships.

The only reciprocity in their interactions is negative; their interactions often involve arguing—even with teachers. Studies differ in their ways of measuring these things, but anywhere from 23 percent to 55 percent of rejected kids have no friends at all. When they do, their friends are also unpopular children, often younger than themselves, and often not even in the same school. Many of their social contacts are with younger children, affording them fewer opportunities to learn age-appropriate behavior. In elementary school, these children spend considerable classroom time not focusing on the task at hand. And their social approaches to other children are more apt to take place in the classroom than on the playground. On the playground, they drift from one possible playmate to another, rarely remaining engaged with anyone for long.

About 20 percent of children are regularly rejected by their peers. Those actively singled out for rejection are not all of a kind. The vast majority fall into two opposite camps—those who are aggressive, such as bullies, and those at the other extreme, the socially inhibited or withdrawn, the painfully shy. They tend to be bullied. Both are the least popular kids at school, but they are very different types, and differ significantly in their pathways to social rejection and in their responses to it—and in their ability to function in the future. Children in both groups don't just behave ineptly; they have underlying personal characteristics that tend to lead to enduring difficulties in peer relations. If there's one thing studies make clear it is that their troublesome behavior is not the consequence of being rejected, it is the *cause* of their unpopularity. These kids, when given the chance to interact with an entirely new group of peers, are invariably rejected anew. But whether they are the perpetrators of extremely negative behavior or the victims, they are at risk for developmental difficulties.

Aggressive-Rejected Kids

Nothing predicts being disliked more than aggression. Children who are aggressive are disliked because they are intrusive, highly disruptive, and cause others pain. They rip toys out of the hands of peers, bite them until they give up a possession, or push kids off bicycles. They spend a lot of time trying to interact with other kids, but their overtures to others are either ignored or rejected and the interactions they do have are marked by aggressive behavior. More than other kids, they are given to rough-and-tumble play, where ambiguous moves ignite misunderstandings and conflict. They start fights easily and "act out." They try to dominate their peers and control them, and are seen as bossy and conflict-makers. They are often mean. In fact, they actively focus on punishing others. These children even rate themselves as quite good at making others feel bad, accomplished at "getting back" at others, and not so skilled at working difficulties out peacefully. Other children rate them as bossy, irritable, likely to violate rules of games, and apt to bother others trying to work.

When, in the course of research, these children are presented with video or verbal narratives of common childhood dilemmas—such as how to enter a group of peers who are already engaged in play, or what happens when someone runs into them and knocks over the tower they were building—they offer unfriendly strategies. They believe in solving problems with force. Once provoked, these children can't seem to find an "off" button; they will even go out of their way to pursue a confrontation.

As distinctive as their behavior is, so are their patterns of interpreting social information. One of the most distinguishing characteristics of these children is the expectations they bring to interactions. Like Alex, they have a pronounced tendency to misinterpret the intentions of other children. Even when peers approach them with good intentions, they label their intentions as hostile. Or they mistakenly view aggression as a suitable way to get what they want. Aggressive children don't just act differently from others; they see the world differently. Many of their aggressive actions are in fact fairly logical responses to their distorted social perceptions. The amazing thing about rejected kids is, they can sometimes function constructively in other, nonsocial situations—for a time.

Despite being rejected, aggressive-rejected kids do not experience particularly high levels of loneliness, at least at first. That's partly because they see themselves inaccurately, and partly because they pooh-pooh feelings of attachment and sadness. It is intrinsic to the distorted way they see the world that they blame others for their own social failure. Despite their general lack of acceptance by the peer group, their other-blaming interpretation of events may shield them from feeling terribly lonely. But it also may be because they do actually have some friends in their classes. As anyone who's been to junior high knows, aggressive kids tend to hang out with one another in school.

Over time, aggressive-rejected children develop a negative reputation that makes it especially hard for them to change their behavior. Because of the reputations they develop, they are blamed when anything goes wrong—even if they had no hand in it. Any good they do is likely to be ignored or dismissed by their peers.

Physical aggression plays a bigger role in the rejection of boys than of girls, and aggressiveness is one of the best predictors of later adjustment problems. Aggressiveness shows up early in life, certainly during the preschool years. By the time boys are eight years old, or in the third grade, those who target aggression at other kids tend to be on a steady course of antisocial behavior. Interpersonal aggression is one of the most stable of all behavioral characteristics. In boys more than girls, physical aggression is linked to an array of social deficiencies. Besides lacking the ability to read the intentions of others, aggressive children come up empty on empathy; they are unable to see the point of view of another.

Children who are aggressive develop problems in adjustment that snowball over time.

Girls Do It, Too

Girls, however, are simply aggressive in a different, more subtle way, especially as they move toward adolescence. Whereas aggression in boys tends to involve overt physical and verbal abuse of others, in girls it shows up as a kind of manipulativeness of others, what psychologist Nicki R. Crick calls relational aggression, as in "I'll be your best friend if . . ." In order to get their way, they threaten to leave other kids out of their play. They give kids the silent treatment. Or they knowingly spread malicious lies about peers, even the ones who are their friends. If aggressive boys misuse physical power, aggressive girls misuse the power of intimacy. For them, the vehicle for intentionally inflicting harm is the relationship itself. This kind of aggression shows up in behavioral repertoires in girls as young as three, and it persists over time.

Most of these girls have at least one mutual friendship, but they are also disliked by many, seen as deliberately mean. Their friendships are highly intimate; in fact, these girls often demand exclusivity in their friendships and talk a great deal about their feelings. But intimacy is their way of getting information to control others. One of the most remarkable aspects of friendship is its ability to protect participants; the reciprocity of liking, the mutuality that suffuses just one mutual friendship, the exchange of emotional support can buffer children against the negative effects of stressful experiences and even other hurtful human relationships with peers and even parents. But in contrast to what happens in ordinary friendships, the friends of relationally aggressive girls are not protected at all from aggression; rather, the friendship itself often becomes a major source of negativity and distress. Their friends often feel betrayed. Over time—even over the course of a school year—relationally aggressive girls are at risk of becoming widely disliked, with few friends available; eventually, others just get tired of their manipulative behavior. Unlike physically aggressive boys, relationally aggressive girls do not gravitate toward one another.

Submissive-Rejected Kids

But aggressive children are not the only ones who are shunned by their peers. Children like least peers at the other behavioral extreme—those who are particularly nonassertive. If bullies make sins of commission, withdrawn children's are sins of omission. They do not stand up for themselves. Others describe them as "easily pushed around." And indeed, they commonly become the target of bullying because they are perceived as being "easy marks." But one thing is clear: they are thoroughly nonassertive even before they become targets of physical aggression. They avoid confrontation, make few requests of others, and when they do are too deferential for anyone's comfort. They give up their position or place at the drop of a hat. They rarely lead their peers in any positive fashion. They do not initiate conversation or make attempts to persuade, or dissuade, their peers. Outside the classroom they spend more time passively playing than interacting, and they pursue solitary activities. These children avoid interaction inside the classroom as well.

Overly compliant children not only miss out on the attention of their peers, they do not get much attention from teachers in the classroom, either. While they may be tolerated by classmates in early and middle childhood, adolescence puts them on a sure path to rejection. The nearer they get to adolescence, the less such children are liked by other kids. Their behavior sets in motion a vicious cycle. The more they shrink from play, the more they are picked on. The more they are picked on, the more they withdraw socially, becoming less and less likable and having fewer and fewer opportunities to learn how to approach others.

Still, it's not just the display of aggressiveness or submissiveness that makes young people disliked by their peers. There are indeed aggressive or submissive kids who are not rejected by others. What sinks them socially is the lack of redeeming characteristics. These students also lack prosocial qualities. They do not cooperate or even focus on other children. Instead, when they are engaged in social interaction, they are consumed with thoughts about themselves; they are worried about being humiliated and rejected. Aggressiveness and submissiveness are strongly negative qualities but they lead to rejection only in the absence of positive social qualities.

Submissive-rejected students feel the aching emptiness of loneliness more than others and are dissatisfied with their outcast status. They hover as passive spectators at the fringes of groups; and while hovering is characteristic of most newcomers to any group, socially successful children use the experience to gather information about their peers' play as a way of getting up the steam to join in. Rejected students just continue to hover passively, avoiding social engagement. And the attempts they do make to join in are often inappropriate to the situation. They may, for example, try to start up social contact while other kids are busy doing homework. Their ineffectual attempts at social interaction earn them the label of "nuisance." Other kids let them know they are not wanted.

Submissive-rejected children believe that rejection results from their own social incompetence, a belief that only deters them from making further attempts to gain acceptance. And it is this belief, in combination with their poor social experience, that makes them feel lonely, lonelier than any other group of children. It is also makes them prime candidates for depression. Rejection by the group doesn't preclude close friendships, but their friendships are typically of poor quality. Even their best friends treat them worse than they do other children.

One distinguishing characteristic that both aggressive-rejected and submissive-rejected students share is the inability to cope with the teasing of peers. Teasing, however, is one of the surefire trials of middle childhood, and a basic social requirement of this age group.

Whether it is the absence of friends or the presence of enemies that does the harm is not entirely clear. But children who are rejected by their peers experience problems of school adjustment. They drop out of school with a far greater frequency than other kids. They engage in criminal behavior. Their troubles are also reflected in later personality development. They have social difficulties throughout life. They are subject to extreme loneliness. And they arrive at adulthood at risk for many mental-health problems. Aggressive-rejected children suffer the most problems of all.

Children's peers, it turns out, are exquisitely sensitive indicators of which children later develop mental and emotional problems. The are the DEWline (Distant Early Warning system) of mental health.

THE NEGLECTED—20 TO 25 PERCENT

These children are not quite as well liked by their peers as are average kids. But they are not actively disliked, either. It's just that their names rarely come up when classmates are asked to identify their best friends or even just to name children they want to play with. In practice, they make little impact and are ignored by most other children their age, even in group settings like preschool or elementary school. Adults, however, both parents and teachers, have a hard time figuring out what neglected kids do that sets them apart from socially average kids.

This is what social neglect sounds like in a sixth-grader: "Today everybody's going to Mary Ann's party in the group. I'm sort of the one that gets left behind. I'm not invited to the party so I won't do anything on the weekend. Anywhere the whole group goes, I don't. . . . I'm just the person that gets left back. Maybe they don't realize that I get left, that I'm there, but it happens all the time."

Although they don't register on the radar screen of general peer acceptance, and spend more school time alone than popular children, they may have good friendships with one or two individual children. What's more, they tend to be satisfied with the peer relationships that they do have and feel no more lonely or distressed than their average-accepted peers, although they do not see themselves as socially competent.

About 20 to 25 percent of children are socially neglected, and this much is known about their behavior: they tend to shun conflict and they rarely act or respond aggressively themselves, even when provoked by those who are not their friends. They are compliant in the classroom. Unlike aggressive-rejected kids, they never brag about their ability to beat anyone up.

Neglected kids do not experience negative treatment by their peers; they are not targeted for aggressive acts. And so they are spared the pain of active rejection. But in their invisibility neither do they receive caring responses from peers, and they may actually be at risk of adjustment difficulties from the lack of positive, prosocial acts by their peers. That may leave them stranded, without help for coping with some of the usual transitions and difficulties of childhood.

What is probably most important is that they have no shortage of ability to take in and mentally process certain crucial social information. They are quite good at interpreting the intentions of others and, even in situations where it's not clear why something undesirable happened—another child tripped and knocked the ball out of their hands—they do not presume hostility in others; they assume other children's intentions are positive. And should a friend act negatively toward them, they tend to overlook provocations; what's more, they let bygones be bygones and do not hold grudges for past transgressions. These children have good social understanding, but they are neglected as long as they do not translate it into action. Still, because they generally believe that peers intend to behave positively toward them, and they carry few grudges, these children often develop good relationships with their peers at some later point.

If neglected kids get less attention from their peers and their teachers, they also get less scrutiny from researchers. Unlike the behavior of popular kids and even aggressive kids, theirs are not acts of commission; their behavior doesn't make much of an impression. A more important reason is that neglected status is often temporary or sporadic, not the product of an underlying way of seeing the world but of a specific situation, and when the situation changes so does the child's social status.

Lucas is a bright and physically agile eight-year-old who attends a private school in New York. This year there are no other kids in his class with whom he is friendly. For starters, there are very few boys in his class. When he first began complaining to his mother that he had no friends, she dismissed his laments as beginning-of-the-year uncertainty. She knew he had friends in the neighborhood, had made friends at summer day camp, and he played well with other kids in Little League. But over the school year his complaints got louder.

Eventually, he began finding ways of avoiding school, like claiming illness—although he always magically improved in time for Little League practice. "Mom, my stomach hurts today" became one of his favorite chants. Although his mother knew and the teachers confirmed that Lucas wasn't picked on by other kids, they couldn't figure out just what was going on. The situation grew so worrisome that Lucas's mom began looking into a change of schools, a move that would be required in two more years anyway when he finished grade school. Somehow, they struggled through the year. Lucas went off to summer camp and had a happy time. But he came back already dreading the start of a new school year. Not only was he anxious about having to get used to a new school, but his expectations for personal success were nonexistent; he was sure he was walking into another year without everyday friends. In spite of all his misgivings, the change of school was simply miraculous. Lucas quickly made many new friends. There were plenty of boys (and girls!) to talk baseball with. Within days, he was looking forward to getting up in the morning. And within a week or two, his mother saw the most important change of all—his self-confidence was restored enough that he was joining in many school-related activities.

Neglected children may have an advantage over other children. At least in the preadolescent years, they seem to shine in some areas where average children—or even popular children—do not. They are far more committed to schoolwork than other children. And teachers like them, although this is a two-edged sword in the preteen years, when their peers are developing a distaste for adult authority. But it is not yet clear whether they are driven to academic studies because of their neglected status, or whether they have a preference for solitary activities that results both in their being neglected and pursuing academic interests.

THE CONTROVERSIAL—10 TO 15 PERCENT

There is another social category of children, the controversial; they are sought out by a fair number of children and rejected by an equal number; few are neutral about them. These children are named as very well liked by a number of children, and actively named as highly disliked by other children. What makes them controversial is that they engage in antisocial behavior as well as prosocial behavior. In fact, in some studies, controversial kids turn out to engage in more aggression even than those who are rejected.

Many of the children in this group engage in a form of aggression that is not physical at all but directed at harming the relationships of others. They participate in mutual friendships, but their friendships are riven with high degrees of conflict. And there is a much greater degree of asymmetry in their friendships than in those among popular children; there is an imbalance in the disclosure of personal information, of intimacies, of the kinds of support and validation that friends typically provide. The efforts made to assist one another flow heavily in one direction only—theirs.

WHEN CHILDREN EVALUATE THEIR PEERS

Social status	Peer nominations	
	Best friend or like	*Do not like*
Popular	xxx	
Average	xx	x
Rejected		xxx
Neglected		
Controversial	xx	xx

Being Alone Is Not Always Loneliness

All children play by themselves, and all children need to spend time being alone and playing alone. Solitary play is important in its own right and as an arena for the exercise of the imagination and the play of the intellect. No one wants to spend all his or her time accommodating the needs of others. Children, like adults, need some time to focus exclusively on their own interests by themselves.

Some children, especially when young, are "asocial"; they isolate themselves. They prefer solitary pursuits rather than social ones. They like to be alone and to play alone. They are not aggressive and not actively rejected by their peers. But neither are they accepted by them, and their isolation puts them at potential risk for missing out on the acquisition of social skills.

What's crucial is not that a child is alone, but whether a child chooses or wants to be alone. Socially competent children can choose when they want to be alone and when they want to be with others. The time they spend alone is usually pleasurable and highly rewarding to them; typically, they are engaged in some positive activity. Unpopular children have aloneness thrust upon them. While they may ultimately find very constructive things to do with that time, especially if they are bright, they are in effect socially isolated. Not only do they experience more loneliness, but their time alone is more often spent in aimless activity or daydreaming.

Sadly, socially lonely children live in a self-perpetuating state of isolation. In one study of twenty-six first-graders, popular and unpopular children are asked how they'd handle everyday peer dilemmas:

- If you were playing with a toy and another child came up and took it off you, what would you do?
- If you were on a swing and another kid came up to you and told you to get off because they wanted to go, what would you do?
- If you were just starting a new school, what would you do to make friends there?

Videotapes, analyzed by researchers who had no idea of the social standing of each child, demonstrated that the unpopular children were likely to spend more time alone. The assessment of their problem-solving strategies demonstrated that they were not simply behaviorally deficient but also lacked the social knowledge to guide successful action. They had no idea what was appropriate, and gave responses that were either directly confrontational—vowing to take the toy back—or totally nonassertive. Which is to say, their negative reactions would only beget more hostile responses from their peers.

Now More Than Ever

Social competence and acceptance by peers have always been important in children's development. But social skills appear to be increasingly important in the lives of children at an earlier age than ever before. As the rearing of children shifts toward preschool, and entrance at earlier ages than ever before, children are in social settings where there is greater exposure to peers for longer periods of time than usually occurs at home. The demand for social skills comes early. At the same time, preschool attendance brings a tremendous opportunity to acquire and practice social skills, too.

What happens in preschool is a reliable indicator of what happens in kindergarten, and that, in turn, is a reliable predictor of what happens in elementary school. Relationship styles begin to gel during the preschool years, and kids with difficulties in peer interaction at that age are far more likely than others to experience academic difficulties and peer rejection or neglect in elementary school; once that happens, they can be set on a dizzying downward spiral, their exclusion virtually guaranteeing they will be deprived of opportunities to acquire ever more subtle and sophisticated social skills. At the same time, the power of negative reputation is such that it can keep them stuck in a stigmatized status even if they should magically learn how better to approach other children.

CHAPTER TWO

The Assault on Sociability

Raising popular kids is a more urgent need than ever. Since the 1970s, children have been losing ground in social competence. According to a national survey of children between the ages of seven and sixteen, kids are spending a diminishing amount of time with friends. And the kids they do play with are getting younger. More children today would simply rather be alone. At the same time, more of them are unhappy, apathetic, unmotivated, and more of them dislike school—all problems related to inability to get along with peers.

Throughout the culture, there are rising pressures against social competence and, more subtly, against valuing social competence. In our "culture of complaint," the notion of teamwork and cooperation has largely been replaced by a process of competing special interests; the process has wildly infected not only politics but the content of education and the conduct of business. The result is a society whose defining quality, in the words of University of Chicago theologian Jean Bethke Elshtain, is "an orgy of mistrust" among individuals. But pressures against social competence are invading every home as well as public arenas.

Why Johnny Can't Play

Consider some of the developments that are placing the social development of all children today under assault. Remember that today's children create the fabric of society in the next generation.

MARITAL DISCORD AND DIVORCE

When parents have problems getting along with each other, their children develop unworkable ways of relating to others. Sociologists Paul R. Amato and Alan Booth have kept tabs on two thousand families whose children have grown up to become part of Generation X. They find that, by itself, divorce does not affect a child's social ties or ability to form social bonds in young adulthood. However, poor marital quality does. When parents are unhappy with their marriages, fight a lot, and "act as if they are going to divorce (even if they do not)," their children "observe and learn poor interpersonal skills, develop personality traits shaped by a sense of emotional insecurity, and internalize problematic working models of relationships," Amato and Booth report in *A Generation at Risk* (Harvard University Press, 1997). They are worried because their evidence shows that marriage is becoming an even more conflicted and insecure arrangement. "Then offspring may be entering young adulthood with fewer social ties and weaker interpersonal orientations now than in the past." Their children will have even fewer social skills.

MOVING

Our society continues to become a mobile one. One in five families moves each year. Any move, even for the best of reasons, is traumatic, especially for a child; adults can maintain contact over distances, but for a child, a move even to a new school district disrupts the entire universe of existing social bonds. It puts new demands on acceptance at the very time a child is feeling most sad and anxious and is also striving to meet new academic challenges.

POST-DIVORCE CHANGES

Further, for a large percentage of children, the disruption of moving is a consequence of parental divorce. The sadness, depression, and generalized family stress that inevitably follow divorce are not usually enduring, but they often play out in withdrawing or aggressive behaviors that beget rejection during crucial transition times; a child may not be given a second chance to gain acceptance into the new peer group. In one important study that specifically looked at children in families experiencing such adversity as divorce, the children were indeed more rejected by their peers.

Add to the mix that most moves following divorce involve the compounded trauma of reduced living standards and perhaps tougher neighborhoods. Children may be unprepared to interact with new types of peers at the same time they are less eager to do so. But what is even more significant is that children are hardly the only ones in the family disrupted by divorce. Without exception, parents are distracted by their own stresses in adjusting to new lives—which means they are less available to help their children over their huge social and emotional hurdles just when the kids need that help most.

ONE-ADULT FAMILIES

The rise of single-parent families deprives children of an important way of acquiring social competence. Through their own interactions, parents are critical for modeling social skills for children.

NO SIBLINGS

Family size is decreasing, so kids have fewer siblings and fewer opportunities to develop or practice social skills. The average family has shrunk from 2.3 kids in 1970 to 1.8 in 1991, according to the U.S. Census Bureau. Yet sibling interactions have been shown to promote the development of social understanding. Even arguments between siblings provide children with valuable firsthand experience, particularly in handling emotionally intense disputes. How siblings resolve their disputes, researchers have found, is echoed in the ways children manage conflict in their outside friendships. Only children have less practice in sharing resources, resolving conflicts of interest, and working in groups. As they grow up, they may not know how cooperation and sharing make all kinds of enterprises run better.

In fact, the more siblings a person has, and particularly older siblings, the more likely he or she is to develop a prosocial orientation to others, to approach others trustingly, with a cooperative style, and to work out solutions to problems where both parties benefit. In a 1997 study of 631 college-age students, Dutch researchers found that those raised in smaller families are likely to have a more self-serving or competitive approach to others.

DIMINISHED FAMILY TIME

Family time—meals taken together, time spent talking—is diminishing. The average family now spends a grand total of seven minutes a day together. There is no time to gain practice in the art of face-to-face conversation or problem-solving. Children first learn to regulate their emotionality, solve problems, argue constructively, and manage conflicts in mutually satisfying ways through parent-child interactions. In their experiences at home, kids pick up skills and enduring behavioral patterns that they take with them to relationships outside. One recent study showed just how enduring those behavioral patterns can be. Using close, in-home observation, researchers found that if mothers handled disputes with their three-year-olds by considering the child's interests (as opposed to defending their own position or not discussing the problem at all) and invoked strategies of compromise, conciliation, and bargaining, the children successfully negotiated difficulties and constructively resolved arguments in their own friendships *at age six*. And make no mistake about it, conflict is a very frequent feature of peer interactions, at age six and later.

From the time they were little, friends of my sons have long been astonished at, and almost always welcome to join, our practice of eating together at the kitchen or dining-room table virtually every night. It's a ritual I started not so much because I felt my children needed it—a belief I have since come to hold strongly—but because I needed it; otherwise, I felt as if I were being spun in a high-speed centrifuge through the day. I needed to experience a *there* there. Now that my sons are grown, most of their many friends on one occasion or another have told us how meaningful—and unique!—it was (and still on occasion is) to dine in the embrace of a family, where they gained a sense of being centered and connected and where difficulties were discussed. Not every meal was a laugh a minute, but many were damn close.

TIME PRESSURES

Time itself is scarce. Despite more timesaving devices, there is wide-spread perception of a time crunch. People are feeling busier than ever. Surveys show that the way Americans cope with time pressures is to devote less time to hobbies, leisure, and being with friends, family, and coworkers. Dr. Philip Zimbardo, Ph.D., a professor of psychology at Stanford University and a pioneer in studying and treating shyness, has been monitoring social patterns for over two decades. He is especially eloquent on the insidious effects of time pressure: "Voilà, you don't have time for me—and about 40 percent of respondents don't—so I am more isolated than previously unless I am willing to put in the effort to scale this temporal barrier between us. It also leads to an increasing perception that social interactions are time-wasters to be avoided or minimized, rather than cherished and expanded."

UNSAFE STREETS

The widespread belief that our cities and streets are unsafe drives parents to prefer their children to play indoors. When you play on the streets or in the sandlots, you might play with anyone and everyone. Kids devise a variety of strategies to deal effectively with diversity, come up with ways to negotiate their own differences, and develop skills in leadership. When you play indoors, you bring home only a few kids—if any at all—and then only those who meet your parents' approval. And that's likely to be others just like yourself. There are fewer frustrations to learn how to handle, fewer differences to mediate.

PERFORMING PEOPLE

As traditional groups and communities break down, people today are accepted increasingly on the basis of personal attributes and ability. Kids have to *perform* rather than *be* themselves at play—and then demand performance from others. Performance goals—how many points Johnny can score, how well Hilary dances—come to overshadow the intrinsic value of being in relationships, learning to participate in them, and enjoying the company of others. Through this process, being a good sport, for example, is sacrificed to winning, individual self-interest takes precedence over mutual interests.

BYE-BYE, BANK TELLER

The opportunities for face-to-face interactions are dwindling by the day. When we do our daily business with a machine instead of a bank teller or gas-station attendant we miss out on innumerable chances to learn how to initiate and maintain conversation, to decode nonverbal gestures and language, and—perhaps most important of all—to experience emotion and learn to manage emotionality in exchanges. That these conversations are informal, inconsequential, and mundane is exactly why we need them—the situations contain extremely low risk of failure yet allow us to learn the rules and rhythms of social interaction and gain experience and confidence in person-to-person encounters. But the longer a person goes without informal social contact, the more awkward it becomes when you have it. What should seem natural seems artificial and becomes a source of tension rather than of pleasure.

COMPUTERIZATION

The use of computers for interpersonal communication is increasing, and among younger and younger kids. While actually promoting many types of communication, computers do keep kids from the kinds of face-to-face interactions where social skills are born and confidence in them is gained. Dr. Zimbardo is alarmed that technology is becoming the hiding place of those who dread or are unskilled at social interaction. The difference is not simply a changeover from human encounters to computerized ones; something subtle happens at the keyboard. As the weight of our experience shifts, so does the value we give to that experience. Ultimately, we come not just to *have* fewer personal encounters but to *devalue* personal encounters. Increasingly, they are seen as inefficient and wastes of time. One piece of supporting evidence: The adult workplace has less and less of a social component. In some companies, you can no longer sit down and chat for five minutes in a coworker's office—there are no offices, just the kind of drop-in arrangements seen in airport VIP lounges.

Particularly striking is the way computers are transforming college life. College is without question the social jackpot of a lifetime—total immersion in a community where everyone is the same age, where every corridor and class provide many opportunities for initiating and continuing conversations, where social encounters are smoothed by the existence of groups organized around almost every conceivable interest. The ease of contact that marks even the most academically intense campus makes college the single most significant source of enduring friendships. And yet computerization is turning campuses into a cluster of caves. In 1995, Dr. James Banning, an environmental psychologist at Colorado State University, surveyed one hundred university housing officers. He was alarmed at what he found. "Universities are saying: 'Oh my god, they're in their rooms. How can we ever build a sense of community in this building if they don't come out.' "

COMPUTER TOYS

The use of computers is zooming not just for communication but for children's play. In his work over the past twenty years, Stanford's Dr. Zimbardo finds that children are increasingly declaring their best friend to be . . . *their computer*. This used to be true of computer nerds and hackers, says Dr. Zimbardo. It is now a widening form of social disaffection. Even when two or more children are in the same room, they often are not playing *together*, or against each other; they are playing against the computer. But the computer is a lot like a coach; it becomes the mediator. It determines the rules. It tells the kids how to play the game. The children don't have to learn cooperation and they don't have to solve problems that come up or work out ways to manage conflict. Or learn to handle troubling emotions—a virtual friend doesn't give you negative feedback.

WHATEVER HAPPENED TO KIDS' PLAY?

Perhaps the greatest pressure against social competence arises from the increasing institutionalization of childhood. Simply, children are being given less and less time for free, child-driven play. The time kids spend in social activities with other kids is shrinking. More insidious, the time that may be spent with other kids usually involves an activity that is monitored by an adult. When adults—whether coaches, instructors, or parents—preside over children's activities, the difficulties and rule violations that are bound to arise get adjudicated by the adults, not hammered out by the children. As a result, children do not learn how to work out their own relationship problems, the greatest social skill of all.

While we live in an age where there are more "throwaway" kids than ever, that is, kids who are too easily dispensed with by parents, there is a subset of kids who are anything but. They represent an exactly opposite phenomenon, what I call "hothouse kids." These are children whose parents invest a great deal of time and energy and expectations in them, and who, as a result, hover over them and become overinvolved in their lives. They leave no room for goofing off.

Hothouse Kids

Parents have never been more involved in their children's lives than they are today. "Parents, especially the educated and the affluent, are becoming more absorbed in their children's lives," observes Jay Belsky, Ph.D., a prominent developmental psychologist based at Penn State University. The parents, for their part, are reflecting new strains and stresses filtering through the culture, through families, and through individuals. Nevertheless, they are transforming the childhood experience in ways that make life less fun.

Because they feel it reflects well on them to have children who perform well, many parents are eager to enroll their children in structured activities that are oriented to measurable academic or physical performance. French lessons. Art class. Gymnastics class. Karate class. Ballet class. Soccer. Not just one activity, but many, are crammed into the after-school schedule. "Lauren goes to gymnastics class after school on Mondays, to ballet class on Wednesday, to music class on Thursday, and to art class on Saturday," reports a friend, relating the standard repertoire of affluence and those who aspire to it. (The music class is new, added in response to recent studies reporting a link between music and intelligence.) And as an at-home mom, at least for the time being, my friend doesn't have the excuse of needing care for her children in nonschool hours. But she does feel competitive pressure.

PARENTAL ANXIETIES

Blinded by their own feelings of inadequacy, many adults see this force-feeding of goal-oriented activities to children as an advantage over the more casual, laissez-faire nature of their own childhood. And a leg up in an increasingly competitive world where, as resources are shrinking, most parents understand the market and status value of a good education and an eclectic repertoire of tangible skills. The concerns of parents are accurately summed up in an advertisement lining the cars of the New York City subway system. The advertisement is for a center that does nothing but provide instruction in how to take tests: tests for getting into elite private schools, tests for getting into elite colleges, for getting into law, medical, and other graduate schools, and tests for entry into various professions. "There's nothing wrong with underachieving," says the ad. "It just doesn't pay very well." What makes such consumer advertising so successful is that it goes to the heart of parental anxieties.

But parents who take their own measure by basking in the performance or praise of their children are not only narcissists, they have it exactly backward. What they don't understand is the normal way that childhood wends its way to adulthood. Or that the competencies of the child's world are not the competencies of the adult world. Children need their own time to experience the world and make it their own. Child's play—where kids initiate and direct their own activities—is the constant acquisition, rehearsal, and refinement of social skills. Acting on their own curiosity, kids discover themselves for themselves. The taking of turns ritualized by kids' games establishes the basic ground rules of all social interaction. It is the scaffolding of social life.

If children are left to their own devices, play normally consumes much time of childhood. That it does so is a sign of how important social skills are and how nuanced they must be to serve for a lifetime of social encounters. In reality, the process of elaborating and fine-tuning these skills continues throughout life.

But misunderstanding the value of social competence allows parents to distort child-rearing in tune with their own anxieties. The irony of the new child-centered family is that it does not serve the child's needs.

"He loves swimming," one mother—we'll call her Andrea John-son—told *The New York Times* not long ago. "But I don't know how serious he is about it."

The child was definitely not as serious as his mother. Mrs. Johnson had enrolled her son in his first swimming class—when he was six months old. But the teacher only dribbled water on Aaron's face, so she enrolled him elsewhere. She didn't like that class, either. "He just played with toys by the side of the pool," she said. "I felt like I was getting no results at all."

Then she heard about a teacher who seemed to get *results*—at fifty dollars a half hour. So she hired him to teach her son. Even so, when she saw her son playing around—*having fun!*—during one lesson, she was moved to admonish him: "Come on now, focus, Aaron."

It's never too early to hurry when adults blame their own insecurities on inadequate preparation for lives they now lead. "I'm not a competent swimmer," another mother said. "If I had the kind of lessons my kids have, I'd be a great swimmer. It's expensive, but I decided it was an investment." Does it matter that the experts—in this case, the American Red Cross—advise against formal swimming lessons before age five? Younger children just don't have the necessary motor skills and do not understand the dangers posed by water.

Of course, if you were to ask these same parents—and I have made it a practice of asking parents—about their own most cherished memories of childhood, you'd hear a remarkable convergence. They focus on idylls and experiences where performance or any other pressures were blissfully banished, where time just melted in the sun or the snow. Yet their own children are afforded no such freedoms.

When classes and formal activities monopolize a child's out-of-school time, they can become velvet isolation-incubators. What's lost can be so subtle that it goes entirely unnoticed. And when problems later develop—loneliness, say, or, in its wake, depression—they can be so consequential that attributing them to a change in child's play can seem, on the face of it, ludicrous. The belief that big life problems, like depression or oppositional personality, have smack-you-in-the-eye causes (the search for trauma is currently popular) is deeply entrenched. But the truth is that the roots of many later life problems are invisible in their ordinariness; they lie in the day-to-day routines of childhood. The power of everyday experience lies in repetition; what it lacks in drama it more than makes up for in frequency. Does an overextended parent yank a disputed toy away from two squabbling siblings and order them to their rooms, where resentments smolder, or does he do a little fact-finding about the nature of the problem from each party and explain their needs to each other so they can see a solution themselves?

But the ordinariness of parent-child exchanges cloaks—and does it so well they are nearly invisible—grand lessons about conflict management, about the value of listening to another person's perspective, about the kindness and trustworthiness of others, about the expression and regulation of emotions, lessons that get woven into a philosophy of feelings and of life and even get transmitted to the next generation. When a parent says, "If you are going to be angry (or sad), then go to your room and sulk," what is a parent really saying? And how will this play out in a child's life, and especially in relationships with peers? If a child doesn't learn how to express and regulate emotions, it becomes too hard to take in information in social settings, especially anything that might be upsetting, and to understand others. If parents do not value the emotions of a child that get stirred up in the process of making friends, they cannot help the child cope with those emotions, and the child is at risk of not learning how to cope with the intricacies of making friends.

One effect of the reliance on structured activities is that children draw their identity from their performance in that group. It is a shallow, unsustainable kind of identity that gives way on a bad night later on. Kids take on a sense of identity—but by essentially forcing others to give it to them. They are set up to feel that only if others applaud them do they exist or have any value. In short, they are groomed for narcissism.

Further, the activity is usually monitored by an adult. "What's worse," says Dr. Bernard Carducci, a professor of psychology at Indiana University Southeast, is that it is adult-*mediated*. "Coaches solve the disputes. Not the kids. And so kids lose their tolerance for diversity and the ability to solve the differences that inevitably arise between people." In one study that looked at just such situations, supervising adults *dictated* the course of action more than 90 percent of the time.

DECLINING SOCIAL COMPETENCE

Such children go through life interpersonally diminished, setting them up for difficulties in all kinds of relationships. The alarming fact is that social competence is squarely on the decline. In 1975, Stanford's Dr. Zimbardo surveyed eight hundred students in several American colleges and found that an astonishing 40 percent considered themselves to be shy. Since then, Dr. Carducci has been informally keeping tabs on Zimbardo's original findings, and may be the only person in the country who keeps a kind of running index of social competence. In his undergraduate classes in psychology, Dr. Carducci asks each new crop of students to fill out a questionnaire about their social confidence. Over the past two decades, the number of persons declaring themselves shy has risen to 48 percent. Both he and Dr. Zimbardo predict that shyness will increase even further as a consequence of the electronic revolution.

A lot of shyness stems from anticipating the consequences of ineptness in social interaction. Dr. Carducci points to growing social incompetence as a major force requiring the increasing intervention of professional mediators in everyday life. Lawyers have become the interpersonal mediators of the adult playground. In fact, Dr. Carducci regards the proliferation of lawyers as a golden index of our social disenfranchisement. Given the sign of growing social disconnection in the escalating rates of shyness, he expects that the need for lawyers in all facets of life will only grow in the future.

All these developments rob children of opportunities to learn and practice basic social skills. So there's reason to believe that just ahead lies a society with a radically different—and greatly impoverished—social character from the one we know today. What will this society look like? Its outlines have already been drawn. There will be an increasing split. On the one hand will be those who are bolder, more aggressive, more outgoing; they will naturally lead others and rise to the top in organizations. On the other hand will be the increasing numbers of the shy or socially incompetent. They will work behind the scenes, in back offices, running the technology.

Stanford's Dr. Zimbardo has seen the future, and it is in a study conducted by Professor Thomas Harrell at Stanford University's business school, a highly selective place to which only the most outstanding candidates are accorded entry. He wanted to find out the best predictors of success in these stellar students. He gathered all their records, transcripts of their grades, their letters of recommendation. Then, ten years after they'd received their M.B.A.'s, he rated their level of success based on the quality of their jobs. Only one variable could predict the success of these students. It wasn't intelligence; they were all bright. It wasn't ambition; they were all ambitious. The critical difference was verbal fluency, a basic social skill. Explains Dr. Zimbardo: The verbally fluent are able to sell themselves in interesting and credible ways, and they are able to sell their services and their company. The people in top management don't necessarily need or even have technological skills.

POINTERS FOR PARENTS

KNOW ABOUT KIDS' PEER COMPETENCE, BUT DON'T MAKE A CAREER OUT OF IT.
In some social strata, parents are already far too involved in managing their children's experiences. Your children can gain acceptance by their peers only by learning to handle their own social lives. That doesn't happen overnight or automatically, but it does occur sooner than you might think.

ENCOURAGE YOUR CHILDREN TO EXPLORE THEIR ENVIRONMENT AND TO ENTER NEW SITUATIONS.
But allow your children to find their own comfortable level of accommodation to the world. The worst thing you can do to children is overprotect them. It confirms their worst fears about themselves and sets them up for a lifetime of anxiety and social withdrawal.

REGARD CHILDREN'S SOCIAL LIFE AS A NECESSITY, NOT A LUXURY.

Bear in mind how important social skills are. They influence children's feelings about themselves and their academic performance. They influence lifelong susceptibility to depression and anxiety. They contribute at least as much to health as antismoking programs do.

VALUE CHILDREN'S SOCIAL PLAY.

Play is both a source of pleasure and a way children learn. From playing catch to playing house to the teasing of adolescence, playing with peers is crucial to children's social, language, emotional, and cognitive development. In the context of play, children figure out how to exchange information, make sense of the world they have to live in, and develop abilities for coping with it. They learn rules and roles, how to govern themselves, and ultimately how to create their own society. In play they acquire a sense of themselves as effective human beings. It's an arena for acquiring, exercising, and rehearsing many life skills.

All children need to spend time in solitary activities, too. Of concern is not how much time children spend alone but whether children are isolating themselves. Is solitude pursued positively, as an expression of interest in some activity—to read a book, even a series of books, for example? Or is a child avoiding peers, being ignored by them, or being excluded from activity with them?

When children spend large amounts of their time playing by themselves, or in parallel play to others, find out why. Talk to your children. They may be avoiding other children because they feel others do not like them or that they themselves do not know how to make a go of it.

SEE THAT YOUR CHILDREN HAVE UNHURRIED TIME TO PLAY WITH PEERS.

Play should be encouraged for sheer enjoyment, with no agenda or ulterior motive. It counts only if the children themselves, not parents or others, are driving the play and deciding the activities. Encourage your children to have friends visit them at home. Find out who your child likes in class and ask your child to invite a classmate to your home for informal play. Especially in the early years, most socializing in school is done in pairs, and familiarity is important. Pretend play and rough-and-tumble play are both important.

PROVIDE CHILDREN ACCESS TO UNSTRUCTURED ACTIVITIES.

Places like community pools, parks, schoolyards, and libraries afford children opportunities to meet and relate with peers on their own terms, and they are filled with suitable resources. In contrast to more structured community-based activities, such as provided by Boy and Girl Scouts, Little League, and 4-H, unstructured activities demonstrably boost children's social functioning. They stimulate children to come up with their own rules, making demands on social skills and encouraging their development. Children forge coping skills for handling peer situations as they arise, and particularly for making school transitions.

"WASTE" QUALITY TIME WITH YOUR CHILDREN.

Spend time hanging out together in a peerlike way, just for the sake of having fun. Let them realize that there is life beyond information exchange, that interaction doesn't always need an agenda. At the same time they will be getting to play with, and possibly even picking up a new trick or two from, a more advanced social partner (we hope). This isn't a time for criticism or even directives. Just follow your child's ideas.

LET YOUR CHILDREN SEE YOU INTERACTING WITH OTHER PEOPLE.

Children learn what they see their parents do. Be sure you make time for your own social life. Since social skills are born and practiced in face-to-face interactions, regard the family dinner as essential, a boot camp for social behavior.

POLISH YOUR OWN SOCIAL SKILLS.

Children acquire much of their social disposition, particularly their inclination to approach others, through their parents. There is evidence that children who have trouble entering peer groups, one of the most important social skills, often have parents who also lack that ability.

Luxury Versus Necessity

How does ballet class get to be seen as a necessity while social life becomes a luxury? It's in part a perversion of the concept of quality time, a sense that important sequences can be packed into slivers of time. Add the all-American belief in the value of self-improvement, not to mention our notorious puritanical streak, which crops up in the oddest places, hounding us to believe that any form of learning takes precedence over any form of play or pleasure. And since for our children we want only the best, we cram their days with "advantages." Six-year-olds have schedules.

Parents sincerely believe they are improving their children's lives over their own by pushing them harder and sooner than they themselves were pushed—indeed, if they were pushed at all. And therein lies the secret. What they are really feeling is a new sense of inferiority, of insecurity, a feeling no Baby Boomer ever had before, and this sense of inferiority has crept up on them in the wake of exposure to the global village/marketplace. Although their children have been born into the new order, and do not feel dislocated in it or have to make the same adjustment to it as their parents have had to, this same sense of dislocation is *assumed* to exist in their children. Parents honestly believe they are doing well in fortifying their children to be at ease in the new order by cramming their heads and their toe shoes with as much as possible.

But parents are overfocusing on the *content* of childhood experience, when it's the *process* of childhood that also creates successful adults. "With our emphasis on achievement and success," observes Wake Forest University psychologist Mark Leary, "anything that doesn't produce tangible, productive outcomes is a bit suspect. In this view, socializing is something that you do after your productive work is done. It's as if people have to 'earn' the right to socialize. Adults looking at the social lives of young people see not only a lack of productive behavior, but often seemingly counterproductive activities. It's bad enough kids just 'hang out,' but often they're smoking or drinking or watching MTV, none of which seems very important to the unenlightened. What people miss, of course, is that the manifest activity is not the important thing; it's the latent agenda of being included."

Child's play appears to be inefficient. So impromptu. Ad hoc. And by some semantic sleight, what appears *accidental* becomes *incidental*. The inefficient-appearing ways of childhood are sacrificed to the adult value of time.

There are considerable reasons to be concerned about today's children. Primarily, today's kids are bearing enormous psychological stress, some transmitted by their anxious parents, some absorbed inadvertently from their exposure to the media. At the same time they have fewer outlets than children traditionally have had. These children may not grow up with a strong sense of self; they may be the ultimate wimps. They may also be very self-absorbed, with little regard for others.

Another child-watcher who is very concerned is Dr. Per Mjaavatn, head of the Norwegian Institute for Child Research, a remarkable organization devoted not just to research on children around the globe but to studying society from the child's point of view. It is a world leader in setting policies for children. "If you look at society from the children's perspective," he told me, "you get a very different picture of results. You recognize that what is good for children is good for adults. By contrast, what is good for adults is not always good for children."

Because the clearest way to get a picture of a nation is to look at its children, I asked Dr. Mjaavatn what his major concerns are. "The growing institutionalization of childhood," he replied. "The less time children have for free play, the more they lag in social development, and the more they lack the ability to solve conflicts. I see this in Oslo as well as the United States. When you take play time and space away from kids, the less socially competent they will be as adults."

He pauses briefly, then assails what could be considered America's growing empathy deficit, because it's one of our fastest-growing exports. "People are getting less competent with prosocial behavior and empathy. There has been negative change in the ability to feel for others. This is a product of adult behavior. It's an alarm that there's a huge increase in violence among children and between children. Something is completely wrong when they hurt one another; under normal circumstances there should be a mechanism in the head to prevent that."

Under Adult Eyes

Clearly childhood under the constant gaze of adults is a new phenomenon. Just as clearly, there are many contributing elements to this behavior. At least a dozen warrant consideration because they collaborate invisibly in many departments of the culture to erode the time individual parents allocate for their children to play.

- Gradually, parenting is being turned into a **specialty**. Childless marriages now carry far less of a stigma than they once did because parenting has become increasingly a choice among married couples. The fact that many couples are aggressively, vocally childless, or at least unabashedly so, puts subtle pressure on those who choose to raise children to demonstrate some form of expertise. What better way than having the children perform as mini-adults in activities where there are observable, concrete standards?

- Parenthood is also undergoing a degree of **professionalization**. Many are approaching parenthood like a career—or instead of a career but bringing career values to it. Scarcely an issue of a women's magazine gets published without an article showing how high-powered women are dropping out of the work force to raise their kids, but using the lessons learned in their careers to drive parenting—rather than applying lessons of parenting to inform their careers. In this case, women are leading the way, teaching men how to overparent. Men, however, have their own reasons. They grew up realizing that they scarcely knew their fathers and are trying to overcompensate with their own children for what their fathers never were with them—involved.

- The **convergence of male and female roles as parents** amplifies the place of children in stabilizing the household. It shifts the center of family life from adult needs to the children's needs.

- At the same time, the **high cost of having kids**—hospital costs, schooling, family housing, food, Air Jordans—leads people to justify, protect, and tightly monitor their investment.

- Toss into the equation parental, especially maternal, **guilt for working**. Parents feel they must make up to their kids somehow for their own diversion of attention. Guilt may be a good motivator, but it is a lousy teacher.

- Of course, the current generation of parents isn't just any old collection of people. They are highly endowed with **narcissism**, which suffuses their approach to parenting; kids—like all other people—are valued only insofar as they make their parents feel good.

- This is as good a time as any to note that **the idea of perfection** has crept into child-rearing, a realm where it has no rightful place. There is diminished tolerance for normal imperfections and for childhood as time of ambling, seemingly inefficient rehearsal.

- The diversion of interest and energy from the public to the private sector continues apace, and so American adults turn from caring about community to caring about their own households. With smaller families, parents **microattend** to the individual child's needs.

- Many parents today find their own lives highly circumscribed. The increased stresses of work and of juggling work and family life have led to a wide curtailing of **the social life of adults**.

That increases the pressures on parents to meet more of their own social needs through their children. Penn State's Dr. Belsky sees parents of only children often seeking a "best friend" relationship with their child. That, however, typically limits the time children have to do what *they* want. Parents who register their children in activity classes often do it for their own social needs; they serve an important function for adults by selecting out and bringing together affluent parents with at least one common interest.

- At the same time, a great many adults are walking around with overinflated expectations for love and self-realization in marriage. **Unfulfilled romantic yearnings** prompt parents to pour their energy into their children's life for emotional fulfillment. Similarly, any failures at self-realization—whether in career, politics, or intimacy—becomes cause for directing parental energy into offspring. It has the added virtue of seeming utterly selfless.

- Because of the way these things tend to get sloganized, simplified, and portrayed in media imagery, an emphasis on **"family values"** gives rise to the idea that everyone in a household must spend lots of time together to be a family. "Family values," says Norway's Per Mjaavatn, "is really a way of throwing away responsibility for children's welfare from the public to the private sector."

- Similarly, there is a widespread misapplication of the ethos of **individualism**. It is often distorted into the notion that the family exists primarily as a venue for nurturing individuals. Parents believe their job is to pour resources into individual children.

- In some quarters, the growing literature on the nature of parent-infant attachment or **bonding** has been wildly misinterpreted. Parents confuse emotion with glue. A highly educated couple I know refuses to leave their three-year-old daughter with a baby-sitter—and even with the child's grandparents—because they believe that time away from their child will weaken her bond with them. Lost in this misinterpretation is the child's need for a variety of relationships, including her own with grandparents, in order to grow securely.

- Even the "experts" misinterpret or overextend the attachment literature. The prevailing tendency among them is to **over-emphasize the importance of parents** as socializing agents of their children. As a result, they underemphasize the importance of peers.

- Not unrelatedly, the mistaken view has taken hold that **parental love** (or attention) solves all problems, or at the very least prevents them. By this logic, the more attention the better; there is no such thing as too much.

- Some factors have less to do with parental dynamics than economic ones. The economic expansion leading to the growth of the upper-middle class fosters a constant battle to maintain status, which parents then foist on their kids. Children become opportunities for conspicuous consumption and **status displays**. Advertisers promote it.

- Rapid change in the instruments of culture—for example, the introduction of computers—does require greater literal **investment by parents**. And increasing material wealth leads to a surfeit of other instruments and toys in which parents have heavily invested for the sake of the children. But heavy investment still doesn't entitle adults to heavy control of children's activities. Nor is it a substitute for good old warmth.

- The double life of computers as both toy and essential office machine has helped confuse parents about **work and play**, a confusion they transmit to their children. Misled by their own technological queasiness—which they mistakenly believe afflicts their children, although numerous studies show it does not—parents are pushing to make their children fluent with technology at an early age. In the process, kid's play translates as skill-building; toys increasingly are seen as instruments not of play but for learning.

- Widely disseminated reports of kidnapping, sex perverts, and other **bad news** drive parents to overmonitor kids zealously. The steady drumbeat of horrors emanating from the world's bloated media outlets distorts perception of the risks of childhood *au naturel*.

- In a world that feels increasingly out of control—chaos isn't just what happens at rock concerts anymore, it's now an official scientific description of the way *all* things really are—people are desperately trying to reassure themselves that the world is in fact orderly. So they take pains to exert a measure of control. But because their lives are already circumscribed, their **needs for control** disproportionately devolve on the personal sphere, specifically on their bodies. And their children.

- There is abroad in the land an increasing **distrust of the natural** course of things. Its most obvious manifestation is the widespread insistence that the body can't manage food intake on its own—therefore it's necessary to diet. By this logic, parents come to believe that every development of childhood requires active intervention. A recent article in a parenting magazine actually tells parents how to teach their child *how to walk*. It is irrelevant that children have learned how to walk on their own since *Homo erectus* came down from the trees. But with active intervention perhaps your child can be walking . . . earlier than the neighbor's kid. Such articles have a strong surreptitious effect. They make parents feel irresponsible and downright neglectful for having entrusted such a key development as walking—*walking!*—to time and nature. After all, if the baby doesn't walk, he can't learn to skate, and then he'll miss out on hockey lessons!

Bad for the Parents, Bad for the Kids

But hothouse parenting is neither good for the parents nor good for the children. Having no time without adult supervision, children cannot lay claim to their own experience of the world. They grow up with no opportunity to acquire a strong sense of themselves, to build and test the power of their own psyches. They are set up to become wimps. At the same time, they are spoon-fed self-absorption and acquire a distorted sense of their own importance. Gradually, there is a cultural slippage that ensnares everyone; the quality of life and general happiness are diminished through an overfocus on goals, as opposed to the *process* of living.

The results can be seen in alarming increases in all kinds of childhood pathology, especially anxiety disorders and depression, childhood suicide, and so-called oppositional disorders (characterized by general defiance) and attention-deficit disorder. The 1990s witnessed a landmark reversal in traditional patterns of psychological pathology. While rates of depression rise with advancing age in those over forty, they are now increasing fastest among children, striking more children at younger and younger ages. Children are being forced to absorb pressures that adults once felt they had to confine to their more mature world. By itself, giving children the power to determine the family agenda makes pseudoadults of children. It also unrealistically empowers children to make other demands, to engage in power struggles with their parents while at the same time resenting them for placing adult emotional burdens on them.

In his famous studies of how children's temperaments play out, Harvard's Dr. Jerome Kagan has shown unequivocally that what breeds anxious children is parents hovering over them and over-protecting them from stressful experience. About 20 percent of babies are born with a high-strung temperament; these children can be spotted even when they are still in utero—they have higher than normal heart rates. Their nervous systems are innately programmed to be overexcitable in response to stimulation. As infants and children they experience stress in situations most other children find unthreatening, and they may go through childhood and even adulthood fearful of unfamiliar people and events, withdrawn and shy.

While innate infant reactivity seemed to destine all these children for later anxiety disorders, things didn't turn out that way. Kagan found to his surprise that the development of anxiety was scarcely inevitable despite the genetic programming. None of the over-excitable infants wound up fearful at age two—if their parents backed off of hovering, set limits on the children's behavior, and allowed their children to find some comfortable level of accommodation to the *world on their own.*

There is in his studies a lesson for all parents: Parents who allow their children to deal with life's day-to-day stresses by themselves are in fact helping them overcome their inhibition and develop more resiliency and better coping strategies.

CHAPTER THREE

Popularity:
Why It Matters

When I mention the subject of "peers" in adult company, I often get a striking response. People seem to think the peer story begins and ends in adolescence. That it has something to do with hanging out. Maybe smoking. Drinking beer. From the bottle. Reckless driving. And stolen sex. There's a decidedly pejorative flavor to the discussion. I'm not sure where this vision comes from. But a mountain of evidence proves that it's totally off course. The peer story actually begins very early. It used to begin as soon as children set foot in school, around age five. It now begins much earlier, about the age of two or three, or whenever children enter day care or preschool. And as a result, peers are becoming more important in the lives of all children. Intense peer contact starts earlier than before and ends later, as children stay in school for more years than ever before.

Peers exert a gravitational pull on kids from the start. In truth, children never grow in a vacuum. In their earliest years, they grow in relation to their parents and their siblings. Then peer relationships shape people. And they never stop. That turns out to be a very good thing indeed. It's good for the mind and good for the body. In this chapter, I will trace the exact pathways by which peer relationships exert their influence on some crucial facets of development. You may be surprised to discover that, to an astonishing degree, whom a child will hang out with as an adolescent is set long before then, in the play areas and make-believe corners of preschool and kindergarten.

Intellectual Development

Being liked and having friends makes children feel good. Important as that is, there is much more to social competence. Those who subscribe to the view that social life is a luxury and not a necessity—and the time pressures besieging most adults, especially parents, almost force that view—may have trouble swallowing this bulletin from the research front. Yet the fact is, social development is really the cradle of all cognitive development.

A great deal of sophisticated perception and intellectual action takes place in a social context. In picking up the patterns of social responsiveness, children get practice reading both clear and indirect environmental cues; they get practice in reading the nuances of responses in others. They learn the subtleties of what to pay attention to, which verbal and nonverbal behaviors communicate meaning. They get practice accessing many sources of knowledge and memories and experience, exercising multiple brain systems. They get practice in reasoning—testing inferences about the behavior of others, predicting the behavior of others, and in making judgments about how they themselves should act.

Take, for example, empathy, the ultimate prosocial skill, which is both an act of the head and an act of the heart. It requires a high degree of understanding—the cognitive wizardry of assuming another person's perspective, inferring the needs of another. Is it any wonder, then, that the skills that are sharpened in developing social relationships are the basis of all cognitive skills?

OUR BROTHERS' (SCORE)KEEPERS

Relational learning is the first learning. The view that cognitive processes develop via social interaction is in accord with recent recognition that some social skills are present in infants right from the start—their preference for the human voice and face, for example. By age one, says developmental psychologist Judy Dunn, children who grow up in close contact with other children, such as siblings, have remarkable social understanding. She has caught them in the act of sharpening their mental powers at home—by keeping score against their sibs.

Dr. Dunn, who is currently based at Cambridge University but is also affiliated with Penn State University's noted department of Human Development, has pioneered observation of young children in the home doing what they usually do. Looking at children in their natural habitat has proved to her one thing: that previous studies of very young children's abilities—usually done by plucking individual children from the family and bringing them into a research facility that contains specially rigged playrooms, where they play alone or in groups—have "seriously underestimated the nature of young children's social understanding." The subtlety of social intelligence that children display in the family context, she says, has totally changed her view of children's abilities.

Her studies show that toddlers are truly their brothers' (score)keepers. They monitor with exquisite sensitivity how much affection, attention, and discipline their parents lavish on their siblings, and the warmth and pride they show in them. They measure what their sibs get, then compare it against what they get themselves. They perform a calculus of caring. According to Dunn, "Children from the end of the first year are interested in the behavior of other family members, and especially in their emotional exchanges," which is to say, arguments. "Children rarely ignore disputes between others, but act promptly to support or punish one of the antagonists."

The experiences of differential treatment inside the home do more than turn family life into a daily drama for tots. They shape kids' personalities for life. And they prime the intelligence pump.

It's in a child's best interests to understand family members and the social rules of the shared family world. In Dr. Dunn's view of the home as a hotbed of social and emotional comparisons, "from eighteen months on, children understand how to hurt, comfort, and exacerbate their siblings' pain; they understand what is allowed or disapproved in their family world and anticipate the response of adults to their own and other people's misdeeds." Through their social relationships they are figuring out the causes and consequences of emotions and sensing what others are thinking. The children with the shrewdest social sense are the ones who anticipate when a sibling will get attention—and then make attempts to draw attention to themselves. "It takes a lot of skill to do," says Dunn. Of course, young children are often highly motivated; in the daily drama of family life, each one is looking for a starring role.

The presence of siblings, then, is central to children's early development of social intelligence. And differences in the quality of sibling relationships help explain why children vary in social competence and in their ability to understand the causes and consequence of emotions and grasp connections between the beliefs and actions of others.

MATH AND LANGUAGE SKILLS

Most people know that academic achievement tends to be a self-perpetuating phenomenon. That's why they take great pains to see that their children get off to a good start in school. What is scarcely known outside research circles, however, is that as soon as kids enter school, their social standing with peers is related to learning progress and academic competence.

In 1991, Dr. Ross Parke, perhaps America's dean of child researchers, began the long-term Social Development Project at the University of California at Riverside. He and colleagues are following the course of 337 children who started in the kindergartens of nine schools in a nearby community. Each year, each child is interviewed and asked to name three classmates they "like to play with the most" and up to three they "really don't like to play with." By tallying these nominations, the researchers determine the social status of each child: popular, average, rejected, controversial, or neglected.

Each year, the teachers and the students also are asked to assess the behavioral characteristics of the children in the class. The teachers get a checklist of prosocial (good at helping, sharing, and taking turns) and aggressive (starts fight, says mean things) behaviors and rate the degree to which each quality is characteristic of each child. The children are asked to nominate up to three classmates for whom the prosocial and aggressive behaviors are characteristic.

In addition, with parental permission, the researchers collected information on each child's school record in the third grade. They looked both at report-card grades in language and math and at achievement-test scores.

Whether report-card grades or achievement tests are taken as the measure of intellectual performance, the children who were classified as more popular in the second grade were significantly more likely to do better at math and language in the third grade than their rejected peers. Even more striking, the academic performance was also predictable from the children's social standing in kindergarten. *Kindergarten!* The children rated popular in kindergarten got better marks in math and language in the third grade than did their classmates.

No matter how popularity was pulled apart and looked at—whether by behavioral characteristics or measures of liking—social standing and academic scores stuck together. The better liked a child was or the more prosocial the child's behavior, the better the grades. The less a child was liked by peers, the lower his or her math and language grades were. And the more aggressive the child was, the lower the language grades.

"The results thus far present interesting findings," psychologist Mara Walsh, Ph.D., reported at a research symposium in 1997. "It is clear that social status may successfully predict later academic outcomes as early as kindergarten. Those children who were categorized as popular in kindergarten performed significantly better than their rejected peers in language and math report-card grades and math standardized achievement test scores. Those children who are rated as popular by their peers are more successful academically than their rejected peers."

Dr. Walsh does not want to create the impression that social incompetence is the *only* factor that puts a child at risk for later academic difficulties; differences in social standing did not account for *all* the variation in academic performance, just a respectable portion of it. Nevertheless, the evidence indicates that social competence begets academic competence in the early years of school because they share an important underlying cognitive mechanism: Both require mental pyrotechnics. Agility in mental processing is acquired and sharpened in social relationships and, depending on motivational and other factors, gets applied in various other spheres of activity.

It is also true that aggressive and, to a lesser degree, submissive behaviors often evoke a negative response from teachers, who provide less help to such students, possibly depressing both children's grades and their motivation to achieve academically. And for some aggressive children the problem is inability to concentrate, as inattention and disruptiveness undermine both academic and social prowess. Socially incompetent kids mistime social overtures in class and spend more time not concentrating on schoolwork.

BETTER THAN PUSHY PARENTS

Even among Chinese children, those paragons of academic achievement, social competence makes a contribution to intellectual performance over and above the pressure of all those ancestors valuing academic excellence and the power of parents and teachers to invoke shame on those who don't do well. Just because of the powerful push Chinese culture gives to academic achievement, three researchers recently decided that China would be the ideal setting for testing whether social competence makes any contribution at all to school performance when the motivation to achieve academically is exemplary to begin with. The researchers—developmental psychologists Xinyin Chen of the University of Western Ontario in Canada and Kenneth Rubin of the University of Maryland, and Professor Dan Li of Shanghai Teacher's University—followed for two years several hundred children in twenty-one classrooms in Shanghai.

In 1992, 245 fourth-graders and 237 sixth-graders rated the social behavior of their peers—they were asked, for example, to name someone who is a good leader, someone who is popular, disruptive, and so on—and nominated those they most and least liked to be with. Teachers rated the students' school-related competencies and problems. School records provided information on the students' academic performance on objective examinations, specifically in math and in Chinese language, and also information on the children's leadership accomplishments. In 1994, the same kind of information was gathered again.

Just as in Western cultures, children's social competence made a difference. Popular children had higher grades than rejected children in language and math two years later. Of all the social-status groups, rejected children had the lowest grades of all. The researchers believe that acceptance gives children a resource bank—a pool of peers to study with and to call on for help with schoolwork if needed. At the same time, academic success enhances a child's standing with his peers.

"Both the social and intellectual aspects of children's performance are important for school education," the researchers conclude. Because of "the social root of academic difficulties," they suggest that to foster academic achievement, it is *necessary*—their word—to improve children's social functioning. And programs to improve children's social skills should also focus on achievement.

The only difference at all between the Chinese results and studies in Western cultures was in the academic performance of submissive children. In the United States, shyness and submissiveness are not valued; such children are socially rejected by the peer group, often victimized, and in general do poorly in school. In China, by contrast, shyness and submissiveness are positively viewed, and these children achieve scholastically. Their academic success, however, does not have any impact on their social standing.

WHY AGGRESSION IS STUPID

Children who are aggressive have a course in school and afterward that is particularly instructive. For nearly four decades, psychologist Leonard Eron of the Universities of Michigan and Illinois has been tracking hundreds of children in New York's upstate Columbia County since they were eight years old—all the third-graders enrolled in 1960. They have put the children (now middle-aged adults) through batteries and batteries of tests at decade intervals. This is one of those very long-term studies that are extremely rare and quite priceless in the view they afford of what really counts. And social status among childhood peers is one of the things that counts for intellectual functioning in life.

The children who were named by their peers at age eight as most aggressive—"who pushes or shoves," and the like—tend to remain aggressive. Their aggressiveness has an effect on intellectual achievement that lasts as long as the subjects have been tracked so far. Childhood aggression, Dr. Eron found, is a more important contributor to adult intellectual failure than it's given credit for.

In very young children, Dr. Eron believes, academic failure or low I.Q. may well stimulate aggressive responses; such children "do not possess the cognitive skills necessary to learn the more complex nonaggressive social problem-solving skills." But after age eight, aggressive behavior disrupts intellectual achievement—regardless of a young child's I.Q. Aggressive children are just not paying attention to academic learning cues. And even if they were to get something right, they are not likely to be reinforced or rewarded because teachers have an implacably negative attitude toward them, courtesy of their general obstreperous behavior.

School Trajectory

School, as every parent knows, is not just a place to learn reading, writing, and 'rithmetic. Because of the regular exposure to peers, as well as the formal instruction, school becomes a powerful socializing institution, among the most influential in shaping the course of development and the expression of personality over the entire life-span. Peer relations shape a child's trajectory through school.

Not every student completes formal schooling. About 15 percent of students drop out before graduating from high school. Few of them leave because they lack the intellectual capability; most, in fact, have average to above-average intelligence. They drop out even though it drastically limits their job prospects and their earnings potential in the short run and over their lifetime.

WHO DROPS OUT

In every study that has looked at the dropout phenomenon, peer problems loom large. Whether investigators look back at the childhood of those who dropped out or whether they follow forward for years the school course of children who are rejected, peer problems and dropping out are troubled twins of the schoolhouse. The numbers vary, but children who are unpopular with their peers withdraw from school at anywhere from two to seven times the rate of children who are popular with their peers. This is the case among girls as well as boys, whether it's the teachers or the classmates who are providing information about which kids are accepted by their peers and which kids are rejected.

Janis Kupersmidt, Ph.D., a psychologist at the University of North Carolina, looked at the social standing of a group of 112 fifth-graders and how that played out over time. Twenty-four of those fifth-graders were rejected by their classmates, while 27 were rated as popular. Six years later, 30 percent of the rejected children had dropped out, versus 4 percent of the popular kids. What makes her study particularly noteworthy is that academic performance in earlier grades was scrutinized—but could not account for the high dropout rates among those of low social standing. That is, the unpopular kids didn't drop out because they were doing poorly in their schoolwork; they weren't all doing poorly. Over the course of the six years, the rejected children were also more likely than the other children to have to repeat a grade and to become delinquents.

Undoubtedly, facing rejection on a daily basis is an extremely stressful experience for anyone, and particularly a child. No one wants to sit next to you in class; no one wants to walk home with you. Even lunchtime is an agony: Walking into the school cafeteria alone is humiliating, a public declaration of how little you are liked, and then injury is added to insult when no one chooses to sit with you. You may even face acts of more overt hostility—other kids laughing or staring at you as you walk by, or "accidentally" bumping into you and knocking your books to the ground. The stress of repeated daily humiliations may keep a child from concentrating on work at school. All by itself stress disrupts the ability to focus attention and to learn. Then, too, rejected children are not likely to have access to classmates for studying together or answering questions about schoolwork.

But for the vast majority of dropouts, schoolwork is not the issue. It is the fact that the academic milieu is one and the same as the social milieu. Leaving school, as two researchers have put it, simply "represents a flight from something unpleasant." For many adolescents, the social milieu *is* the point of school and exerts school's holding power. Dropping out is "an unambiguous rebuke of the school's academic and social setting."

JUST ONE TIME

Here's the most remarkable thing about being unpopular. Although the psychological impact of rejection is generally greater the more persistent the rejection is, peer hostility doesn't have to be enduring for it to affect negatively some facets of development. Even a single episode of rejection by classmates can have an effect on a child's schooling. In a later study of 622 children followed over the course of four years, Dr. Kupersmidt found that those who experienced peer rejection *just one time* were still absent from school significantly more often than those who never had any brush with peer rejection. Moreover, the absenteeism did not necessarily follow immediately after the rejection incident. Not everyone rebounds from one encounter of rejection. That may be all it takes for some children to feel the school atmosphere so unpleasant they sooner or later start avoiding it by not going.

Peer unpopularity travels closely with poor academic achievement. But it's a very two-way street. Rejection leads to academic stumbling, and academic failure leads to peer unpopularity. Still, there may be another, more indirect route from peer rejection to academic failure. Dr. Kupersmidt's studies highlight absenteeism as a major way that peer rejection lowers academic performance. It leads kids to avoid going to school whenever possible.

Although peer unpopularity creates an unpleasant environment that leads both males and females to drop out of school, it also starts them down more circuitous paths to withdrawing from school as well. Because girls value relationships more than boys do, peer rejection may have a particularly harsh effect on them. Adolescent girls who have few friends are more likely to become pregnant, either because they see a child as a potential source of companionship or because they are more willing to compromise their own standards. A sexual encounter may beckon as a way to break their isolation, ingratiate themselves, and improve their social standing. Among boys particularly, unpopularity and humiliations at the hands of peers may lead to feelings of frustration that find expression in increased aggressiveness, and that aggressiveness may compound their unpopularity.

IT STARTS IN KINDERGARTEN

If peer relations are a potent precursor of later school adjustment, it is reasonable to ask, Just when are the signs of later school adjustment first reliably visible? The answer that science has to offer is a bit shocking: in the peer experiences of kindergartners. When a group of researchers opened up kindergarten doors of schools in three U.S. cities, they found that 12 percent of 585 children were rejected by their classmates. They then tracked the children into first grade and found that 12 percent of kids again were rated unpopular with their peers. However, only about half of those children—7 percent—were rejected in both grades. Still, children who are rejected over a two-year period, researchers know, are *consistently* rejected. The source of the problem is not in a classroom situation but within them; they have adopted a behavioral style they carry with them. (From detailed interviews with the youngsters' mothers and in-home observations of parental behavior, the researchers pinpointed hostile discipline methods as likely contributors to the kindergartners' peer incompetence, particularly among the boys. They are discussed in more detail in Chapter Seven.)

Because early classroom peer relations are a precursor of later school adjustment, Dr. Gary Ladd, an educational psychologist at the University of Illinois at Champaign-Urbana, has been looking very closely into the adjustment to school that kindergartners make. "We ask them about how they feel in school, whether they like it, whether they would rather be someplace else. It's pretty clear that kids feel unhappy in school when they are being victimized, and there is an impulse to get away from that. But what will they make of themselves in the long run? So we are looking early on to stop this kind of experience."

In his studies, he can see that peer relations make a difference to children's school adjustment by the second month of kindergarten. When he studied 125 children just entering kindergarten, then two months later, and again at the end of the year, he found clear effects of social competence. Children who had a larger number of friends *in the classroom* at the beginning of the year had a more positive view of school two months later, and those who were able to maintain their friendships liked school more and more as the year progressed. The more that the children made new friends, the better they did in school over the year, progressing in academic readiness.

Friendship empowers children to cope with the demands of a new environment, Dr. Ladd finds. It is vital to kids at times of transition, such as entering school. And some elements of friendship are particularly helpful. In kindergarten, Dr. Ladd notes, what kids want from other kids is validation, that is, positive feedback and support (affirmation and ego support: Does Jenny tell you that you are good at things you do in class?) Also, to the degree that a friend provides assistance (such as in problematic social situations: If some kids at school were teasing you, would Jenny tell them to stop?), children liked school better as the year progressed. Children, and especially boys, whose peer relations were marked by conflict had a particularly difficult time adjusting to school. They felt lonely and avoided going to school more than other children.

FRIENDS HELP FRIENDS

Friendship fosters school adjustment because, says Ladd, it furnishes resources that "affect the quality of children's emotional life in school. Friends who offer higher levels of personal support or interpersonal aid enhance children's feelings of competence and security at school." And having such good feelings rubs off on the surroundings; they prompt children to form positive views of the environment they arise in. Rejection by peers hinders children's adaptation to school because it is a major stressor at a time when the transition to school poses its own set of challenges.

If there's any surprise to Dr. Ladd's studies, it's that children as young as five are already connoisseurs of friendship. They can make sophisticated judgments about such relationship qualities as companionship, validation, and exclusivity. Although what five-year-olds want or need out of friendship is different from what twelve-year-olds need (see Chapter Four), they still have a clear-eyed view of their own friendships. And what they get out of friendship influences their adjustment to school.

Good-quality friendships help children all the way through school by serving as a problem-solving resource. When ten-year-olds were monitored while writing stories collaboratively on a computer, those who worked with friends performed better in many ways. Although it might be assumed that they would talk more, they didn't; what talk they had focused more on the task, more on the content of the story, and more on the vocabulary they would use than did the talk between nonfriends working together. Friends posed alternative suggestions and elaborated on them more often than nonfriends. They truly collaborated. The upshot was, they wrote better stories, particularly because language use took a big leap forward.

POINTERS FOR PARENTS

TEACH, MODEL, AND VALUE PROSOCIAL BEHAVIOR.
The single most outstanding feature of socially competent kids is their proclivity to engage in prosocial behavior.

- Cooperate.
- Share things.
- Offer toys to other children.
- Help another with problems.
- Make your child aware of the feelings of others: When upsets occur to others, take the time to ask, "How do you suppose he feels when that happens?"

FOSTER YOUR CHILD'S VERBAL SKILLS.
In the dynamics of development, effects become causes and causes effects. That helps explain why social competence both hinges on verbal ability and kindles verbal fluency.

- Even before they can talk to you, talk to your children. They won't understand what you say, but they will acquire the fundamental rhythm of conversation.
- Then, when they start talking, engage them in conversation frequently. From these interactions children effortlessly pick up how to approach others and initiate conversations themselves. Social interaction will seem like the most natural thing in the world.
- Verbal fluency encompasses more than the art of conversation. It requires the ability to label and describe feelings and experiences. Name objects in the environment as you encounter them. Children come to understand that experience can be described.

TEACH YOUR CHILD HOW TO DEAL WITH SOCIAL FAILURE.

Everyone's best efforts at acceptance will sometimes be rejected. Rebuffs are a fact of life for even the socially popular. As a matter of general principle, adults make a huge contribution to children's social (and general) confidence by helping them cope with reversals and rebuffs.

- **Defenses.** Social rebuffs often arouse defenses. Some children blame others for their failures, believe their peers are deliberately trying to harm them, and so, feeling they have little control over their own social efforts, seek to get back at their peers; they focus on their own needs and endorse aggression as a way of saving face. But that, of course, only leads to generalized dislike by their peers.

  Other children blame themselves; they attribute any failure to enduring internal causes (I'm unlikable, I'm just no good at making friends), which make them feel helpless; they walk away as if nothing happened. To avoid additional painful contact with peers, they withdraw, and carve for themselves a life of social isolation.

- **Attributions.** Children should be encouraged to attribute setbacks to lack of effort—"I need to try harder"—and to pursue prosocial goals.

- **Hurt feelings.** It is crucial to acknowledge and respect children's negative feelings ("I know you feel disappointed . . .").

- **Trying again.** It is at least equally crucial to encourage them to try again (". . . but I'm sure you'll have another chance tomorrow").

- **Counterproposals.** Studies show that when faced with failure, children who are well liked by peers respond by saying things like, "Well, can I play next time?" They turn a negative response into a counterproposal.

- **Resilience.** Well-liked children don't blame others or themselves; they don't engage any defenses—they put all their energy back into the process of play. Children who know that rebuffs are expectable, and who believe that failure is remediable, that it results from lack of effort rather than inadequacies or lack of ability, are not debilitated by setbacks. They are resilient. They are motivated to try again so they can get better at it, and they focus on maintaining contact with their peers. They persist, but not intrusively.

NIP TROUBLE EARLY.

Children who are disliked by their peers tend to develop social problems early. Due to the self-perpetuating nature of social problems, peer difficulties make it progressively harder for children to learn the social skills they will need for future relationships. Besides, rejected children tend to become more defensive as they get older, making them less open to change.

- Problems that develop in preschool bear very close watching.
- But don't pounce on every social upset.
- Use rebuffs and difficulties as opportunities for encouraging children to try harder and coaching them how to do it. Your children need experience handling the reversals of everyday social life—that builds confidence, too.
- But do be on the watch for *persistent* or *chronic* problems with friendlessness, shyness, victimization, manipulativeness, or, especially, overt aggression.

Mental Health

Peers count for more than fun and excitement and motivation for going to school; they are the architects of each other's general adjustment and psychological well-being. For years, researchers have been accumulating evidence that children who have problems getting along with their peers are at risk for serious emotional problems later in life. In one study, how a child was viewed by peers from first to third grade proved to be a better predictor of mental-health problems eleven years later—better than I.Q., school achievement, teachers' ratings, nurses' ratings, personality test scores, or absenteeism.

LONELINESS IS THE LINK

Even when young, children who have friendship problems must deal with the ache of loneliness. That seems to be what places them at high risk for "internalizing" disorders, conditions of psychological distress such as depression, anxiety, and deeply negative self-views.

Make no mistake about it, children experience loneliness much as adults do. Psychologist Steven R. Asher, of the University of Illinois, is a kind of bard of loneliness. For over a decade, he has been interviewing children, listening to their accounts of inner emptiness, and writing about it in scientific journals. He is particularly struck by the degree to which elementary-school children can feel the full emotional pain of loneliness. They describe themselves as "feeling unneeded," "you feel like you're an outsider," or, as one child captured the penetrating desolation, "like you're the only one on the moon." They know what is missing, like companionship ("having no one around you can do things with"), emotional support ("no one to share your private thoughts with"), and affection ("without anybody to love you"). And they know what kinds of situations give rise to loneliness, such as moves, being ignored, being rejected. Even kindergartners understand loneliness and paint it as a feeling of sadness and aloneness.

Most children experience loneliness at some point in their lives. But it is usually a very temporary experience imposed by a specific set of circumstances, such as a move, entry into a new school, or the beginning of summer camp. When he was eight, my son Gabe returned for his second year to summer camp in Massachusetts, which he had very much enjoyed the year before. Within a week of his departure, the following letter arrived:

> Dear mom
> sum times camp is not wat you think it is like.
> Sum times kidds hate me. I am very home sick.
> evry nite I cry because I am home sick.
> Otherwise I am fine.
>   Love Gabe
>   p.s. hear is a pikcher
>   of me at nite.

The picture showed a little person with a big round face in bed with tears falling from his eyes. I cried and I laughed as I read the letter. Gabe's loneliness stabbed me. I could laugh only because I had eight years' knowledge that Gabe was truly a well-liked child and a hunch that the queasiness was a momentary blip, that he was probably having a grand old time even as I was reading otherwise. That little sketch was so touching—it unerringly captured Gabe's mop top and almond eyes, complete with tears. Oh, that spelling! Then there was the hilariously swift turnabout—otherwise I am fine—from the excruciating to the reassuringly mundane in a single breath. Of course, I called the camp just to make sure. I saved the letter, had it framed, and hung it on my bedroom wall. Gabe is now grown. The bittersweetness still pinches every time I read it.

To an unpopular child, there is no "otherwise." Children who are consistently rejected by their peers feel enduringly, deeply lonely. They are at least twice as lonely as popular children, and significantly lonelier than children of all other social-status groups. Rejected children really suffer two tiers of loneliness and disconnection, one that's diffuse but pervasive, the other more intense. Actively disliked by their peer group, they swim in a big sea of negativity and alienation. Others deliberately avoid them. Purgatory. But they also have few friends in school and lack close companionship. And that turns out to be a special kind of hell.

The two rungs of rejection have extremely destructive effects on the way children learn to see themselves. To navigate in a sea of hostility is treacherous enough. But to lack a close friend is to be minus the very thing that for children serves as a major source of ego support and enhancement. That is one of the primary functions of friendship; a friend is someone who values and encourages you. Children who are rejected by their peers and who lack close friendships not only get a double dose of loneliness and the stress of rejection, they have no way out of negative feelings about themselves. That may make depression virtually inescapable, particularly when it coincides with a self-blaming view of social failure and hopelessness about changing their social standing. The sad part is that rejected children establish a pattern of internalizing the negative views others hold of them. The tragedy is that the tendency to internalization becomes entrenched over time in the face of continued negative peer experiences.

SUBMISSIVE-REJECTED CHILDREN

One of the most curious features about unpopular children is that those who are rejected because they are submissive have a very clear-headed view of themselves. They are quite accurate in estimating their social rejection and are keenly aware of how little they are liked. By the time they are in the fourth grade, nine years old, they already expect that other children will put them on the "least liked" list (although they get even more negative nominations than they expect). These children put up few psychological barriers to negative feedback about themselves. They are, in a word, *nondefensive*. They do not shield themselves from reports of peer dislike. One reason they are widely disliked and frequently victimized is that they are extremely unassertive; they don't stand up for themselves to peers. But the deeper truth is that they don't stand up for themselves *to themselves*.

Indeed, one of the hallmarks of clinical depression in adults is the ability of those who get depressed to take in unpleasant feedback about themselves pretty much unblinkingly; the rest of us, by contrast, do backflips and otherwise contort harsh truths so as to maintain a positive view of ourselves. Researchers now have evidence that depressive adults don't merely accept negative feedback from others, *they go out of their way to elicit it*—by behaving badly, by not meeting the expectations of others—in order to *maintain* a negative view of themselves. They seek self-confirming feedback.

For many submissive-rejected children, the path to an internalizing style of interaction is more constitutional. They are born with a so-called inhibited or anxious temperament; as a way of coping with a highly reactive nervous system, they withdraw from new and unfamiliar situations. In short, they are shy. All animals are built to be on guard in new environments; it's a survival mechanism. But shyness, experts now say, is a fear response to novel environments that becomes overgeneralized to all social situations. The shy and withdrawn have a head start on vulnerability to anxiety and depression. They don't have to internalize negative views others hold of them; they generate those views all by themselves. The shy, it turns out, are consumed by the worry that they will make all kinds of blunders and the fear that others are constantly evaluating them negatively. That is why they go out of their way to avoid social interaction when they can. (But even biology isn't destiny, and an anxious temperament can be overcome; parents are the crucial link in whether an anxious temperament is transformed into the inhibited behavioral style that sets children up for victimization. See Chapter Six.)

Studies of submissive-rejected children show that they are significantly lonelier than aggressive-rejected children. And they express more dissatisfaction and distress with their social status. They may forge yet another route to depression via the way they attribute blame and praise for their social successes and failures, and of course they experience mainly failures. In now-classic studies of learned helplessness as a path to depression, the role of explanatory style stands out. Lonely and depressed adults consistently ascribe success to causes that are outside their control and circumstantial in nature; they attribute failures to causes that are not only inside themselves but are enduring and unfixable: "Nobody likes me because I am unlovable." Researchers have now shown that children who are not popular with their peers make similar interpretations of their experiences. They blame themselves—not circumstances, not lack of skills, but their very being. And the more they blame themselves, the lonelier they are.

AGGRESSIVE-REJECTED CHILDREN

Aggressive-rejected children, on the other hand, report less extreme feelings of loneliness—at least at first. A large body of evidence suggests that's because they incorrectly interpret the social signals of others and overestimate their own competence. In a clever set of studies, researchers at Duke University recently showed that aggressive-rejected kids are perfectly capable of sensing and even calibrating degrees of social rejection—when it's other kids who are being rejected. They simply can't read cues of rejection when the negative feedback is directed at themselves. Which is to say, they mentally handle evidence of peer dislike in a highly self-protective way. This ego-defensiveness helps them maintain a pretty positive view of themselves: Any problems they have are due to the hostile intentions of others. Simply, they are unaware of how little they are liked. It is a great protective device that keeps them—in the short run—from feeling lonely and isolated.

Unfortunately, what works for them in the short run exacts a high cost; it subverts them in the long run. Their strategy of denial fools them into thinking they are okay the way they are. In short, it perpetuates their aggressive behavior. But continuing aggressive behavior sets off a vicious downward spiral that lands them in adulthood with a multitude of problems, including depression. Continued aggression lowers their social status and progressively marginalizes them because it increasingly contrasts with what their peers are doing. They may hang out with a few other aggressive kids, but they weave an outcast life of antisocial behavior with a high risk of delinquency and even trouble with the law. As they deploy their aggressive behavioral style and stance, their classmates are not standing still; rather, they are growing toward far more sophisticated ways of managing social interaction through languages—body and verbal. Aggression becomes less and less acceptable. The gulf between the groups widens. For the aggressive kids, the pool of potential cronies shrinks, and they often hang out with younger and younger kids—wannabes—those who might still be impressed by tough behavior. One danger of such age imbalance is that it can provide aggressive kids with ample opportunity to solidify techniques of dominance and control.

By adolescence, aggressive kids not only are locked into externalizing patterns of interaction, blaming others for their difficulties, they are largely locked out of close friendships. Fewer than one in five has anything resembling a really close friend—just when both boys and girls take a great leap toward intimacy in their friendships and romances. The aggressive-rejected kids are now not only further and further behind, but further and further estranged. They have no peer source of ego support (unless, of course, they hook up together and form a gang). They begin developing internalizing problems as well. And as adults, they are heavy users of mental-health services of all kinds.

One way the ego-defense mechanism of aggressive-rejected kids works is to lead them to deny altogether their own feelings of sadness and loneliness, the importance of friends, and the value of attachments in general. Jennifer T. Parkhurst, Ph.D., an educational psychologist at the University of Nebraska, recounts a response she got when administering a questionnaire to students. The questions were aimed at probing how upset they would feel about various kinds of events, including losing a friend. One eighth-grade student blurted out in class, "What a stupid question. Big deal if you lose a friend. Anybody who gets upset if they lose a friend is really dumb. You just make another one."

Lack of acceptance by peers, lack of a source of self-support, a sense of isolation, an acute sense of peer incompetence—each element delivers its own blows to a sense of self. Researchers now believe that these feelings combine in distinct ways in rejected children—depending on gender, temperament, and probably other factors, too—expanding and generalizing their negative self-perceptions from the social realm to other spheres of the self. This spreading stain on the core sense of self deepens and darkens as rejection endures. Children who year after year have no friends to confide in may experience the most extreme forms of loneliness and feelings of worthlessness. The intensely felt lack of support as a child goes a long way to creating a lifelong vulnerability to depression.

WITH FRIENDS LIKE THIS . . .

Even generally rejected elementary-school children, who are widely disliked by the peer group, may be saved from extreme feelings of loneliness and devastation to their self-worth if they have just one mutual friendship in class. In reality, however, few of them do; in one study, only 20 percent of unpopular children, far more of them girls than boys, had a best friend. And then, not just any friendship will do.

All children expect a friend to provide validation and caring, to offer help and guidance, to minimize conflicts, to exchange intimacies, and to be loyal. In the very best friendships, children also have a safe place to explore their fears and their fantasies. But unpopular children, alas, tend to have friendships that are unreciprocated and inadequate, lacking in one or more major relationship features. In one study of nearly 227 children, only 77 percent of unpopular children had at least one reciprocal friend—compared with 98 percent of popular kids. But their friendships are often laden with conflict, they get little help and guidance, little self-validation and few signs of caring, and they sometimes face deep betrayals. Most typically, the friendships they form are with children who don't have the sharpest social skills, those who are also poorly accepted or, at most, of average popularity. To the degree that children have a "best friend" who fails on any count, they are still likely to feel considerable loneliness. In fact, like rejected children without friends, children with poor-quality friends experience both tiers of loneliness—the loneliness that comes from not feeling a part of the general peer community, and the loneliness that comes from having no friendships at all.

NEGLECTED CHILDREN

Neglected children do not report feeling especially lonely. After all, children who are neglected at one point or in one context during their school years do not necessarily remain neglected. Yet the experience of neglect contains elements that render it particularly damaging to some children and may jeopardize their future mental health. In one important study, neglected girls were twice as prone as rejected girls to report later feelings of depression. The study took pains to measure symptoms of depression when the children were in the fourth to sixth grades, two years after social status was calculated; these were not fleeting feelings. Popular girls were the least likely to report feelings of depression (only 3 percent of them did), while 12 percent of rejected girls and a whopping 27 percent of neglected girls did. The researchers concluded that peer rejection sets children up for a range of problems of which depression is but one, and though neglected girls may be spared other adjustment difficulties, the lack of same-aged school friendships creates a specific risk for depression. After all, one of the most powerful functions of close friendships is to provide validation and bolster the sense of self-worth. Not to get it puts a child in jeopardy.

Why only neglected *girls*? Numerous studies have shown that close friendships are valued more highly by girls than by boys. The failure to get support and validation may be a more deeply negative experience and have a disproportionately self-depleting effect on girls, even if they are not generally disliked by their peer group. Then, too, neglected children do not feel socially competent. That may not only compound the wound to self-esteem but also lead them to depression by making them feel helpless, incapable of ever getting the support and companionship most of them desperately desire.

The arithmetic is simple. One high-quality close friendship may be all it takes to buffer a child from feelings of loneliness. And that is crucial because loneliness creates the vulnerability for depression. A single good friendship, then, could be looked on as *minimum* standard of social competence. Some researchers contend that it is also an index of *maximum* social competence because it embraces all the social skills a child needs for sustaining relationships with other less intimate peers.

Whether a single high-quality friendship is the floor or the ceiling, there are many ways parents currently influence their children's social ability; they are detailed in Chapter Seven. And the many steps parents can take to help their children achieve any level of social competence are highlighted in Pointers for Parents in each chapter, as well as the bulk of Chapter Eight.

Reality Check

Loneliness is not only the midwife of depression, it is the handmaiden of paranoia. The ability to maintain social ties is crucial also in fostering accurate self-perception and keeping people sane. Social relationships provide a reality check. They keep our ideas from running away with themselves. In the absence of people with whom they can share feelings and fears, isolated people allow their fears to fester or even escalate, explains Stanford University's Dr. Zimbardo. What's more, they are prone to paranoia; there's no one around to correct their faulty thinking, no checks and balances on their beliefs, no one to keep them grounded in reality. ''We all need someone to tell us when our thinking is irrational, that there is no Mafia in suburban Ohio, that no one is out to get you, that you've just hit a spate of bad luck,'' he says. When children are not accepted, when they are outside these major sources of socialization and support, they likely spin lines of thought and weave webs of behavior that are more and more idiosyncratic.

Social Progress

Social competence is like a dance to music that never stops. It's forever turning, turning, evolving. What children need in their relationships, and therefore what counts as social competence, at age two is
already outdated by age five. And what children need at seven will
no longer suffice at ten. As children grow and develop in complexity,
so must their social abilities. The way children pick up the beat is by
working the steps out with their peers. Children who are rejected not
only are denied admission to the dance hall, they miss out on a major
developmental process that is hard to pick up later. They are deprived
of future learning opportunities with peers.

Once children enter the world of peers, continuing social acceptance is essential for progress in social and even general development.
Peer acceptance is the cocoon in which children acquire all the social
skills that will serve them for a lifetime. Here is where they gain
experience in cooperation and sharing, gain resourcefulness in initiating social activities, the *sine qua non* of social interaction. Here is
where they learn and practice how to solve problems and handle
conflict, not only a skill essential for maintaining all relationships but
perhaps the single most important skill in sustaining later intimate
relationships. Children who are excluded from peer interaction at any
age, and most especially at an early age, lose out on opportunities to
learn and rehearse ever more sophisticated social skills. Rejection impairs development.

Gradually, scientists in general, psychologists in particular, and
even hard-nosed biologists are rethinking the view that our genes are
the be-all and end-all of development, dictating our health, our talents, and personalities as well as our hair color. There is a move toward
a new, far more complex and dynamic view of human development.
"A gene makes a protein and that's about it," biologist Brian Good-
win told *The New York Times* recently, in an article headlined, SOME
BIOLOGISTS ASK "ARE GENES EVERYTHING?" "It doesn't tell you
how proteins interact, how cells and tissues communicate . . . how an
immune system forms, or how evolution works." Note the words
interact and *communicate*. Individuals take shape at least as much from
the context they grow in as from innate endowment, the chromo-

somes contained in every cell. Personality is not neatly wrapped up in a packet of DNA but emerges from the ongoing interaction of an individual with situations and with others around him or her.

If adults have even a vague notion of human development at all, it probably includes the view that each child is a more or less self-contained little creature who, with the blessing of good genes and pushed off by good parenting, sets forth on an individual voyage of discovery of the world. By powers arising strictly from within, the child figures out the meaning of things, and a child's broadening reach in the world is a splendid measure of individual achievement. But that doesn't even begin to capture the emerging picture of things.

Much as we need an individual focus to understand ourselves, we also need a contextual focus, one that takes into account the relationships we are embedded in. "Human development is basically a social process," says Dr. Mette Gulbrandsen of the University of Oslo's Institute of Psychology, who is studying girls' friendships. That means that "the child is *constituted as an individual* through the interactional processes she is engaged in." [The emphasis is Dr. Gulbrandsen's own.]

EVERYDAY MIRACLES

In her studies, Dr. Gulbrandsen gets a very detailed picture of social networks by talking to children about their daily life and recording those conversations. Development, she takes pains to point out, is not something that happens in the abstract. "It is going on in everyday life."

Dr. Gulbrandsen found that while best-friendships can, to the untrained eye, look like tightly closed and highly restrictive relationships, a great variety of social experimentation and learning is really going on, even among young children. She cites the example of Heather and Helen, who were best friends since they met as toddlers in kindergarten. Now, at ages eight and nine, respectively, they went to school together almost every day, were in the same class, met during breaks, and played together in their neighborhood after school. Sometimes just the two of them played, but often they joined larger groups of kids. Both quite athletic, they were even welcomed as fellow players by older boys in the nearby football field. As with Heather and Helen, most private friendships serve as a launching platform for entering larger social galaxies and gaining experience with a diversity of peer groupings and ways of deciding on activities.

From a close-up look at Alexandra, whose exclusive allegiance shifted from Paula to Maria during the course of her study, Dr. Gulbrandsen came to see how even the most intimate of friendships is not claustrophobically confining but fosters remarkably broad understanding of social rules and diversified social intelligence. "Especially among girls," she said, "there is lots of discussion and reasoning within the friendships of the social meaning of their actions. They are always trying out how to do things." Alexandra gained know-how in exploring the opinions of others, developing strategies for dealing with conflicting interests, promoting her own ideas, making joint decisions, and negotiating common solutions.

"When I asked," said Dr. Gulbrandsen, "Alexandra explained the breakup with Paula by Paula's stubbornness. 'She was always the one to decide,' Alexandra said. With Maria it was quite different. 'We became friends the first time we played together.' When I asked how she and Maria decided what to do or where to go, Alexandra said that they just came to an agreement. 'We always want to do the same things.' However, exploring her stories further, I came to see several strategies of negotiating and developing common ideas about what to do." There were straight solutions, like giving priority to Maria's wishes first and Alexandra's afterward—a "one to you" and "one to me" principle. There were games designed to produce a decision, like drawing lots or "zero–fifty–one hundred." In this game, one of the girls proposed an activity and the other would answer "zero" if she completely disagreed, "fifty" for maybe, and "one hundred" for complete agreement. "This was a way of signaling your opinion without really pushing it," says Dr. Gulbrandsen.

All told, Alexandra and Maria, like the other girls she interviewed, had created "informal well-balanced strategies of influence" in their best-friendships. But they also talked about interactions with peers based on other principles of decision-making. There were rules to be followed in skipping rope, playing hopscotch, or even football with the boys. They joined loosely knit groups for skating and skateboarding. "The girls talked about quite varied forms of social activities and relationships," says Dr. Gulbrandsen. "They obviously gained experience with several forms of social organizations. But the most intimate best-friendships provided an arena where social sensitivity and advanced strategies of negotiations were developed and refined."

DUOS OF DEVIANCE

The effects of friendships and peers, of course, are not automatically positive. Exhibit A could well be the story of Christian Oberender. On February 16, 1995, in the dead of Minnesota winter, Christian, then fourteen, along with his best friend, Donald First, also fourteen, ambushed and killed his mother—in the family room of the Oberender home—then took off in her red Taurus station wagon. According to newspaper reports, Christian had been "difficult" for a long time, and had numerous learning difficulties. Within the past year, he and a stepbrother got into trouble; they not only took the family car without permission but wrecked it. He allegedly carried a gun. In school, Christian was lonely and disliked, the frequent butt of teasing. "He'd get pushed around," a peer said. "He couldn't really help himself. He was kind of skinny." Although his mother openly considered her son "difficult," she had an "excellent" relationship with her daughter. His father was an upstanding member of the local school board.

Christian, it was said, had no friends. And indeed, troubled children are more likely than others to be friendless. But Dr. Willard W. Hartup of the University of Minnesota Institute of Child Development takes pains to point out that he actually had two friends. The one with whom he committed the murder, says Hartup, was another troublesome child. The two considered each other "the best of friends" and spent a great deal of time together. They admitted to planning the ambush, and were armed and waiting when Christian's mother came home from work. "One conclusion seems relatively certain," Dr. Hartup said in a 1995 presidential address to the Society for Research in Child Development; "this murder was an unlikely event until these two antisocial friends reached consensus about doing it."

Friendship is generally a good thing. Cooperative, friendly—that is, popular—children, have a wide array of choices for friends. Rejected or aggressive children have a more restricted pool to choose from. When troubled kids have friends, they are often also troublesome children. Truth is, all children become similar to their friends by interacting with them—what psychologists call "mutual socialization." Ordinary children model acceptable behavior for their friends and at the same time get reinforcement from them. When antisocial friends get together, their undesirable behavior escalates. They become more deviant over time. Even in laboratory settings where they are being videotaped, antisocial kids engage in "deviant talk" with their friends, and they manage their differences by using coercion with one another. Ordinary kids may freely criticize and engage in persuasion with their friends, but they rarely strong-arm them.

The moral of the story, says Dr. Hartup, is that troubled children may get a kind of emotional support from hanging around with one another, but it isn't positive and it doesn't foster development. That's the thing about friendship: It both reveals and promotes children's social understanding. Positive support in friendship bolsters popularity, school involvement, achievement, self-esteem—in short, it is the springboard to further growth. Having friends isn't good enough; it matters that the friends also have some social skills.

Life and Health Insurance

In the long run, the ability to maintain social ties is probably the best kind of life and health insurance. This has already become part of the wisdom of the culture. Medical studies tell us that having friends, even animal ones, improves physical health among the sick, the disabled, and the elderly. For example, older men who lose their wives, whether through death or divorce, do not live as long as other men; they lose not merely the attention, companionship, and cooking of their life partner but the whole social network she tended to be responsible for maintaining (given the traditional division of roles).

Reams of new research show that social ties have the power to affect our biology. Loneliness and social isolation—or, most astoundingly, just the *implied threat* of social rejection—lead to physical as well as mental decline, even hastened death. Virtually all the work has been done with adults. But there's every reason to believe that children's bodies respond the same way. Consider just a smattering of the evidence:

- Researchers at Ohio State University gathered ninety newlywed couples still in a state of marital bliss. Each set of partners was asked to resolve an issue—any issue—on which they didn't quite see eye to eye. The nature of conflict is such that the videotapes captured many individuals defending themselves by directing sarcasm or nastiness toward the spouse, or being dismissive. The more partners resorted to such tactics, the more compromised was the immune system of both parties, specifically the activity of the natural killer cells (T lymphocytes) that normally ward off viruses and tumors.
- Women diagnosed with recurrent breast cancer started meeting once a week in groups of eight to share their fears, their tears, and advice for coping with a terminal illness. Forty months later, a third of them were still alive and talking, a Stanford University psychiatrist found. By contrast, among women who received the same anticancer agents but were not assigned to a discussion group, there was not a single survivor.
- A group of 276 men and women underwent medical tests in a Pittsburgh hospital that certified them as healthy. Then they were given nose drops containing one of nature's great nuisances, the common-cold virus, technically called rhinovirus. The ability to resist infection turned out to depend most closely on the extent of ties to friends, family, work, and community. With astonishing precision, the more diverse people's social network, the fewer the colds.

THE BODY HAS ARMS

These findings provide growing proof of what John Donne observed in 1623—"No man is an island, entire of itself." Today, scientists would amend the statement to "No *person* is an island." But otherwise they'd agree wholeheartedly. In fact, they're busy working out the details. A whole new wave of studies is demonstrating the physical power of social connections. They are recognizing that we are built for relationships; the body doesn't function correctly when they are absent or in any way undermined. We are so structured for sociability that when we don't get it, our bodies begin to fall apart. In short, not only does the body have a head, the body has arms.

"What's normal is that we are socially connected," says James Pennebaker, Ph.D., professor of psychology at the University of Texas. "We see this from infancy all the way through life. The infant is socially connected to the parents. When this social fabric is threatened or weakened, it's massively stressful. The body reacts with changes in immune function, hormone function, cardiovascular activity. There's an increase in the probability of illness."

Loneliness is downright lethal. In fact, University of Michigan sociologist James House, Ph.D., has estimated that the lack of social relationships constitutes a major health risk "rivaling the effects of well-established risk factors such as cigarette smoking, blood pressure, blood lipids, obesity, and physical activity." Socially isolated persons have two to five times the overall risk of dying as do persons who maintain supportive relationships. Women who lack supportive, confiding relationships are three times more likely to have complications during pregnancy.

The news from the lab is that it isn't just the presence or absence of relationships that matters; the quality of a relationship deeply registers in our physiology. Having a spouse or a friend is good for you to the extent that you get positive indications of caring.

And when you don't, the body reacts as if it is, in the words of Dr. John Gottman, on the cusp of catastrophe. Professor of psychology at the University of Washington, Dr. Gottman describes the massive stress of loneliness—and especially being lonely *in* a relationship— as kicking off diffuse physiological arousal that wears down multiple systems. On the one hand, he says, the feelings of helplessness and loss activate the neuroendocrine system to produce cortisol, the well-known stress hormone that prepares the body to fight or flee. On the other hand, feelings of anger stir up the stress hormone adrenaline, which sends the cardiac system into overdrive.

Scientists have known for some time that social behavior can affect the endocrine system and its many hormones. In the 1980s, researchers discovered that women who frequently interact, such as college roommates, experience a synchronization of their menstrual cycles. What then looked like a quirk of physiology now appears to be a general principle.

IMMUNITY IN COMMUNITY

While scientists are working out the intricacies of exactly how social relationships affect the body, most of the evidence gathered so far chronicles the damaging effects of negative social interactions. Janice Kiecolt-Glaser, Ph.D., professor of psychiatry and psychology at Ohio State University, has been counting the ways.

In her earliest studies, she found that couples suffer rapid rises in blood pressure when contempt, or hostility, surreptitiously creeps into their attempts to resolve everyday conflicts. In later studies, including the one of newlyweds, she has pinpointed weakening of immune response and disarray in the neuroendocrine system. Dr. Kiecolt-Glaser now focuses on the immune system, but the same stress-related neuroendocrine changes that disrupt immunity also drive cardio-vascular hyperactivity, implicated in heart disease. The endocrine system, she says, is ''an important gateway'' for relationships to affect health.

Strikingly, the newlyweds' rosy descriptions of their marriages suggested they were totally *unaware* they were engaging in any of the negative behaviors captured on videotape—and in the test tube. Still, the signs of physical deterioration set in quickly. All it takes is six to twelve minutes of stressful conflict.

What's more, older couples in longer-term happy marriages experience similar vicissitudes of physiology when their arguments involve negative behavior toward each other. People do not grow any more used to hostility over time.

Rapid and fleeting as many of the immune and endocrine changes are, some are also quite enduring. In one set of studies, Dr. Kiecolt-Glaser found that relationship stress dramatically prolongs wound healing. The researcher carried out a punch biopsy, which created a wound the size of a pencil eraser, among a group of people who were providing care to a spouse or parent with progressive dementia. Among those in conflicted caregiving relationships, it took forty-five days for the wound to close, versus thirty-seven in the others. When trouble in a relationship becomes chronic, so does the disturbance in body processes.

If health hinges on the quality of our relationships, it also depends on the size of our social universe. Dr. Sheldon Cohen, a psychologist at Pittsburgh's Carnegie Mellon University, recently reported on a study in which he deliberately exposed volunteers to the common-cold virus. He calculated a social network index assessing each subject's participation in twelve types of social relationships—with spouse, parent, in-laws, children or other close family members, neighbors, friends, workmates, schoolmates, fellow volunteers, members of social groups, and members of religious groups. For a relationship to count, subjects had to speak to a person, face to face or by phone, at least once every two weeks.

"People who participate in more types of social relationships have less susceptibility to rhinovirus-induced colds," Dr. Cohen found. "This association is graded, although the risk is greatest among those with the fewest types of relationships."

It's not yet clear why diversity of social relationships should prove so important. Having different types of social roles "may influence people's self-concepts and their feelings of control and self-esteem," says Dr. Cohen. Maybe that minimizes the impact of problems elsewhere, such as at work or at home. "When people have less diverse networks, they suffer a much greater threat to their self-concept if something happens in that fairly constrained network."

Dr. Kiecolt-Glaser studies marital conflict precisely because marriage usually *is* the central social relationship in adults' lives. "In many ways it blocks access to other relationships," she observes. "And if it's a bad relationship it's a major stressor. So in place of support you have stress, plus impaired ability to go look for other folks."

WHAT'S IN A SNEER?

Why is relationship conflict so harmful even when it's just in the very subtle form of sarcasm or a sneer? Perhaps when we dish out contempt to a social partner, all that negativity suggests something far worse—that just waiting in the wings is out-and-out rejection. And people may be especially vulnerable in what is likely the most central relationship in their lives. The evidence indicates that rather than contempt, we need social partners who regularly communicate *acceptance*. This seems to be the case particularly when one or the other person is dishing out unsettling information, which is what marital arguments are all about in the first place ("Can't you remember anything? You didn't take the garbage out—again").

Another kind of unsettling information is involved in the disclosure of troubling thoughts. Confiding is an important component of friendship and all by itself it turns out to be hugely powerful emotionally and physically. For several years, Texas's Dr. Pennebaker has been studying people's need to disclose disturbing thoughts. He has found that it is essential for healing all kinds of trauma. Writing about painful experiences is helpful, he finds. Talking about them is even better—provided that the listener is nonjudgmental and accepting. *Accepting,* opposite of *rejecting.* That, of course, if the very definition of a friend: someone you can trust enough to confide your deepest thoughts to without disabling fear of disapproval or rejection.

"The way we talk or write about disturbing experiences is critical," says the Texas psychologist. "You have to be able to organize it, make a coherent narrative." And when people are unable to disclose troubling thoughts, they don't get a handle on them and they also suffer disruptions of the immune system. They experience a drop in action of T lymphocytes, Dr. Pennebaker finds. They also experience psychological distress. Unfortunately, he says, "social threats make talking to someone else a high-risk proposition." But being around a person who accepts you is, ipso facto, stress-reducing.

Acceptance, John M. Gottman, Ph.D., confirms, is downright magical in relationships. His studies show that even in everyday disagreements we need constant acknowledgment of the bond. And when we get it, our bodies, not to mention our relationships, do a virtual tap dance.

The world's de facto dean of relationship studies, Dr. Gottman has what is probably the most startling new evidence on the physical power of social ties. He finds that communicating acceptance while telling a partner how ticked off you are not only prevents marital conflict from bogging down in gridlock, it boosts immune function. "We have the first data that positive aspects of the relationship creates immunoenhancement.

"Positivity has to do with interest, affection, humor, and fondness and admiration for one another. It's the opposite of contempt. It's friendship—*the friendship part of marriage.*" The skills that make friendship work are the same skills that make marriage work.

What makes the findings so astonishing is the fact that our perceptual, emotional, and immune systems seem much more attuned to pick up negative signals than positive ones. Mildly negative events, like a look of disapproval from a friend or lover, register far more strongly than even moderately positive ones. A single look of contempt, Dr. Gottman has found, outweighs five good acts.

The Active Ingredient

Social bonds are fragile; they can be ruptured with a glance. But the fragility of social relations is not to be confused with their power. What is the "active ingredient" in social ties that makes them so potent a medicine? "Acceptance or inclusion is the important thing," insists psychologist Mark Leary, of Wake Forest University. He regards a longing for stable relationships as a fundamental human need, right up there next to food. It has only two requirements: regular contact and *persistent demonstrations of caring.* People need constant indications, little reassurances, that they are accepted. "That's why a lack of responsiveness by a friend or partner even to our mundane mutterings sometimes hurts. It seems objectively minor, but we are programmed to be sensitive to any indication that we might be excluded."

Dr. Leary views many of our basic emotions as essentially social emotions designed to signal when we are having problems with our relationships. He regards anxiety and depression as responses to real, imagined, or feared rejection, as is jealousy. "Even grief, which I view as the epitome of depression, clearly emerges from the sense of interpersonal separation that accompanies death, long-term separation. Our emotional system seems keyed to make us feel badly when exclusion looms."

With every muscle twitch, every blink of an eye, every heartbeat, we need to belong—and to be reassured we belong. The need for social acceptance is built in, right down to the very marrow of our bones.

Just how sensitive are people to indications of rejection? Even playacting rejection on a regular basis can tear away at the body. Michel Stuart was an actor who appeared in the original Broadway production of the musical *A Chorus Line*. He died in 1997, age fifty-four, in an auto accident. In the musical, there is a show within the show. Stuart's character was not chosen for the cast of the show within the show. "Being rejected night after night for almost two years," he once told an interviewer, "my legs started bothering me. My phlebitis started to kick up. Nature was telling me something."

Peer relations and social acceptance—among children or adults—are not incidental to or an accessory to life. Relationships are an integral part of psychological and biological functioning. Popularity in children is absolutely crucial to healthy development in a wide range of areas, from personality style to school adjustment, from general intellectual development to accurate self-perception, from a sense of self-worth to susceptibility to depression and anxiety.

All of us, at every age, even in infancy, help construct the way we are treated by others. Social competence, perhaps even more than attractiveness and intelligence, influences how we are judged by others and how they behave toward us. Children—adults—who are socially skilled elicit favorable treatment from others, who feel positive toward them. Hence it has a major impact on the everyday climate they dwell in. Rejected children hold attitudes and behave in ways that alienate others. Social competence does more than help people build satisfying relationships and protect mental and physical health. It is a major determinant of happiness in life.

The evidence adds up to an overwhelming rationale for understanding and supporting the social life of children. Making room for kids' play—pure, unstructured time for kids to be together—is the very first step.

CHAPTER FOUR

The Anatomy of Social Competence

The following conversation took place in a classroom of preschoolers.

Benjy runs into Max with a wagon. Max starts to cry and bystanding Jesse approaches.

JESSE: Hey, Benjy and Max, can we settle this? Benjy, why did you run into Max?

BENJY: Because he threw sand in my face.

JESSE (turning to Max): So if you don't throw sand at Benjy, then he won't hit you with the wagon.

> When I was eight years old, I moved and went to a different school. Moving for most children that young can be traumatic, and it was for me as well. My mother told me that I was basically a little angel. I always had a smile on my face and always did what I was told. I think this gave the other schoolkids the opportunity to pick on me and tease me.
>
> Every morning we had to line up before the bell rang to signal the start of school. While we were waiting, I was incessantly teased and harassed. I never fought back because I was so afraid to get into trouble. That was something I had the greatest fear of: getting into trouble. It got to the point where I was trying to figure out how to get to school as late as I could without being tardy.
>
> Today I am thirty-seven. I still think about the bullying and wish I could have stood up for myself.—T. F.

Social competence doesn't spring full-blown in children the minute they walk into school. Nor does it look the same at every age. It develops gradually, from early infancy, through adolescence. When Jessica wants to play with Joshua simply because he has more toys than all the other kids in the neighborhood, she is being a perfectly sociable two-year-old. What constitutes popularity at ages two and three—the one who has the most toys wins, quite literally—is different from what works later on, but it is a necessary stage in development. At every step, important social skills are being acquired.

Social competence is becoming more important earlier in the lives of children. Children are getting to flex their social skills earlier—and needing them sooner. As both parents work, children are together with other children for much if not most of the day, starting at a very young age in day-care centers and preschools. This is not at all a bad thing. Peers always play a huge and probably undervalued role in socializing age-mates. Peers can actually accelerate children's development. Of course, there is no need for parents to jump ship just yet. The early movement of children into preschool experiences in no way displaces the family in creating social competence. If anything, it shifts into the home even more importance on the subtle and not so subtle ways the foundation for sociability is acquired first in the family experience.

This chapter looks at some of the major elements of social competence and then draws as comprehensive a picture as possible of what constitutes sociability and popularity at every age, from preschool to adolescence. It throws into relief the major social challenges children must master at each age. When children spend time gossiping at age twelve, for example, they aren't being trivial or malicious; they are using it as a vehicle for understanding themselves, which is a huge function of friendship at that age. It also becomes clear that children have differing perspectives on their peers' behavior at different ages. For example, children who are withdrawn become increasingly disliked and rejected over the school years. Peers aren't being arbitrary or mean; they have a knack for zeroing in on skills needed for later life adjustment. Children like children who speak up for themselves, their needs, their goals. Whether they let them in the game any one time or not, they like children who ask, forthrightly, "Can I play?"

To both describe the elements of social competence and construct the much more dynamic road map to social relations throughout childhood, I have waded through the findings of literally hundreds of studies of children and adolescents. There is no precedent; no one has pulled the information together this way before.

The Elements of Social Competence

SOCIABLE DISPOSITION

The inclination to approach people positively, initiate contact, and be sociable with others may rest partly on biological makeup; a child who is fearful in new situations is hardly likely to approach another child. A child who is temperamentally easy is more inclined to initiate peer interaction than a difficult child. However, approaching a peer also requires the expectation that others can be counted on to respond positively themselves—in other words, trust. Exactly how this trust is transmitted to the child is not clear, but it appears to be acquired at least in part through the early parent-child, or caretaker-child, relationship. A parent who is attentive and responsive to an infant's needs breeds a sense of security and safety in the child, a sense that relationships are satisfying and reliable, and a belief that the world is dependable, a place that can be trusted. The parent-child relationship then serves as a "secure base" that allows the child to explore the world and build other relationships. What's more, it also creates expectations that others will be responsive, a precondition for making friendly overtures to others.

PROSOCIAL ORIENTATION

Prosocial orientation reflects the tendency to approach people cooperatively and consider the well-being of others, as well as of oneself, and to respond to their needs. It suggests an intuitive recognition of interdependence in relationships. Children with a prosocial orientation are given to sharing, doing nice things for others, helping people, and cheering people up; they expect others to act cooperatively toward them—until experience proves otherwise. What most distinguishes well-liked children from all others is the presence of positive qualities, such as prosocial behavior, rather than the absence of negative qualities.

Generally, the tendency toward prosocial behavior increases with age over the life-span, but it exists even in children as young as two. Research indicates that engaging in positive prosocial behavior plays a bigger role in the healthy social and emotional adjustment of girls than of boys.

Prosocial orientation is the root of empathy, the ability to feel for others. It manifests early on as the inclination of a child to help a peer in distress.

Because temperamentally easy children have lots of contact with their peers, they become practiced at identifying, interpreting, and responding to their peers' emotional flare-ups. Besides, they have lots of friends, and they're highly motivated to help their friends when they are emotionally distressed. Social involvement with peers breeds prosocial behavior, among boys as well as girls.

Nevertheless, prosocial orientation is acquired in part from early social experiences in the family. It is linked to both security of attachment to early caretakers, and to having siblings while growing up, whereby children learn the value of sharing and of acting in a collectively beneficial manner. Children acquire some prosocial responsiveness by imitating the actions of parents and caregivers toward them. Through modeling the behavior of others around them, even children with difficult temperaments learn to respond with kindness to peers' problems.

Direct naturalistic observations of young children in preschool show that kids in a caring setting become caring themselves—evidence that kids are constantly monitoring the actions of those around them, especially in emotionally charged situations. In one study of fifty-two preschoolers, it was the frequent criers who became frequent suppliers of relief to others in distress; what was tendered to them by teachers and by peers they in turn applied by helping others and mediating unpleasant incidents.

The researchers in that study clocked 248 crying incidents in forty-eight hours of observation of three preschool groups during free play. Accidents accounted for 45 percent of the crying incidents; peer aggression was the runner-up, instigating 26 percent of incidents. Disputes over sharing possessions or territory sparked 19 percent of the crying episodes.

Children rarely ignored their peers' distress; they responded even when teachers or supervisors did not. Not one child failed to make some response to a child's distress, and some children responded as many as thirty-one times. Most often (40 percent of the time), children reacted with simple curiosity, just by approaching and watching another child in distress. But 22 percent of the times, peers actively offered comfort, and 19 percent of times they offered comments. Occasionally they ignored a peer's distress (10 percent) but just as often they jumped in and mediated the cause of the problem, as Jesse did in the opening vignette.

Other researchers access prosocial behavior by asking children to name their peers who are most helpful. Typical questions might include: Name someone who

- will try to help someone who has been hurt.
- shows sympathy to someone who has made a mistake.
- offers to help other children having difficulty with work in the classroom.

Prosocial responses make children extremely well liked by their peers and successful at establishing close friendships. Popularity, pure and simple, correlates with prosocial behavior, as well as high levels of social interaction and initiative. And the lack of prosocial responsiveness is what distinguishes aggressive children and makes them disliked. The lack of a prosocial outlook allows them to cause pain to others. And it keeps them from knowing how to relate to others in nonaggressive ways.

Researchers debate whether boys and girls are equally empathic and prosocial. The problem may be that they demonstrate empathy in different ways. In one study, males were more likely to help out strangers, while females were more likely to help others in close relationships.

EMOTION REGULATION

Social situations are incredibly complex and dynamic. A child—or adult, for that matter—has to pay attention to all kinds of verbal and nonverbal signals in any situation, such as a peer's facial expression and voice tone, interpret their meaning accurately, generate possible responses, decide on the best response for the situation, and then carry out that response—all in a matter of microseconds. No one can pay attention to or correctly interpret what is going on, let alone act skillfully, without a reasonable degree of control over his or her own emotional states, especially negative emotions such as anger, fear, anxiety. Yet these are the very emotions that usually arise in situations of conflict. Or in response to any social information that is upsetting, even the painfully ordinary "No, you can't play with us."

Recently, studies have begun to look more deeply at children who are inclined to spontaneously prosocial responses. They show that such children tend to have a distinctive emotional makeup. They are emotionally well regulated. They can focus attention on social situations and other children's needs because they are particularly good at modulating their own negative feelings of fear, anger, and frustration in response to the demands of any situation.

It isn't that these children hide their emotions and grin and bear it, or that they overcontrol and internalize all their negative feelings; they are perfectly capable of expressing emotion. There are physiological systems involved in the experience of emotion, and competent children have learned to decrease their own internal emotional arousal; they do it by shifting attention away from distressing stimuli toward positive aspects of a situation. In other words, they have excellent coping skills early in their development. The ability to regulate emotions, because it allows children to focus their attention, is one reason kids who are socially competent also do well academically.

The capacity to regulate oneself this way develops during the toddler and preschool period. But it begins in infancy. One of the major functions of parents and caretakers is to limit the infant's exposure to emotionally stimulating events, help the infant modulate arousal, and alleviate the infant's distress and frustration by soothing him. Consider, for example, what happens in the typical play between mother and young infant in face-to-face encounters.

In the earliest stages, the mother leads the game, reaching over to draw her baby out: "Hey there, pumpkin, give me one of those goofy-doofy smiles." Gradually, the baby essays a few smiles, throws out a few vocalizations, and starts up the game himself. He reaches out to get her, she brightens to his overtures, feeding him talk and facial expressions—the elements of communication—until, over-loaded with stimulation, he averts his head to recover himself, before beginning again.

Throughout, the mother serves as a protective "envelope" for her baby, screening out the background noise of the world, letting through only as much stimulation and information as she learns to expect he can handle, enlarging the envelope as her baby signals his readiness for more, before he turns away. The infant is learning to use the presence of his parent for emotional regulation in stressful circum-stances. Gradually, children shift from external to internal ways; over the preschool years, children rely less on Mom and more on them-selves and mental strategies they devise to manage emotional upsets.

Long-term studies show that to the degree that young children can regulate their own emotions—calming themselves by reaching for their favorite blanket, avoiding situations that scare them—they will be popular with their peers (and physically healthy and high achievers). When children cannot, they get into trouble. They be-come overwhelmed, overly reactive to the negative emotions of oth-ers, and either resort to aggression, as a more or less automatic reaction to their own emotional state, or withdraw from social contact. Chil-dren who are unable to regulate their own emotional arousal are less likely to help a peer in distress. Emotional arousal hijacks attention, crimps perception, and prevents children from taking in information and processing it intelligently.

READING EMOTIONAL STATES

Children's social ability is more than a bag of behaviors; it depends on the ability to perceive social cues and interpret them. Enter the emotions. Emotions are not only experienced internally; all the basic human emotions wear facial expressions that instantly communicate to others what one is feeling. They are universally recognizable social signals. Children recognize the expression of emotions before they can pin verbal labels on them.

The ability to label emotional expressions is a prerequisite for detecting and understanding a peer's thoughts, feelings, intentions, and viewpoint. Children begin to decode these signals by becoming aware of situations that give rise to their own emotions, by correctly labeling their experience, and, based on their own experience and emotional expressions, by inferring what others must be feeling. Even toddlers are capable of reading others' emotional states.

Whether they realize it or not, parents are actually teaching their children about the expression and regulation of emotion all the time. How parents respond to children's feelings of sadness, anxiety, and anger has a huge influence on children's abilities to understand feelings and read them correctly in themselves and others. Parents who dismiss feelings ("Oh, pussycat, that's nothing to be sad about),") derogate them ("Anger is the devil's emotion. There'll be no anger in our house"), or punish ("If you want to be angry, then go to your own room") children's display of emotion, however well meaning, are setting up kids for problems with their peers, and worse.

Empathy hinges on the ability of children to read and label the emotional states of others, to assume another's perspective, and to respond. It also requires such classy cognitive skills as the ability to make inferences. Having the ability to infer the needs of others helps make children popular with their peers generally and successful in close friendships.

INITIATING INTERACTION

Children who take the initiative in extending a verbal invitation to play to another child or in starting a conversation are popular with their peers. In toddlers this might take the form of simply offering another child an object. Popular kids also know how to accept or politely turn down an invitation—always by providing a reason or offering an alternative (or turnabout) idea.

GROUP OR GAME ENTRY

Entering a group of peers who are already at play is a fact of everyday playground life, and it is a challenge for any child. Even the most socially competent children get rebuffed a good portion of the time. And yet, whether the attempt to enter a group is successful or not, what a child *does* to try to enter always counts. It's what peers use in judging other kids.

First, socially competent kids pay attention to the interests of their peers and devise a way to go with the flow of group activity. If the answer to "Can I play?" is "No, we don't have enough blocks," a competent child might counter with, "Well, I can be the guard."

Aggressive children make *more* attempts to join others but are *less* successful at it than children of average status, because they use inept tactics. They do things that call attention to themselves, rather than find a way to fit themselves into the ongoing group activity. They might throw a ball into the middle of a group and disrupt the ongoing activity, or they might respond contentiously to a question asked of them, or start off with unwelcome demands ("Gimme one of those"). Withdrawn children often hover at the edge of a group without saying anything—and then walk away.

Some researchers have found that children who have trouble entering a group have parents with similar problems.

Nevertheless, rebuffs are a fact of life even for socially competent kids starting at a very early age. Children must learn ways of dealing with them and the negative feelings they generate, such as how to calm themselves and soothe themselves. "Unless parents teach their kids to handle rebuffs, kids fail to learn how to change bad feelings to good ones," says Auburn University's Jackie Mize. "If they get upset, they will stay upset. If there's one thing that characterizes social competence, it's the ability to make positive responses to others even in the face of negativity."

When socially competent kids are on the receiving end of others' attempts to gain group entry, they find a way to accommodate others into the group. "You can be the baby." Or "You can back up the catcher." They are flexible, having the ability to consider others kids' ideas for play. And they know how to say no to others' desire to join—in a positive way. "You can join us later when we need a daddy. You can come and be him."

RESPONSIVITY

Like little detectives, socially competent kids scan the scene for important information to guide their actions. They tune in to interactions, are on the alert to ways and times to make their interests mesh with those of their peers, and get their behavior in step with that of their peers. They make relevant comments to their peers, responding in a connected way to what was said to them, and smile at appropriate times. Their comments are appropriate to the social situation. They monitor others' reactions to their own behavior, and then make adjustments in their own performance. Socially incompetent children are ignored or rebuffed because they make play suggestions to peers who are focused on other activities, such as classwork, they mistime responses as well as overtures, and they disrupt ongoing activity or shift attention to unrelated matters.

PAYING ATTENTION TO RELATIONSHIPS

To get along well with others, children not only need social skills, they need to pay some attention to relationship matters in whatever situation they are in. "Social situations are complex and often ambiguous," observes Dr. Steven Asher of the University of Illinois. "They present a context for the pursuit of many different goals. A child playing a game, for example, might focus on one or more goals, such as getting along well with the other children, winning, assuming control over the situation, improving his or her skills at the game, or avoiding humiliation. The child's behavior will depend in large part on the goals he or she pursues." A child interested in getting along with the other children will probably try to be a good sport. A child who focuses on winning might cheat, sulk, or quit when losing—or show off and brag when winning. Any of these is bound to alienate others, even though a child really intends to hold on to friendships. Dr. Asher's observations of rejected kids indicate that they do not pay enough attention to relationship goals in many situations.

HANDLING PROVOCATION

Provocations ignite many peer conflicts, but by no means do all children fight fire with fire and respond to a deliberately hostile remark by reciprocating negativity. In fact, differences in handling provocations distinguish popular kids from aggressive-rejected ones. And consider this: The ability to decelerate negativity makes kids popular, and it is the very same quality that researchers find accounts for happiness between partners in marriage!

MANAGING DISAGREEMENTS WITHOUT FIGHTING

Conflict is part of life, and coping with peer confrontations turns out to be one of the most critical of social skills. Disagreements are common even in close friendships, inevitable in all relationships. Two (or more) people mean two (or more) perspectives. There's a direct clash between one's own interests and those of another. Positions harden. One person tries to overcome the other's opposition. It's not the degree of conflict that sinks relationships, but the ways children resolve them. Disagreements, if handled well, can help children know themselves better, develop language skills, gain valuable information, and cement their relationships. Kids often can benefit from strategic help in managing conflict; adults, however, tend to be more interested in peacemaking and stopping it outright.

Children who are socially competent find ways to preserve involvement and positive feelings despite disagreeing. Managing conflict without aggression requires skills in listening, communicating—arguing, persuading—taking the perspective of others, controlling negative emotions, and problem-solving. Most of all, socially competent kids stop conflict from escalating; they apologize, suggest a compromise, propose a joint activity, offer a toy, or negotiate. And sometimes they just change the topic.

There are kids who are inclined to oppose others, insist on their own way, and escalate conflict to the point of coercion by aggression. They may be acting on frustrations from the early parent-child relationship, by which they come to expect others to be unfair and not take their needs into account. Or they may be activating a kind of "basic training" from home; through exposure to high levels of family conflict they may come to believe that aggression and victimization are simply normal aspects of a relationship. Children who resort to aggression to solve conflicts do get what they want—but they also quickly become unpopular with their peers.

NEGOTIATING DIFFERENCES

A simple way to resolve conflicts without fighting is for one child to yield to another's demands. But compliance and submissiveness violate the equality and reciprocity basic to healthy peer relationships—and a sense of self-worth. As children gain in social competence, they try to accommodate the needs of both parties through negotiation. Essentially, they give voice to their different interests and perspectives. Researchers have found that when children state their reasons for disagreeing—"You can't play with my dinosaur 'cause he's sleeping"—they are in essence making a conciliatory move, and that opens the door for a partner to offer a suggestion that ends the conflict. It deescalates the conflict. A distinguishing feature of friendship is that both kids devote considerable time negotiating solutions to problems.

POINTERS FOR PARENTS

ENCOURAGE A SENSE OF HUMOR.
Humor is a most prized social skill, the fast track to being liked—at all ages (it's what adults most want in a mate). Laughter, and especially the ability to laugh at oneself, physically relaxes people; it creates a safe environment.

Rejected children seldom smile or laugh; they lack a sense of humor. Submissive children actually admit this. Yet humor works even in threatening situations because it defuses negativity and disarms bullies.

There is no recipe for creating a sense of humor; in fact, the surest way to kill humor is to lunge after it. But you can look at the funny side of things and help your children to do that, too.

- Cut out funny pictures from newspapers and magazines and share them with your kids.
- Tell them about funny things that happened to you during the day.
- Tell (clean) jokes to your kids and let them tell you ones (be sure to laugh; at least smile).
- Read funny stories, nonsense poems.

- Take your kids to funny movies.
- Encourage and appreciate occasional bouts of silliness.
- At least sometimes make a silly face at your kids when you are angry at them.
- Every family needs a set of private signals for use in public when one has made a fool of himself or stepped over some line; choosing a funny but subtle expression takes the sting out of silent reprimands.
- Remember that little humorous acts done often produce big changes in the climate of relationships.

RESPECT TEASING.
Children who are hypersensitive to teasing are disliked by their peers. A highly prominent characteristic of submissive-rejected kids is that they can't take teasing—and their typically emotional response is one thing that sets them up for victimization. Aggressive-rejected kids see teasing as provocation.

- Help your child see the positive value in teasing. Much teasing is good-natured, designed to provoke gently. Much teasing is a highly ritualized form of insult. Boys will tease each other about relationships with girls, and girls will tease each other about having crushes or, later, budding relationships with boys.
- Assure your child that every child is subjected to some teasing—it is a way of testing each other for abilities they will need as they go through life.
- Coping with teasing is a necessary skill, a test of emotional development and especially emotion regulation; it teaches children to put a lid on emotional intensity. In the rituals of development into which teasing fits, no response—being cool—is probably the safest response.
- Help your child develop a repertoire of fun comebacks. Responding to teasing with humor is categorically non-reinforcing to aggressors.

- Have your child repeat teasing comments that peers have made, or role-play to reenact the episode. Allow your child to think up responses. And gently coach your child. "What else can you say? What's a funny thing to say when someone says that? Okay, so you get red in the face when a girl talks to you. What are you going to say the next time one of the other boys teases you about that?"

PAY EXTRA ATTENTION, AND PROVIDE EXTRA SUPPORT, AT TRANSITION TIMES.

Peer problems may especially emerge at these times, and children may need extra support and help.

- The start of a new school, a new school year, even a change of classroom—all make extra demands on children's social skills.
- So do transitions that do not originate inside the school—family moves, divorce, remarriage, to name but a few.
- First grade is particularly important for children to secure their long-range success in school.
- Middle-school entrance marks a dramatic expansion of the school experience with multiple classrooms and teachers—and the increasing influence of peer groups.
- The transition to middle school and to high school presents all children with new ways to feel small and powerless.

STAY OUT OF SMALL PEER DISAGREEMENTS.

Conflict has its value. It's a crucial learning laboratory for kids. Conflict actually helps children develop and sharpen their identity. Children learn to assert their own perspective. Children need not less conflict but strategies to curb negative emotions, the ability to listen effectively, and creative ways of resolving the underlying problem. Allow children to handle conflicts by themselves—as long as one child is not being harassed or threatened or the conflict doesn't escalate dramatically into a nasty fight. If you do intervene, listen well to both sides before acting.

The Road Map of Social Competence

By definition, social competence is a moving target. From birth to adolescence, it is constantly evolving. Not that it stops there; social development, any self-respecting adult knows, continues throughout life. Still, the landmarks are laid out largely by adolescence. A rough sketch of the territory looks like this.

THE FIRST YEAR

Babies come into the world with an amazing readiness for social interaction. They orient themselves to sound, and prefer the sound of the human voice, especially the high pitch of the female voice. They choose to look at faces over other objects and will follow with their eyes the turning of a nearby human face. They may imitate facial gestures, such as sticking out a tongue, and they synchronize their body movements to the rhythm of the human voice. Most of their early social life consists of meeting the gaze of Mom, taking in her verbal sallies, and smiling and cooing in response—incredibly important exchanges that frame some of the basic rules of social interaction: eye-to-eye engagement, paying attention, turn-taking, synchronizing behavior, responding contingently. For the first year at least, adults are a baby's primary playmates, and they have the responsibility for initiating episodes of play.

Children develop their first positive interest in other children at about six months. At this age infants might look at each other, touch and imitate each other's actions, vocalize, and smile at each other. But their social advances tend to be brief—so brief they may not even be recognized as such by the other child. Being exposed to skilled partners such as a parent or older sibling at age six months, engaging in such sophisticated activity as cooing by turn-taking, pays off. Infants who spend more time interacting with parents at six months devote more time to other nearby tots by nine months.

Although children do not utter their first word until ten to fifteen months of age, they are sensitive to the sounds of speech from birth on and through social interaction with those around them are busy learning language and acquiring the ability to deploy it later. The richer the linguistic environment a child dwells in, the more expressive the language parents use with their children, the more finely tuned a child's language development will be, allowing the child to master the foundation of social interaction—the ability to communicate in a way that is contingent upon the situation and relevant to it. Ultimately, verbal fluency is the handmaiden of social skillfulness.

Parenting styles and practices at this early age can already predict with reasonable accuracy which children will develop later problems with aggression.

TODDLER YEARS, AGES ONE TO TWO

Toddlers solve some personal dilemmas in a very social way that demonstrates just how skilled they are in understanding emotional expression. They are already adept at what is known as social referencing; in ambiguous situations—say, they fall down but don't hurt themselves or someone snatches a toy from their hands—they check out the facial expressions of their caretakers for cues on how they themselves should feel and respond. This is one way young children use the presence of a parent or caretaker to learn to manage their own emotional distress.

Even among children this young, researchers can discern the popular—so-called sociometric stars. They make more overtures to other children, initiate more contacts, and respond more contingently to play offers from other children. Children who initiate play become the agenda-setters. Toddlers practice synchronizing their behavior with others through turn-taking exchanges such as hide-and-seek. Still, they show clear preferences for some children, and friendships start forming.

Prosocial behavior emerges naturally at this age. Toddlers have been observed displaying a repertoire of comforting behavior—hugging, kissing, or patting someone who is crying or injured. They also make empathic gestures, such as sad or concerned expressions when someone else is sad or crying, or offer objects they know are comforting, such as their own teddy bear. They may even bring a crying child to their own mother. Toddlers offered toys by their caretakers are more likely to offer toys to their peers.

Aggression as a way of solving problems is common in children at two years of age, and does not have the meaning it does later on.

In fact, physical aggression steadily increases from nine months of age to a peak at age two, when humans are more likely to be the victims of aggression than at any other age. Physical aggression begins to decline as children learn that it hurts to be attacked, as adults intervene in aggressive episodes and indicate aggression is the wrong behavior, and as language skills increase and children learn to express themselves that way. Language skills—developed through reading to children, talking to them, and naming objects as they are encountered—play such a huge role in social competence that in at least one study absence of language skills predicts later criminality. The transformation of early aggressive behavior into bullying depends in large measure on the responses adults make to the child's aggression. Not all children will grow out of the terrible twos on their own.

Two-year-olds direct aggression at objects, not people, and their aggression is most common after conflict with parents. Their conflicts revolve around the sharing of toys and other objects. And conflicts are common; in one study, among ten toddlers in a group-care setting, there was one bout of conflict between two toddlers every 2.6 minutes! Still, the more opportunities children have to interact, the less aggression there is.

Even at the age of two, the peer group is important to children. And children begin forming friendships. Toddler friendships are based almost exclusively on similar levels of development, temperament, and styles of behavior. Although they do not have the vocabulary to talk about their feelings for another child, toddlers' friendships have many of the features of later, more sophisticated relationships—for example, they provide emotional support for one another. From observations made at their laboratory school, researchers at Ohio State University have identified many elements of friendship in children this young.

Typically children this age signal friendship by closely **imitating** each other. For example, in one well-bonded pair, one girl, while running through the play area, began tugging at her pants because they were too big and began falling down. Her friend, following her, reached back and tugged at her own perfectly fitting jumpsuit in exactly the same way. This kind of nonverbal synchrony is typical of popular children. They also **help** each other. In one instance, when one toddler hurt her hand, a friend found her bottle and blanket and handed them to her, and stood by with the teacher until the friend calmed down. Another characteristic of friendship is **intimacy**, and the researchers were surprised to find that children at this age engage in intimacy much the way older friends and lovers do—they separate themselves from the group and go off to a corner to play by themselves.

Among two-year-olds, friends consistently play certain games with each other. They are **loyal** to each other and **support** each other in the presence of others, and they **share** with each other, although often one partner in the pair does more sharing than the other.

PRESCHOOL, AGES THREE TO FIVE

Children begin to shift more interaction toward their peers than to their parents. If you have any doubt, just ask any parents who have ever moved from one part of the country to another when their kids are this age. The children start bringing home the accent of their friends in preschool, even if they spend only half a day there.

Around age three, the word *friend* enters the vocabulary of children. Boys this age average 1.7 friends, and girls 0.9 friends. Girls' friendship networks are smaller and more exclusive, and they stay that way until adolescence.

Social understanding develops rapidly over the preschool years, and that underlies a whole series of shifts in patterns of interaction. While both preschool boys and girls spend time in group activities, they can generally sustain play with only one other child. As a result, most of their socializing is done in pairs, where one child is engaged in the same activity with and actively, reciprocally communicating with one other child, even within the larger group. Boys and girls at this age interact *à deux* with equal frequency, although girls spend more extended periods of time in their couplings.

Familiarity counts. Children like other children based on their past experiences with those children. A preschooler selects play partners based at any given moment on some mix of factors, including liking of another child, the nature of the activity, and just who happens to be available. Especially at age three, contacts and friendships are very fluid and largely defined by the play situation; they are more moment-to-moment and lack intimacy. Still, more than half of all preschoolers establish stable, reciprocal friendships that last throughout the year. In fact, over the course of each year in preschool, children become much more selective about their companions. They spend more of their time with fewer children, playing in smaller groups and having more stable, more reciprocal friendships at the end of each year than at the beginning. Throughout preschool, children are developing clearer peer preferences and more established friendships. Their friendships are based largely on common interests and enjoyment of common activities, and when conflicts arise, they are typically about wanting the same plaything or privilege.

Even at this age, reciprocity is a defining feature of friendship, although among young children it is expressed in concrete ways, as in friends giving each other things. What gets reciprocated in friendship changes over the course of childhood and adulthood, based on developmental challenges of the age. But any way it's delivered, reciprocity accounts for the sense of well-being that friendship provides at all ages.

Even among preschoolers, there's more to social competence than just acting in a positive manner and limiting aggression. They are learning how to be sensitive to others, figuring out what are appropriate social contexts, understanding how to focus on and interpret social cues, and building a repertoire of behaviors that will carry them through an expanding array of situations.

From age three to the time they enter school, children are busy with a supremely serious social task—through trial and error, they are learning how to play together. The emphasis is on *together*. It's fun, but it's also challenging. What makes this such a landmark achievement is that to play together as friends, children have to coordinate their actions, their thinking, their understanding. To do this, they must master what is really the most basic social ability of all—carrying out connected conversation. That is, they must be able to engage in contingent speech, make statements that are logically related to the other child's utterances and that continue for a number of turns with that playmate, who is also responding in a related way.

By age four, a single pair of children may average 232 connected turns of conversation in forty-five minutes of play! However, even at this age, children vary enormously in their ability to connect verbally with a friend, and while some children can conduct even more sustained dialogues, others can muster only much shorter exchanges. The degree to which children can sustain a volley of connected conversation at around four years of age rests on a quite sophisticated ability to understand the thoughts and feelings of others. Even at this tender age, children are remarkably capable of being "tuned in" to each other, adept at actually "reading" each other.

In one study, thirty-eight children were tested at age three and a half to see how well they could figure out the intentions of others and generally understand how the mind works. Researchers tapped in to this skill by measuring the children's responses to others, actually puppets, acting on patently false beliefs. For example, the children watched a puppet searching for an item, say a Band-Aid, in a logical place, such as a box labeled BAND-AIDS, when they knew the item was not there but in an unlabeled box. The children were asked to predict how the puppet would act on the false belief that Band-Aids were in the Band-Aid box and to explain the puppet's behavior. The more explanations the children generated about the puppet's actions in terms of its mistaken beliefs—"Because he thinks there's a Band-Aid in it"—the better they scored. When the results were tallied, the better the children scored at forty months of age, the more connected their conversation was with a close friend seven months later.

Children, in a sense, become tiny psychologists, tuned in to the thoughts and desires of a playmate, so that they can regulate and coordinate their interactions—in short, so they can make friends and play together as friends. The same skills children use to mesh their play, researchers find, make them popular with all others and also lay the groundwork for the development of empathy and prosocial behavior.

Child's play has a hierarchy. And the most sophisticated form of play activity is fantasy or pretend play, where children engage in make-believe. It makes the most demands on social responsiveness, requires the most coordination. Children constructing a fantasy together have to maintain clear communication, manage the level of conflict, and shift continually from one child's perspective to the other's. Such coordinated play not only magnifies the fun; it helps children learn how to manage their emotions.

Increasingly over the preschool years, children spend diminishing amounts of time in mixed-sex contact and their peer groups become segregated by gender. However, at least at first, they are more likely to *say* that opposite-sex kids are icky than to stop playing with them. Three-year-olds do not sort out their companions and their friends by gender. But by age four, kids begin saying they dislike, and ultimately excluding, children of the opposite sex—even if they had previously been friends. This dramatically influences the makeup of peer groups and the pool of available playmates, especially important to remember if a child is having problems. A child's peer experiences and peer status are influenced not only by the nature, behavior, and social understanding of the child but by the character of the social milieu. A very quiet boy who finds himself unpopular in a setting where there are only a few boys and they are high-spirited ones may have a far different daily experience in a group that has more boys, with presumably more diverse character, to associate with. By the same token, children who have happily enjoyed cross-sex friendships may feel stranded as the centrifugal forces of gender division descend on preschool, ready to exert a virtually irresistible pull in middle childhood.

The more exposure kids have to peers, the greater their preference for engaging in social play rather than spending time alone or with adults. As they progress through preschool, children spend more of their time interacting with peers, especially same-sex ones. Still, solitary play is important and necessary, and it is not in itself a sign of lack of social skills. It may spring from interest in a particular activity rather than avoidance of or rejection by schoolmates.

Social status is associated with approaching others positively; with positive behaviors such as giving gifts or attention; with offering play suggestions to peers; with asking questions of peers; with showing affection and making positive helpful comments; and with commenting to peers on ongoing activities. Children show more positive behavior to friends than nonfriends. Children who are later judged as popular at this age attempt to enter groups of other children by joining the conversation rather than by changing it or making irrelevant statements. Shy, withdrawn children have higher rates of absenteeism from nursery school than do other kids.

By the time they are five years old, children's peer standing is already starting to gel. Children who are popular tend to remain popular. But with far more certainty, children who are unpopular, especially among the boys, are on a well-worn path to remaining unpopular. Not only do early difficulties in social interaction tend to persist, but a negative reputation encrusts around those who engage in negative behavior, such as aggression, that turns off their peers. Children who are rated unpopular with their peers in the beginning of the school year—and there is no faster way to be disliked than by being aggressive—are even more apt to be rated negatively by peers at the end of the preschool year. It seems to be one of the essentials of our makeup: Negative social behavior registers rapidly, deeply, and durably. And it becomes progressively more difficult for children to learn or develop new social skills.

When conflicts develop, they rarely get settled without one child giving in to the other or without the aid of an adult.

Around age three, children struggle with parents and siblings over autonomy issues. This is an important if not critical arena and a crucial time for picking up conflict-management skills. What children learn in their early family relationships they later transfer to other relationships. For example, long-term observational studies show that when mothers consistently employ reasoning that focuses on the child's needs or interests at thirty-three months (for example, "You have to pick up your toys now so you can have more space to play"), children deploy more successful negotiation strategies in their own disputes with friends at age six. They resolve conflicts more quickly because they know how to argue constructively and incorporate the other person's perspective into their negotiations.

Relational aggression first rears its ugly head in preschool, especially among girls, and leads to rejection now and in the future. Reactional aggression also starts in preschool, reflecting emotional volatility and problems in emotional regulation that also manifest themselves in attention problems and impulsivity. Even in preschool, children who are aggressive don't simply engage in negative, harmful behavior—they also fail to engage in prosocial behavior.

Unlike at later ages, aggression at this age is fairly visible to teachers and observers; preschoolers are not yet likely to inhibit aggression in the presence of adults. If at age two aggression is directed largely at objects, by age four it is aimed to hurt someone or someone's feelings, and is most common after peer conflict.

"Preschool is an important time," observes Auburn University's Jackie Mize. "Very firm foundations are laid by pre-school. Things have a self-perpetuating feature. If negative attitudes toward a child exist, he or she is already at a disadvantage. Unless steps are taken to actively change them, they will become more firmly established. Negative attitudes towards a child solidify at pre-school." Further, because of the self-perpetuating nature of social problems, children who have problems with their peers at this age will find it progressively harder to develop social skills later on.

KINDERGARTEN, AGES FIVE TO SIX

Kindergarten heralds a major transition in the lives of young children. Kids have to get around new school buildings, learn new school and teacher expectations, and gain acceptance into new peer groups. The value of friendship in helping people through life's challenges shows itself at this age; children who have friends make the adaptation to school easily and well. Friendship gives children emotional support, the wherewithal to explore their environment, and lots of tangible help and assistance—all needed for feeling secure in the new and vastly larger environment of elementary school. Kids, and especially boys, whose friendships are marked by conflict have a hard time making the adjustment to school and start off already looking to avoid it.

By this age, about three in four children is involved in a close friendship with another child. Three out of ten children have more than one close friend.

Kids who are popular with their peers at this age are more successful academically five years later. What constitutes popularity at this age is prosocial behavior. Popular children put the *kind* in kindergarten. By age five, children can understand the social situations that cause distress in others.

As more preschoolers attend child-care programs, kindergarten curriculum has shifted to a more academic orientation. Still, play is extremely important, not only for enjoyment and the release of frustrations but for the development of social competence. Pretend play, which assumes a major place in kindergartners' lives, helps them experiment with new roles.

Around this time, boys develop a preference for interacting in large groups rather than in pairs. In contrast to girls, they spend increasing amounts of time in coordinated group activity, in which they are all engaging in the same activity and integrating their actions with the other members of the group. Still, the groups are fairly fluid.

By the time children enter school, it is harder to excuse aggression and withdrawal as forms of immaturity.

MIDDLE CHILDHOOD, AGES SIX TO TEN

Social acceptance by peers takes a giant leap forward in importance. Children now shift from playing in pairs to playing in groups. The ability to enter a group at play is crucial.

No longer is social status determined merely by the behavior of the individual child. Group dynamics play a large role, and the peer group forms opinions and reputations of children based on their behavior. Children this age are highly conscious of and influenced by the reputations of their peers. That's one reason elementary-school children who are unpopular remain rejected from year to year; even if their behavior changes, the peer group continues to see rejected children in a negative light.

Rejected and neglected children make just as many approaches to initiate social contact as do other children, but the approaches of popular children are more positively received. Unpopular children make overtures that are inappropriate to the situation; they try to join others by calling attention to themselves, talking about themselves, inserting their own opinions and feelings, and asking informational questions, or they may bother others who are trying to work. At this age, even popular children may brag about their ability to beat up everybody.

By first grade, children are making accurate judgments about the social competence of their peers. Now that the basis of acceptance is norms set by the larger peer group, children are spending a great deal of time analyzing social relations and trying to figure out "what to be like" in order to be accepted by the peer group and to find a place in it.

Children begin distinguishing different spheres in which they are competent—such as social, scholastic, appearance, athletic, and conduct domains. Specifically, they begin weaving the positivity or negativity of their social experience into their perceptions about themselves. By the time children are in the third grade, they can accurately judge their own social status. How they are treated by peers is increasingly reflected in children's sense of self-worth.

As peer groups grow in importance, withdrawn behavior becomes more clearly defined and more disliked, increasingly a basis for peer rejection. Among children who are withdrawn, self-worth is doubly assaulted, not only by hostile treatment from peers but by their own dispositional style of blaming themselves, attributing social failure to causes that are internal to them and unchangeable. Hence, faster than all other children, they begin rolling down a path to loneliness and depression.

From a study of 189 sets of parents and 331 teachers, Swedish researchers were able to identify twenty-five components of social competence among eight- and nine-year-olds, all twenty-five equally applicable to boys and girls. The behaviors of social competence arrayed themselves into two distinct groupings, which the researchers dubbed prosocial orientation and social initiative. They defined prosocial orientation as "an inclination to behave smoothly in normal social interactions, coupled with abilities to perform adequately in more troublesome situations." One way to think of prosocial behavior is the ability to provide social support. Social initiative represents a social style of active participation.

PROSOCIAL ORIENTATION, LISTED IN THE ORDER OF IMPORTANCE ATTRIBUTED BY PARENTS:
    Has capacity for generosity to peers
    Has capacity to be helping/altruistic
    Has capacity to sympathize with peers
    Criticizes peers (This factor was strongly negatively associated
    with Prosocial Orientation.)
    Helpful with adults

Helps peer tidy up/search for lost items
Shares his or her belongings
Good at preventing conflicts
Comforts peer who is upset/sick
Includes shy children in play
Has ability to decode peers' feelings
Tries to intervene in peers' conflicts
Gives compliments to peers
Finds solution when in conflict
Has the capacity to play/work well with peers
Can give and take in interactions
Shares peers' joy

SOCIAL INITIATIVE:
Leads play activities
Makes contact easily with unfamiliar children
Suggests activities to peers

THESE FACTORS WERE RATED STRONGLY NEGATIVE ASPECTS OF
SOCIAL INITIATIVE BY PARENTS AND TEACHERS:
Socially withdrawn with peers
Hesitant with peers
Spectator while others play
Shy/hesitant with unfamiliar adults
Dominated by peers

Both prosocial orientation and facility with social initiatives make popular kids popular, the researchers found when they compared the behaviors as ranked by adults with those actually displayed by popular children in peer activities. And the lack of prosocial skills is what gets rejected kids rejected. By contrast, it is a failure at social initiation that keeps average kids from being more popular with their peers.

Children's peer groups and play partners become highly sex-segregated during middle childhood; cross-sex avoidance is so much the norm that boys and girls are increasingly rejected by children of the opposite sex and prefer same-sex classmates. While 35 percent of preschoolers have a best friend of the opposite sex, that's a very rare event among grade-schoolers. So stringent are gender expectations at this age that elementary-school children who do not fit rigid, gender-stereotype patterns of behavior are also at risk for rejection by their peers. Whatever gender-role socialization processes are going on, having same-gender friends during middle childhood forecasts the ability to have romantic relationships during adolescence.

There are many sex differences in interaction style, but just what they mean or how they have come about is a matter of intense debate; this much can be said with impunity: Boys tend to play in larger, more extensive groups, girls in smaller, more intensive groupings. Boys are more aggressive than girls and engage more in rough-and-tumble play, and girls are more verbally fluent, although there is a great deal of overlap between the genders.

Despite increasing gender segregation, the more popular children are, the more likely their widest network of pals is likely to include children of both sexes and many ages. Their close friends are likely to be age-mates, but they maintain contact with a wide array of others.

By age ten, new sensitivities emerge in social interaction. There is a new capacity for embarrassment. The hallmark of this age is the sudden emergence of boy-girl teasing. Think of it as a supreme test of emotional regulation. Being "cool." "You have to act as if you've had an emotion-ectomy," says the University of Washington's John Gottman. "You solve social problems better." Hypersensitivity to teasing increasingly makes kids disliked. Neither aggressive- nor submissive-rejected kids can take teasing.

At this age, children make a large distinction between friends and nonfriends. Aggression gives way to sharing and cooperation, as children learn to communicate better. Children are also becoming far more proficient at attributing intentions and distinguishing accidental from deliberate acts. As children become more sophisticated cognitively, their conception of friendship evolves. Disclosure of private thoughts and feelings—the hallmark of intimacy—gradually increases in importance in the development of relationships.

According to the University of Illinois's Dr. Steven Asher, children are always considering six core questions as they choose their friends:

- Is this child fun to be with?
- Is this child trustworthy?
- Do we influence each others in ways I like?
- Does this child facilitate, and not undermine, my goals?
- Does this child make me feel good about myself?
- Is this child similar to me?

However, different questions are more prominent at different stages of life. Young schoolchildren are particularly interested in having a friend who is fun to be with.

When children mull over these questions, they consider the characteristics of peers. Here's how peer qualities fare in leading to acceptance and rejection:

Core Question	Acceptance	Rejection
Is this child fun to be with?		
	sense of humor	aggressive/mean
	resourceful/skilled	disruptive
	participatory/	
	readily involved	bossy/domineering
	cooperative	withdrawn/apprehensive
		low cognitive skills
Is this child trustworthy?		
	reliable	aggressive/mean
	honest	dishonest
	loyal	betrays confidence
Do we influence each others in ways I like?		
	cooperative	aggressive/mean
	responsive	bossy/domineering
		resistant/rigid
Does this child facilitate, and not undermine, my goals?		
	cooperative	disruptive
	helpful	impulsive

Core Question	Acceptance	Rejection
Does this child make me feel good about myself?		
	supportive/kind	insulting/demeaning
	responsive	nonresponsive
	likes me	dislikes me
Is this child similar to me?		
	common values	different values and interests
	respect for peer conventions	nonconformity to peer conventions
	same gender, race, age	superior manner handicapped

Similarity is still important in friendships, especially similarity in social behavior. It's not that kids conduct a rational search for others like themselves. But the likenesses emerge through a "shopping" process in which children establish relationships with those who "feel right." Cooperative, friendly, nonaggressive children have the widest array of choices. Schoolchildren average three to five "best" friends. About two thirds of schoolchildren have at least one mutual friendship.

Social support also becomes a growing feature of friendships. Supportive friends help each other cope with difficulties such as divorce and other stresses. Where toddlers turned to their caretakers for support in times of stress, school-age children look to their friendships with peers. In fact, throughout middle childhood, young people look more to their peers for everything. Including their own appraisals of themselves. They begin comparing themselves with others, rating their appearance, their talents, aptitudes, possessions, and families against those of their peers.

Peer relationships and friendships are the context in which children now begin learning how to manage conflict, which no longer centers on objects but is focused on social matters. Friends are likely to explain the basis of their disagreements. Friendly rivalry or competitiveness may develop, but it arises out of the ability to make social comparisons, which children use to make a realistic estimate of their own capabilities.

During the elementary-school years, children spend a great deal of time in games with fixed rules of play; they are learning how to balance competition and friendship, how to maintain positive feelings despite competition. No surprise, then, that behavior during some rule-governed game, where winning or losing is at stake, is the most common cause of fighting at this stage. By age nine, children have had many opportunities for negotiations, and they are getting clever at it.

Children are gaining great skill at "reading" the emotions of others. Those children who are most adept at this are also those who are most popular among their peers.

When aggression takes place among children this age, it happens largely outside the scrutiny of adults, including teachers. It often arises in the context of active rough-and-tumble play, where the line between fun and aggression is fine to begin with. Hitting and name-calling are the major forms of aggression at this age.

Age eight marks a kind of turning point in aggressive behavior. By then, aggressive behavior patterns appear to be firmly set—and hard to give up. Aggression starts interfering with school achievement. Peers' negative expectations of an aggressive child lead them to behave more negatively toward the child, setting off a downward spiral of behavior that leads to increasing outcast status. Aggressive-rejected children begin looking further and further afield for social contact. By third grade, it is possible to predict who will be future delinquents based on lack of peer acceptance. By the end of elementary school, half of all bullies are not in their age-appropriate class.

However, to some kids, it looks as if bullies are having a good time, albeit at someone's expense. Among children living in inner cities, aggressive behavior after age eight may bring about an increase in popularity in the short run, as children living in a violent environment may see the value of having some aggressive friends.

Children who are popular in early elementary school tend to remain popular through late adolescence, and the most popular kids are always the least aggressive.

Beginning around age ten, and continuing to about age fourteen, peer victimization is most intense. Children themselves regard these as the worst years for bullying. Victimization increasingly brings on rejection by peers; victimized children who are also aggressive, so-called reactive aggressors, are the most rejected in any grade.

LATE CHILDHOOD, PREADOLESCENCE, AGES
ELEVEN TO TWELVE

As children move from the fixed classrooms and consistent peer groups of elementary school to the movable feast and multiple class-rooms of middle or junior high school, their social world expands exponentially. It can be a very stressful time. Not only are friendships that endured elementary school now often disrupted, youngsters are thrown on their own devices to construct a new peer network and find a new peer group that accepts and supports them.

Bullying and victimization become less widespread but more intense. Popular children and those who have friendships that are highly supportive have an easier time adjusting to middle school than other children. Those who are aggressive or rejected face increasing difficulties in adjusting to school; they are three times more likely to be poorly adjusted at the end of the first year of middle school than are other young people.

Neglected children also have a hard time making the transition both to middle school and to high school. Their social problems flare up the first year of middle school and the first year of high school.

Friendship has a huge buffering effect on preadolescents. Those who have friends not only make a better school transition, they experience a rise in self-esteem—at a time when self-esteem comes under assault. They also have better relationships with their families. Particularly for preadolescents, friendships provide a safe place for exploring and developing personal strengths.

Children this age themselves say that prosocial behavior is what makes kids popular. Their definition of prosocial behavior moves beyond cooperation, however, to the supreme kindness of including others in relationships, such as inviting someone to join a group of peers. Showing respect for self and others—having manners, being polite, listening to what others say, having a positive attitude, being open to others, being yourself, enhancing your own reputation, being clean—rates high, especially among girls.

Through their exposure to many others, popular children are gaining a great deal of social knowledge. They are picking up and practicing an expanding repertoire of strategies for making overtures to others and establishing friendships. Studies show that it is no longer enough to know what to do to achieve social success; it is especially important for boys to know what *not* to do—engage in negative behavior, such as breaking promises or verbal abuse.

Gossip takes up residence in the lives of young people, especially girls. It becomes a way to test the depth of the waters of friendship, to see whether it's safe for disclosure of private thoughts and feelings.

The new emphasis on the judgment of peers catapults some children into social withdrawal. Whereas in younger children most shyness is believed to stem from inborn temperamental traits, in combination with parenting practices, this age sees the rise of a different, more psychologically based form of shyness, sparked by acute self-consciousness in social situations. Young people become painfully aware of how they are being evaluated by others. For some, this awareness of self-awareness—called meta-awareness—can be overwhelming, unpleasant, and lead to obsessive worry about being humiliated or even teased. Yet research shows that coping with teasing is a necessary rite of passage, as children at this age are learning to distinguish teasing from ridicule.

In some children, the hyperawareness of social performance can bring on social anxiety and insecurity and the full flush of shyness symptoms, as well as a new image of themselves as shy, anxious, and awkward around others. During social encounters they engage in a lot of negative self-talk—"God, I'm doing terribly, why don't people like me better? What's wrong with me?"—and they come away from social interactions feeling dumb, defeated, and blaming themselves. They then anticipate negative consequences of social interaction and begin avoiding it.

Among preadolescents, aggression is becoming less overt. Girls increasingly see relational aggression as an appropriate response to anger at peers. Themes of social exclusion begin to loom large among girls in their conflicts with peers.

Bullying shows itself as part of a more general antisocial attitude and rule-breaking behavior pattern. Among boys named as bullies in grades six to nine, 60 percent had at least one court conviction by age twenty-four.

EARLY ADOLESCENCE, AGES THIRTEEN TO FIFTEEN

The search for a stable individual identity plays out through social identity—with a vengeance. Young people build at least part of their identity through their peer-group affiliations. They seek out groups that will satisfy their need for inclusion but at the same time provide them a measure of distinctiveness. They figure out how to behave by monitoring the behavior of those in the social group they belong to, or aspire to belong to. "In group" versus "out group" comparisons help adolescents build a sense of self-worth.

Friendship undergoes great changes. It's not just that it moves into the shopping mall or monopolizes the telephone. The big wall that discourages cross-sex friendships starts to come down, and it happens first among the most popular children. They have enough social competence and, probably, confidence to penetrate differences in interaction and communication styles. Also, young people now begin to accord their peers more flexibility in carrying out gender-based roles. Boys will be boys and girls will be girls, but the rules of acceptable behavior for each gender now accommodate more individuality.

Still, same-gender friends are crucial. Having same-gender friends during adolescence forecasts romantic relationships in early adulthood.

The need for intimacy takes a leap to center stage and is first filled through friendships. Some 80 to 90 percent of teenagers have mutual friends; this usually includes one or two "best friends" and several "close" or "good" friends.

Self-disclosure to peers, the sharing of thoughts and feelings with them—at the expense of disclosure to parents, particularly fathers—increases dramatically, especially among females, and plays a key role in relationships. The reciprocation of self-disclosure is the beginning of intimacy, so important for adult relationships. It is also a leading indicator of relationship status.

Reciprocity now centers on mutual understanding and loyalty.

The confiding that adolescents do among peers leads them to emphasize and expect trustworthiness in their friendships. Violations of confidences become serious breaches of friendship. A sense of commitment is growing.

At all ages, similarity reduces conflict between people, and peer relationships at this age are based most strongly on similarity of attitudes—especially attitudes to drugs—and behavior. Similarity in attitudes to school and achievement is also important, and in attitudes to drinking, dating, and sexual activity, especially among girls. Adolescents not only select friends based on such similarities, they socialize each other to become more alike—and one way they do it is by the free airing of their disagreements. Adolescents do not necessarily choose friends based on similarity of personality.

Closeness counts more than ever. The newfound intimacy among friends escalates their expectations for trust and loyalty. Early adolescents make a big distinction between close friends and casual acquaintances; their expectations of friendship are such that being called a name or "stupid" by a classmate may elicit a certain amount of anger, while the same act by a friend would launch not only a great amount of anger but a whole host of negative emotional reactions, including sadness over the threat to the relationship and distress over the state of the relationship.

Intimacy, closeness, supportiveness—all this takes time. Adolescents spend 29 percent of their waking time among friends. By contrast, their parents spend no more than a paltry 7 percent of time interacting with friends. But time with friends pays off, apparently. In studies of adolescents, supportiveness between friends correlates with school involvement and achievement, with popularity and with self-esteem, with lack of identity problems, avoidance of delinquency, and absence of depression.

The emphasis on emotional control of middle childhood gives way to mature social problem-solving in which emotion and social reasoning now become integrated. Increasing maturity also brings the ability to make finer distinctions in the social behavior and acceptability of their peers.

Teasing remains a socially useful test. Those adolescents who lack a sense of humor and can't take a joke are disliked by their peers.

Children are increasingly intolerant of aggressive behavior in others as they get older. By ninth grade, bullies are isolated from their peers and experience more and more negative consequences.

Students who have the most difficult time relating to peers also have the most difficult time relating to teachers. Most adolescents who engage in juvenile crime have a history of persistent peer rejection when younger, because of aggressiveness. The lower their social status with peers, the greater the risk of delinquency. Children who become runaways also usually have experienced severe problems with peer relations.

Bullies are more apt than other kids to start drinking earlier and to become inebriated; they are especially likely to develop problem drinking. They start sexual intercourse early, by age fourteen.

SIBLING RIVALRY—OR SOCIAL INCOMPETENCE?

Parents, studies show, have a number of misconceptions about the social development of kids. One of the more basic ones is that sibling rivalry is a big, bad problem. While sibling conflict may distress parents, the new view is that—as long as there is no physical aggression—it also promotes development and helps kids work out their individual identities.

Sibling conflict is in reality a kind of in-home training ground for learning to cope with negative emotions and for solving problems that are basic to many social situations. After all, siblings are often contending for finite resources—there's only so much attention to go around, just so many toys a parent can stock up on. How kids work out these problems has enormous repercussions for how they work out problems with their peers.

And, in fact, focusing on ways to stop siblings from fighting can be counterproductive. As one team of researchers recently found, telling kids stories about sibling problems and showing them videotapes that dramatize such problems—even for the purpose of correcting such behavior—inadvertently presents kids with opportunities for rehearsing and refining the negative points of sibling relationships. Kids exposed to these common methods for stopping sibling rivalry actually wound up getting along *worse* with their sibs than when they started. Those who got along better had been given direct training in positive prosocial skills, such as how to approach another child to initiate play and how to see things from the perspective of the other.

When parents lament the way their children get along, they are misattributing to sibling conflict or to competition what is really a lack of prosocial skills—the same skills that underlie popularity among peers. Such as the ability to show kindness and affection, sharing, playing together, even talking to each other. Of course, conflict and anger are easier to see and hear than lack of warmth.

And what helps siblings is not a lifetime of refereeing by parents, or intervention by a parent to stop the fighting, unless it is severe, but strategies that focus on enhancing social competencies. These include such basics as learning how to approach another child and deliver, accept, or politely decline invitations to play, or how to look at situations from the perspective of the other child.

That increases the warmth between siblings. It gives them a way to open a conversation about a troublesome issue.

The sibling arena is especially crucial for kids who have trouble getting along with peers. Left to its own devices, sibling rivalry tends to escalate and can be a breeding ground for aggression. Just as aggressive kids minimize their own aggression and blame their peers for starting fights, so do they blame their siblings. Teaching all siblings positive social skills turns the cycle around and gives children ways of deescalating negativity without coming to blows.

CHAPTER FIVE

Big. Bad. Bully.

The name was conferred by strict family tradition—Windy, short for Windham. No one could have foreseen how uncannily descriptive of this child's nature his nickname would be. Blond, adorable—it's those killer dimples—and well dressed, always with a dress shirt when others go to school in T-shirts, ten-year-old Windy looks as if he stepped out of a Ralph Lauren ad. Articulate and polite with adults, he's thought by parents the perfect playmate for their children. But not for long. He's a hurricane of a human, and a child's room is likely to be littered with the debris of broken toys and shattered expectations by the time Windy leaves. He can look the resident adult in the eye and plead earnestly, "Please don't tell my father," evoking whatever is left of sympathy for the harshness he is apparently dealt at home.

Then, too, he can stir up trouble between kids who are friends, telling David that his best friend Danny really says bad things about him behind his back. When they realize what is going on, other kids don't so much confront him as sidestep him—after all, as an aggressive kid, he is something of a threat to others. Kids soon stop bringing him over to play after school.

Windy has it tough; he's alone and unsupervised much of the time. So he roams the streets of his upscale urban neighborhood, gravitating to its rougher edges, looking for excitement. He usually finds it, even if he has to taunt kids into going along with him. The kids he runs with seem to be getting younger and younger.

By the time he's twelve, Windy's busy parents—both lawyers—muster some concern over their son's growing isolation from other kids whose parents they know and over the reports of misbehavior that filter back to them. Since they see the problem originating exclusively in Windy—after all, his younger sister is much better behaved—they pack him off to a military academy. There he will receive the rigid discipline his well-to-do family believes is the appropriate corrective for "boisterous" boys like their son.

Like about half of all children who are rejected by their peers, Windy is highly aggressive. These kids are the playground bullies. They create pain for others. They tend not to take rejection to heart, but eventually develop problems of externalization, such as delinquency, drug abuse, and alcoholism. They blame others for their problems, hold unrealistically positive views of themselves, deny their own discomfort or maladjustment, and minimize their behavioral difficulties, which are highly visible to others.

Sadly, they are filled with negative emotional reactions that they don't know how to defuse or dissipate. They may suppress these feelings inside their own home, but they seek outlets outside, where they apply the hurtful ways of expressing powerful emotions such as anger that they absorbed at home. These children pick up unproductive ways of solving problems, and do not have alternative ways of dealing with the inevitable conflicts that develop among people, even friends: They are likely to have many negative, conflictual relationships. These children overestimate the value of aggressive solutions to social problems. They are more punitive than other children, and less forgiving. They start fights, they disrupt the play of others, and they bully other kids.

Aggression is a particularly strong contributing factor to rejection among boys. Children who are rejected because of aggressive tendencies are not "bad." They are unable to decode or "read" emotion effectively, so they misperceive and misinterpret social signals in others; they don't process social information the way other kids do. To events that other children might regard as neutral or ambiguous—say, being bumped into by another child running after a ball in the playground—they often attribute hostile intentions.

Still, being overtly aggressive puts Windy at significant risk for snowballing behavioral problems and social maladjustment. In addition, Windy displays another form of aggression, social or relational aggression. It is more typically found in girls, but occasionally coexists with overt physical aggression in boys. In either gender, the harm is intentionally inflicted by way of manipulating the relationships of others. And it will just intensify Windy's adjustment difficulties.

On the first day of spring in 1993, honor student Curtis Taylor took his seat in the eighth-grade classroom he had grown to hate at the Oak Street Middle School in Burlington, Iowa. For three years other boys had been tripping him in the hallways, knocking things out of his hands. They'd even taken his head in their hands and banged it into a locker. Things were now intensifying. The name-calling was harsher. Some beloved books were taken. His bicycle was vandalized twice. Kids even kicked the cast that covered his broken ankle. And in front of his classmates, some guys had poured chocolate milk down the front of his sweatshirt. Curtis was so upset he went to see a school counselor. He blamed himself for the other kids' not liking him.

That night, Curtis went into a family bedroom, took out a gun, and shot himself to death. The community was stunned, said the news reports. The television cameras rolled, at least for a few days. Chicago journalist Bob Greene lingered over the events in his column, and then he printed letters from folks for whom the episode served not as a stimulus to social action, as in Norway, but largely as a self-focused reminder of their own childhood humiliations at the hands of bullies.

Months later, in Cherokee County, Georgia, fifteen-year-old Brian Head grew tired of the same teasing and deeds. The denouement was only slightly more remarkable. He shot himself to death—in front of his classmates. He walked to the front of the classroom and pulled the trigger. The Georgia death came on the heels of five bullying-related suicides in a small town in New Hampshire. Within days, the story got lost in the cacophony of other breaking news.

Just over a decade earlier, in late 1982, a nearly identical series of events unfolded in the northern reaches of Norway. Three boys between the ages of ten and fourteen killed themselves, one newspaper reported, to avoid continued severe bullying from schoolmates. But the story would not die. Nor would it wither into self-pity. An entire nation erupted. The following fall, scarcely nine months later, a campaign against bullying was in full swing in all of Norway's primary and junior high schools, launched by the minister of education. And its architect, Dan Olweus, Ph.D., a psychologist who had already pioneered research on bullies, now professor of research psychology at the University of Bergen, became something of a national hero.

The difference between the American and the Scandinavian experience could arguably be summed up in four words: Mighty Morphin Power Rangers. A nation whose toys are given to slashing robots in half seems to have more tolerance for violence as a solution to problems. Most Americans—even school personnel, a surprising finding since most bullying takes place in schools—do not take bullying very seriously. If they think at all about it, they tend to think that bullying is a given of childhood, at most a passing stage, one inhabited largely by boys who will, simply, inevitably, be boys.

"They even encourage it in boys," observes Gary W. Ladd, Ph.D., a professor of psychology at the University of Illinois and one of a growing cadre of American psychologists studying the phenomenon. "That's what parents always ask me," says psychologist David Schwartz, Ph.D., of Vanderbilt University. "Isn't it just a case of boys being boys?" The same parents harbor the belief that kids should somehow always be able to defend themselves—to "stand up for themselves," "fight back," "not be pushed around by anyone"—and those who don't or can't almost deserve what they get. Bullying is just good old boyhood in a land of aggressive individualists.

Nothing could be further from the truth.

First in Scandinavia, since in England, Japan, the Netherlands, Canada, and finally, the United States, researchers have begun scrutinizing the phenomenon of bullying. What they are finding is as sad as it is alarming:

- Bullies are a special breed of children. The vast majority of children (60 to 70 percent) are never involved in bullying, either as perpetrators or victims. Early in development, most children acquire internal restraints against such behavior. But those who bully do it consistently.
- Their aggression starts at an early age.

- It takes a very specific set of conditions to produce a child who can start fights, threaten or intimidate a peer ("Give me the jump rope or I'll kill you"), and actively inflict pain upon others.
- Bullying causes a great deal of misery to others, and its effects on victims last for decades, perhaps a lifetime.
- But the person hurt most of all by bullying is the bully himself, though that's not at first obvious, and the negative effects increase over time.
- Most bullies have a downwardly spiraling course through life, their behavior interfering with learning, friendships, jobs, intimate relationships, income, and mental health.
- Bullies turn into antisocial adults, and are far more likely than nonaggressive kids to commit crimes, batter their wives, abuse their children—and produce another generation of bullies.
- Girls can be bullies too. The aggression of girls has been vastly underestimated because it takes a different form. It is a far more subtle and complex kind of meanness than the overt physical aggression boys engage in.
- Both kinds of aggressive children are lacking in two things other children have: prosocial behavioral skills *and* an ability to inhibit destructive behavior.

To understand the behavior of bullies is to see how aggression is learned and how well the lesson is taken to heart. The existence of bullies tells us that the social needs of human beings are vastly undervalued, at least in Western culture. For the social life of kids, often thought of as an accessory to childhood, turns out to be crucial to healthy development. In the long run, bullying can be a way—a desperate and damaging way—for some people to maintain a circle of human contacts.

And bullying always has a very long run. Bullying may begin in childhood, but it continues in adulthood; it is among the most stable of human behavior styles. A child who is a bully by age nine or ten— and possibly long before then—is probably going to stay a bully.

What's a Bully and Who Is It?

There is no standard definition of a bully but Dan Olweus has honed the definition to three core elements—bullying involves **aggressive behavior** with **negative intent** directed from one child to another where there is a **power difference**. There's either a larger child or several children picking on one, or a child who is clearly more dominant. (This is distinct from garden-variety aggression, where there may be similar acts but between two people of equal status.) By definition the bully's target has difficulty defending him- or herself, and the bully's aggressive behavior is specifically intended to cause distress. What's more, the bully's actions are perceived as hurtful by the victim.

And, observes Dr. Olweus, the behavior is repeated over time. The chronicity of bullying is one of its more intriguing features. It is the most obvious clue that there comes to be some kind of a social relationship between a bully and his victims—and most bullies are boys, while victims are equally girls and boys. And it suggests that, contrary to parents' beliefs, bullying is not a problem that sorts itself out naturally.

The aggression can be physical—pushes and shoves and hitting, kicking, and punching. Or it can be verbal—name-calling, taunts, threats, ridicule, and insults. Bullies not only say mean things *to* you, they say mean things *about* you to others. Often enough, the intimidation that starts with a fist is later accomplished with no more than a nasty glance. The older bullies get, the more their aggression takes the form of verbal threats and abuse inflicting psychological harm.

Figures differ from study to study, from country to country, and especially from school to school, but from 15 to 20 percent of children are involved in bullying more than once or twice a term, as either bullies or victims. In a study conducted in Canada, 15 percent of students reported that they bullied others more than once or twice during the term. According to large-scale studies Dr. Olweus conducted in Norway in 1983, 7 percent of students bullied others "with some regularity." But since then, bully problems have increased, he says. By 1991, they had gone up a whopping 30 percent.

Bullies, for the most part, are different from you and me. Studies reliably show that they have a distinctive cognitive makeup—a hostile attributional bias, a kind of paranoia. In social situations, they have trouble reading intent. They perpetually attribute hostile intentions to others, so they see the world as a scary place. They make a defensive response to a perceived provocation, perhaps even a preemptive strike. The trouble is, they perceive provocation where it does not exist. That comes to justify their aggressive behavior. Say someone bumps them and they drop a book; bullies don't see it as an accident, they see it as a call to arms. And their own response, then, is a defensive maneuver to relieve the threat. These children respond aggressively because they process social information inaccurately. They endorse revenge.

That allows them a favorable attitude toward violence and the use of violence to solve problems. Whether they start out there or get there along the way, bullies come to believe that aggression is the best solution to conflicts. They also have a strong need to dominate others and derive satisfaction from injuring others. Bullies lack prosocial behavior—they do not know how to relate positively to others. No caring, helping, cooperative—prosocial—attitudes hold them in check; they do not understand the feelings of others, and therefore come to deny the suffering of others.

Bullies are also untroubled by anxiety, an emotion disabling in its extreme form but in milder form the root of human restraint. What may be most surprising is that bullies see themselves quite positively—which may be because they are so little aware of what others truly think of them. Indeed, a blindness to the feelings of others permeates their behavioral style and outlook.

Every attempt to trace aggression to its roots indicates that it starts sometime in the preschool years and thrives in elementary and middle school. Up to grade six, Dr. Olweus reports, bullies are of average popularity. They tend to have two or three friends—largely other aggressive kids. And it's their physical strength that other kids admire. As they get older, though, their popularity with classmates wanes; by high school they are hanging out only with other toughs. They may get what they want through aggression, and be looked up to for being tough, but they are not *liked*.

If their self-confidence survives increasing rejection by peers, it may be because bullies are unable to perceive themselves correctly in social situations, part of their social blindness. Reports child psychologist Melissa DeRosier, Ph.D., of the University of North Carolina: "Bullies are clueless as to how little they are liked. They are out of touch with what kids think." As something of a threat to others, they are not likely to learn just exactly how other kids feel about them. And with their deficits in social cognition, they certainly don't see the impact of their own behavior on others.

But it isn't simply that aggressive kids receive somewhat muted signals of dislike because others fear physical retaliation. That does happen. What is also clear is that bullies distort the negative social feedback they do get about their own behavior. The evidence points to a very self-serving, narcissistic form of social insensitivity. First of all, when put to the test—asked to name "Who really likes you?" among classmates and "Who really does not like you?" and their answers compared with those of other kids—they overestimate their social competence. They get far more "like least" nominations from classmates than they expect. Similarly, they actually get far fewer "like most" nominations than they anticipate.

The funny thing is, when the tables are turned and bullies are asked the same questions about their classmates, they are extremely capable of assessing the social status of their peers. Psychologists Audrey L. Zakriski, Ph.D., of Brown University, and John D. Coie, Ph.D., of Duke University, went to great lengths to determine that aggressive-rejected kids have trouble interpreting social feedback only when negative messages are targeted to them. The researchers created carefully scripted videotapes of two kids playing a new card game. In one vignette a card player was up against a peer who delivered monosyllabic feedback that was neutral in tone; in another vignette the card player got negative feedback from a much more begrudging peer in response to his questions. The researchers showed the two videotapes to fifty-six boys, eighteen of whom were aggressive-rejected kids, and asked them to evaluate how much each player liked the other. Then they put each of the boys in turn in real-live situations paralleling the two videotaped vignettes, in which peer-actors delivered the same two kinds of ambiguous and openly negative feedback. (All the boys thought the goal was to personally road-test the card game.)

The aggressive boys have highly accurate acceptance- and rejection-detectors when it comes to other kids. They are fully capable of reading rejection cues—provided the rejection is happening to someone else. Their social judgment is impaired only with regard to themselves. The responses of the aggressive kids were in stark contrast with those of submissive-rejected boys; the latter were remarkably accurate and nondefensive in detecting rejection directed at them—one reason they may grow up feeling so lonely and depressed.

"Aggressive-rejected children possess specific difficulties in processing social rejection cues only when the self is involved," reported Drs. Zakriski and Coie. Because rejection is a very painful experience, the aggressive boys defend themselves against the dislike of their peers by actively distorting it in a self-protective way. In short, they engage in denial.

The researchers conclude that bullies feel less lonely than other rejected children because their insensitivity to negative feedback directed at them allows them to truly believe they are disliked less than they are in reality. This lack of awareness also preserves their self-esteem. Studies show that bullies actually esteem themselves more highly than others do.

But denial has its costs. What serves as a way of coping with chronic rejection also keeps bullies locked in to their progressively isolating behavior. Lacking awareness of how much they are actually disliked, they are not likely to make any effort to change their behavior. So they go on doing what keeps getting them rejected.

Mark Leary of Wake Forest University has an added perspective. Everyone, he argues, has a fundamental need to belong, to be accepted. There are many routes to social inclusion, and most of us choose the "social desirability" one—that is, we try to be nice people whom others want to have around. "But others try to be accepted primarily on the basis of their appearance, or their competence, or their adherence to group norms (the ultraconformist). We all use each of these sometimes, but have our personal favorites. Some people even seek acceptance at the cost of being liked, and the bully is one of them."

Power is one way of promoting a tenuous sense of inclusion, Leary adds. "People may not like me, but liking isn't the important thing; it's only one route to inclusion. If I'm intimidating, I can at least eke out an odd sense of respect; people will be afraid to explicitly exclude me too often, and at least a few kids (who hold me in fearful awe) will think I'm pretty cool and hang out with me. It's a pretty poor alternative to being adored for being a wonderful person, but as an inclusion strategy of last resort, it's an option for those with poor social skills but the capacity for intimidating.''

HOW TO IDENTIFY A BULLY

- Pushes, shoves, hits, kicks, and/or makes fun of other kids, says mean things about them, or calls them names.
- Meanness may take form of manipulating relationships of others.
- Aggression starts early—as early as preschool years.
- Believes aggression is acceptable way to solve conflicts.
- Is quick to interpret accidents and other neutral events as deliberate acts of hostility.
- Gets into fights—but blames others for starting them.
- Lacks understanding of pain in others.
- Aggression is part of general rule-breaking stance.
- Has a need to dominate others.
- Has two or three friends—who are also aggressive.
- Feels no anxiety.
- Generally feels well liked by other children.
- Does not feel lonely.
- Hangs out with increasingly younger children.

An Increase in Aggressive Fantasies

It's possible that bullying is not the same in all the world's cultures and that American children may suffer more severely at the hands of bullies—a suggestion borne out by the fact that bullies register less popular with peers here, especially as they get older, than they do in Scandinavia. There may be an intensity to bullying here that does not exist elsewhere. Dominance may be more valued; competition may be more accepted. Victimization may be more extreme. This intensity has many observers worried because aggression is worsening in violence in the United States and other countries, particularly among the young. While that doesn't necessarily mean bullying is getting worse, there are disturbing signals. "Clinically, I see an increment in the aggressive fantasies kids now bring to therapy," confides Vanderbilt's Dr. Schwartz. "They talk about their dolls tearing the skin off each other." The age at which children are displaying ruthlessly violent aggression is steadily decreasing. In April 1998, an eight-year-old was arrested for toting a loaded gun to school in his backpack.

Bullying exists, to greater or lesser degrees, in virtually every Westernized culture. It is a serious problem in Japan. It happens in China. No one knows for sure, because the same methodology has not been applied in every country, but there may be more bullies per capita in the United States, England, Canada, and Ireland than in other countries. And bullying is not partial to cities; if anything, it's more common in the one-room schoolhouse than in urban settings.

But no matter where they live, bullies find one place especially congenial to their nefarious activities: school. Most bullying occurs on the school playground, especially its unsupervised corners, and in the long and crowded corridors of most schools. Above all else, says Norway's Dan Olweus, bullying is a school problem.

It's not that bullying worsens at adolescence—in fact, it tends to lessen. But that's when sensitivity to rejection by peers takes a painful leap forward. Curtis Taylor probably could have told us that.

Danse Macabre

Increasingly, researchers are coming to see bullying and victimization not only as the products of individual characteristics but also as outgrowths of unique interactive chemistry. Over the course of time, bullies and their victims become a twosome—a dyad, in the lingo of social science. Like husbands and wives, mothers and infants, and other lovers and also close friends, they come to have an ongoing relationship, they interact frequently, and there is a special dynamic operating.

What makes normal dyadic relationships so enthralling for both parties—and for infants it is the very medium in which growth takes place—is the intricate pattern of exchange, of action and response, the *recitative*, the synchrony of give-and-take that gets established. It sets up its own gravitational field; it draws the two together and validates each as a very special person. If that's not quite how it goes with bullies and their victims, still these children develop a history with each other, and the behavior of each reinforces the other. Call it the bully-victim dance.

That's how Debra Pepler, Ph.D., sees it. "There is a relationship. There is a repeatedness over time. Then a glance or comment can work, setting up a whole terrifying sequence of emotions such as anxiety," where once there was the verbal threat of aggression, or even the real thing. Then the submissiveness signals to the bully that his aggression is working. Once selected for aggression, victims seem to reward their attackers with submission.

Other researchers describe victims who actually pester the bully. There is, for example, the kid who runs after the bully: "Aren't you going to tease me today? I won't get mad." Both bullies and victims are disliked by their peers; they may be seeking each other for social contact—just because no one else will.

An Underground Activity

Bullying inhabits a covert kids-only world—right under the noses of adults. "Teachers tell us it doesn't happen in their school or classroom," reports the University of Illinois's Dr. Ladd, "when in fact it does"—a point he teases out by giving separate questionnaires about such behavior to students and teachers. "To some degree the teachers simply don't want to admit it. But there is also a fair amount of evidence that kids know just how antisocial their behavior is and often choose corners that are out of the ken of their teachers. Teachers just aren't as accurate as the children in reporting instances of bullying."

Nor do most parents know about it when their kids are victimized. Like Curtis Taylor, kids often think it is their own fault. So there is deep shame and humiliation. Moreover, the fear of reprisals keeps kids from saying a word. And tragically, says Dr. Ladd, the pace of parenting today doesn't leave a whole lot of room for parents to sit down every evening with their children and find out how their day went, to talk about how they are being treated by their peers.

He wishes they would, because when he asks, he hears. "In our interview procedure, we ask kids to tell us something fun that happened at school. Then we ask, 'Tell us about something that happened at school that was nasty.' Out pour stories about harassment, exclusion, rejection, victimization. A lot of the parents look like they're hearing about it for the first time."

When Toronto psychologist Debra Pepler wanted to get a detailed glimpse into the world of bullies, she planted a video camera in several schools and trained it on the playground, where the kids were monitored by remote microphones. In fifty-two hours of tape, Dr. Pepler, a researcher at York University, documented more than four hundred episodes of bullying. They ranged from brushes of mild teasing to thirty-seven solid minutes of kicking and punching. The average episode, however, lasted thirty-seven seconds. Teachers noticed and intervened in only one out of twenty-five episodes.

The child in the thirty-seven-minute episode, says Dr. Pepler, is repeatedly kicked and thrown around by two kids (although in the vast majority of instances, bullying is one on one). "What's so strange to me is that *he stays in it*. There are lots of opportunities for him to get away. At one point a teacher even approaches and tries to break it up, and *all three* of them say, 'Oh no, we're just having fun.'

"In talking to other kids about it and showing them the tapes, I confirmed what I felt—it's so important for children to be members of a social group that to receive negative attention is better than to receive no attention at all. It's actually self-confirming. There's a sense of who I am; I am at least somebody with a role in the group. I have no way of identifying myself if nobody pays attention to me. Who am I? I have no one to relate to."

Although Dr. Olweus insists that not everything she's taped truly represents bullying—there's not always repeated behavior, he observes—Dr. Pepler's studies suggest that bullying is far more common among children than most adults either observe or admit. According to Dr. Pepler, it occurs once every seven minutes in a moderately sized school. And 4 percent of bullies are armed, at least in Toronto, one of the most ethnically balanced cities in the world.

Probably because bullying is such a covert activity, schools seem to have a hard time figuring out what to do about it. There are only scattered efforts in U.S. schools to institute any antibullying programs, and, unlike in Scandinavia, rarely have they been tested for effectiveness.

Bullying may thrive underground, but it is a psychologically distinctive experience. It's painful. It's scary. Victims feel a great loss of control. Ask anyone who's ever been victimized even once—the memory tends to survive well into adulthood.

Not All Bullies Are Alike

Until recently, a bully was just a bully. But researchers are turning up differences among them that provide strong clues as to how the behavior takes shape. For the moment, there seem to be two distinct types of bully, distinguished, in part, by how often they themselves are bullied.

To make matters slightly more complex, different researchers have different names for them. There are those bullies who are out-and-out aggressive and don't need situations of conflict to set them off, called "proactive aggressors" in some studies, "effectual aggressors" in others. Classic playground bullies fall into this camp. Their behavior is motivated by future reward—like "get me something." It's goal-oriented, instrumental. These bullies not only want something—and that something is usually a toy or an object, not a friendship—they make an active decision that they can get it. Or perhaps these bullies have high thresholds of arousal and need some increase in arousal level. These bullies see aggression as an effective means of getting what they want—because peers are likely to submit to their aggressive acts. In fact, their aggressiveness may actually increase over time as they experience its effectiveness. Hard as it is to believe, these bullies have friends—primarily other bullies. What they don't have at all is empathy; cooperation is a foreign word. They are missing prosocial feelings.

Then there are those bullies who are sometimes aggressors and sometimes victims—"reactive bullies," "ineffectual aggressors," or, in Dr. Olweus's lexicon, "provocative" or "collaborative victims." Regardless of who starts a fight, these kids prolong the battle, says David Perry, Ph.D., professor of psychology at Florida Atlantic University in Boca Raton. They get angry easily and escalate conflict into aggression, but end up losing. Their behavior is motivated by perceived provocation or threat.

Dr. Perry claims that half of all bullies are such hotheads. Any way the bully pie is sliced, these highly reactive aggressors are the worst off. They engage in the highest levels of conflict—they give it and they get it. Like all other bullies, they perceive provocation where it does not exist. And they place great value on controlling their adversaries. But their emotional makeup is distinct: They are easily emotionally aroused and can't handle conflict. They don't give anyone the benefit of the doubt. Once these kids make a hostile interpretation of a situation, researchers believe, the interpretation and the emotion preempt any further mental processing of the situation. They don't stop to evaluate, the way nonaggressive kids do, whether their response is even workable under the conditions.

"Peers are good at describing their characteristics," Dr. Perry reports. "They get emotionally upset, they show distress easily, they are quick to become oppositional and defiant. They are quick to cry. And they are named most likely to lose fights amid exaggerated cries of frustration and distress."

And they are the least liked. Of all children, they are the most rejected in the peer group. What's more, the hostility of their peers toward them tends to grow. The cognitive distortions reactive bullies make lock them into an ever-expanding negative cycle in which they attribute hostile intent to peer provocateurs and retaliate aggressively, the peers then respond with increased hostility, and they then interpret their peers' hostility as confirmation of their earlier interpretation. Rejection puts them at risk of developing the kinds of externalizing, antisocial problems bullies develop and the internalizing problems, like anxiety and depression, common to victims. Whether these bullies have the most trouble in life isn't clear, but they do have the fewest friends.

Why do they keep at it, when they always lose? Most of all, says Dr. Perry, they have problems of emotional regulation; they have low thresholds of arousal in the first place, and they can't soothe themselves, calm themselves down once conflict starts. They get invested in their fights. Their high level of arousal keeps them from recognizing it's time to get up and walk away when they are clearly losing. "Their emotions may be preempting their cognitions or arousal may be distorting their cognition," Dr. Perry says.

Perhaps best of all, they are targets because they're fun for other bullies to pick on; they provide lots of theatrical value. They get provoked because they react in ways that are rewarding to bullies—*they get a response*. Getting a response from another human being is the bully's ultimate reward.

These hotheads, says Dr. Perry, seem to have a low threshold of irritability. "They seem to exist in a mood state of readiness." They frequently take an oppositional stance in situations.

Monkey Business

The ineffectual bullies bear an uncanny resemblance to psychobiologist Gary W. Kraemer's monkeys. Dr. Kraemer is an associate professor at the University of Wisconsin and a researcher at the famed Harlow Primate Laboratory, where Harry Harlow conducted his famous studies of maternal deprivation among monkeys reared with mothers made of cloth. Dr. Kraemer is working with two of the lab's populations of rhesus monkeys. One group is reared from birth by their monkey mothers. The other is nurtured by lab workers for the first month after birth, then reared with their monkey peers.

Human "mothers," Kraemer finds, do a swell job of raising physically robust monkeys. But only the monkey moms raise socially competent ones. The human-reared monkeys are either impulsively aggressive or inordinately reclusive—and their behavior varies unpredictably. They have a collage of changes in the way they see the world, deficits in cognitive problem-solving that endure no matter how much social interaction with their peers the monkeys later get.

"Peer-reared monkeys can't anticipate what is going to happen next in social interactions," says Kraemer. "They look like a wild cannon. Something will set them off. And they have no 'off' button. Once in agonistic encounters, they have a hard time stopping." These monkeys not only display unregulated aggression and antisocial behavior, they contribute to the instability of the whole group. They just don't "get" the rhythms of relationships.

In addition to behaving like reactive bullies, they have an array of enduring neurochemical changes in the brain. There is chaos in specific neurotransmitter systems—the serotonin, norepinephrine, and dopamine pathways. "The norepinephrine system is not developed at all," says Kraemer. "The serotonin system is strange." While some studies have shown that disturbances in serotonin levels are related to violence in humans, Dr. Kraemer finds that the disorder is not limited to one neurotransmitter.

To Kraemer, these monkeys are proof that social relations—specifically the early caregiver-infant attachment process, the *dance* of mother and child—actually structures the developing nervous system. It gets incorporated within, a kind of internal map, and becomes the prototype, the guide for all social behavior. In the connection between mother and infant lies the pattern, the desire, and the ability for connecting with others. Through the child's internalized image of the way the world interacts, the social environment itself plays a role in regulating the behavior of individuals.

The studies, says Dr. Kraemer, clearly demonstrate that there is a biological underpinning to violence. But "biological" does not necessarily mean it's genetic. "We find that these monkeys have biological changes," he says. "The changes are due to early rearing experiences and interactions in the social environment." And so the later problems the monkeys face stem from early rearing experiences.

"To the degree that caregivers are unpredictable, random, and asynchronous, then social behavior is not likely to be internally regulated," Dr. Kraemer says. "Social activity is not an accessory in life; it's reproduced in your brain." That's one reason, he believes, that aggression begins at an early age and winds up being so durable an approach to life.

Of the human-reared monkeys, he says, "You can give them all the Prozac in the world but you can never get them back on the usual trajectory. It will reduce the duration and frequency of repetitive behaviors, but it doesn't increase the proportion of social behavior. The entire system is dysregulated. You can make a symptom go away, but that doesn't restore normalcy. The neurobiological changes that are important occur in the context of purposeful social interaction. That is the therapeutic medium.''

In the normal course of events, says Dr. Kraemer, human children develop dominance hierarchies, although they are not very rigid. Aggression enables people to create space around them; usually that's a stabilizing influence. But in bullies, the process becomes supervening. Even when failure is evident, they continue. ''There is certainly a dysregulation of something. Bullies and victims are breaking the normal harmony. Theirs is a different dance.''

If his studies suggest that aggression begins in the early parent- or caregiver-child interaction, there's an arsenal of human research making the very same case. ''In human cultures,'' he says, ''there is a great diversity in caregiver behavior. What proves to be important is the fact that adults make an investment in their children, and that the investment is structured, not haphazard or neglectful. There is a dance, and there must be synchrony. How kids are reared has a potent effect on how kids will be.''

Aw, C'mon— Isn't It Just Boys Being Boys?

Sure, lots of boys engage in all kinds of competitions and rough-and-tumble play; those are nonthreatening physical ways of establishing dominance hierarchies, a goal that actually promotes social stability.

But the line between fun and fisticuffs gets erased only when there's a bully in the pack; the bully misconstrues some borderline gesture or movement as intentionally hostile. When push turns to shove, when meanness intrudes on play—when someone selects a target and inflicts pain and the payoff is someone else's humiliation—then it's outright bullying.

And that's not a healthy way of interacting, not for the victims, but especially not for the bullies. There are huge costs to them. It is the first and perhaps most identifiable stop on a trajectory that leads almost directly to criminal behavior. Bullying is just another word for antisocial behavior, and it's part of a more general rule-breaking stance. According to long-term studies conducted by Norway's Dr. Olweus, 60 percent of boys who were named as bullies in grades six to nine have at least one court conviction by age twenty-four.

Kids who are aggressive in childhood are aggressive in adolescence and later. In a decades-long look at boys in London, those who were bullies at age fourteen were bullies at age eighteen—and at thirty-two. In a classic long-term study that is still ongoing, University of Michigan psychologist Leonard Eron, Ph.D., and colleagues have been following 518 children in New York's upstate Columbia County since they were eight years old. All are now in their forties. The most astonishing finding is that the kids who were named by their peers—*at age eight*—as most aggressive commit more crimes and more serious crimes as adults. They have more driving offenses. More court convictions. More alcoholism. More antisocial personality disorder. More use of mental-health services.

When young, says Dr. Eron, these kids have intelligence levels equal to those of their normal peers. But by age nineteen, aggressive behavior gets in the way of developing intellectual skills. At age thirty, they and their spouses were interviewed. "There is significantly more abusive behavior," says Eron, who's girding for another round of assessment. "They don't achieve socially, economically, or professionally. They never learned prosocial behavior, and that interferes with every activity." Their work histories are erratic, at best—the same behaviors that make them troublesome among peers make them disruptive among coworkers. "The longer the haul, the more the bully suffers.

"Parents should be concerned about bullying," notes Dr. Eron. "These kids are not just harming others—they're harming themselves."

Downward Drift

"Over time, aggression is a marker of every negative outcome that there is," adds Vanderbilt's Dr. Schwartz. Bullies get locked into patterns of aggressive and hostile response that are very rewarding to them—but that sharply circumscribe whom they get to hang out with. As they go through high school, increasingly their behavior is acceptable only to others like themselves, and, fortified with their hostile attributional style and growing contempt for the values of others, they spin their way to outcast lifestyle. Bullies develop conduct disorder and become delinquents in adolescence.

There's sex, drugs, and booze to keep them busy—and they take up with all of them earlier than most other kids, studies show. They drop out of school, hang out with aggressive peers, and that drives further deviance; the link with others like themselves may be what turns a bully into a criminal. However criminals are made, the point cannot be clearer—bullies' social style drives their downward drift through life.

Eventually, such children are likely to experience adjustment problems at school and become socially isolated in adolescence. As a result, their attitude toward school is scarcely favorable, they do everything they can to avoid going, and they do not perform well when there. These children are at risk to become school dropouts; adolescents who feel socially isolated appear to strike out in reaction to their feelings of anger and frustration. Once in this position, they are set up to carry out the role of social outlaw.

As if things aren't bad enough, the presence of antisocial behavior in these children does not eliminate the risk of developing internalizing disorders. Their maladjustment puts these children at risk for multiple mental-health problems in adulthood. They are prone to depression as well as to drug abuse and alcoholism. They invariably wind up with lower socioeconomic status than they started out with.

Double the trouble for girl bullies. When girls are overtly aggressive, they are essentially engaging in a form of behavior that boys approve of more than girls do. Their participation in activity that is not characteristic of their gender compounds the opprobrium and rejection they are already subject to because of aggression, and that magnifies their adjustment difficulties.

If bullying is bad for those who give it as well as those who get it, then just exactly why do kids do it? "It's a great strategy for getting what you want," says Illinois's Gary Ladd. You push the little girl off the tricycle, you get the tricycle. "A lot of aggressive kids think aggression works. They think about one outcome, but not about the others."

People do have a need to control their environment, and perhaps some enter life with differences in that need, as occurs with other traits. The great psychological benefit to bullying, says Dr. Ladd, is that bullies feel powerful, in control. "They've picked a little micro-cosm in which to exert control." But it's a hell of a way to get your own way. Having to win through intimidation does not make them feel great about themselves.

"These kids are experts at using short-term payoffs," says psy-chologist Gerald R. Patterson, Ph.D., a founder of the Oregon Social Learning Center in Eugene, and a pioneer in family studies of ag-gression. "They're not very good at long-range things that are in their best interest."

For all those boys who engage in bullying as a way of gaining status in the eyes of their peers, the last laugh is on them. Their trophy is a sham. What looks like power and status turns out not to be that at all. The proof is in their testosterone levels.

Richard E. Tremblay, Ph.D., is a psychologist at the University of Montreal who has been conducting long-term studies of more than a thousand bullies and other aggressive kids. Among one group of 178 kids that has passed the threshold of adolescence, Dr. Tremblay decided to check out hormone-behavior links by measuring the boys' levels of testosterone. What he found set him on his ear. The boys rated (by their peers and their teachers) most physically aggressive from ages to six to twelve had lower levels of testosterone at age thirteen than ordinary peers. The "multiproblem fighters," or hot-head bullies, proved to have the lowest testosterone levels of all.

How could these consistently aggressive boys register so low on testosterone? Isn't aggression an extreme of masculine behavior, and wouldn't the testosterone levels of aggressive boys be high? Tremblay admits to having been puzzled. The mistake, he realized, is all those direct extrapolations from animal studies of dominance in which tes-tosterone equals aggression. He has come to believe that testosterone levels really reflect not brute force but social success. "Physical ag-gression that is not accompanied by social well-being and social success—being designated a leader by peers—does not appear to be associated with high testicular activity.''

Among animals, physical aggression leads to dominance. Among humans, he says, dominance and physical aggression are not the same thing. Physical aggression leads increasingly to rejection by peers, by parents, and even by the school system.

"They are losers," he states emphatically. "Their testosterone status at puberty reflects the fact that they are not dominating their environment. The human behaviors of dominance are not the same as animal ones," he insists. In humans, even in beefy boys, social dominance has less to do with physical aggression and more with language. "While aggression is important for attaining high social status," says Dr. Tremblay, "it is not the only strategy. And when sustained, it is not decisive at all." And that is precisely where bullies are weak. While their general intelligence starts out more or less on a par with that of other kids, studies show that their verbal intelligence is low.

POINTERS FOR PARENTS

PROVIDE A SAFE AND STIMULATING ENVIRONMENT FOR GROWTH.
Children need stimulation, with books and toys to play with. Children with a more stimulating home environment are more socially competent and less aggressive.

Suggest positive activities that your child can do alone, such as:
• doing puzzles—(have on hand wooden-piece puzzles for very young children, books of mazes for older ones)
• making up a comic book
• playing Nerf basketball (the basket affixes by suction—put it on the back of a door; a narrow hallway will do)

Suggest activities your child can do with one or more other children. For example, some activities minimize the possibility of disputes over objects:

- word games
- a request to hear the scariest/funniest/silliest story
- assigning a cooperative creative task, like making a video. Companies like Fisher Price make inexpensive childproof equipment. Cooperation is built in: One kid has to work the camera while another acts. After a set amount of time, they can switch places. They can then view themselves by turning on the TV. In one fell swoop, children are forced to collaborate, exercise creative powers—and get behavioral feedback.

See that kids in groups have plenty of things to do. Provide play materials. Buy a soccer ball. Paint a hopscotch pattern on the sidewalk. Bullying flourishes when kids are together and have nothing else to do.

Make sure your child has outlets for physical energy.

RECOGNIZE THE DANGER SIGNS OF BULLYING.
Bullies are always getting into scrapes, but minimizing their own contributions. It's always someone else's fault. They exaggerate the role of others. "He started it." "She pushed me." "He was acting dumb." "He wasn't going to let me get a turn." Don't fall for it.

TACKLE PROBLEMS EARLY.
There is a large set of children for whom aggressive behavior starts early, in preschool. And by age eight, it is firmly established.

Once aggressive kids enter school, their coercive style of interaction generalizes to interactions with teachers and peers, and achievement suffers. Parents often have trouble relating well with the school regarding the child's academic and behavioral adjustment, which exacerbates the problem at school—and provides additional fodder for parent-child conflict at home. Not only do aggressive kids have few social relationships, but by early adolescence there's a high likelihood of alcohol and drug use, school dropout or failure, and risky sexual behavior. The later intervention begins, the more problems to treat.

BUT DON'T OVERREACT TO NORMAL BEHAVIOR.
Physical aggression and oppositional behavior typically reach their peak around thirty months of age. Thereafter, children learn to curb aggressive impulses as they respond to consistent parental monitoring and express themselves through language rather than, say, grabbing. Between ages two and three, children and their parents normally come into conflict an average—an *average*—of three to fifteen times an hour, and most of their interactions focus on prohibitions.

BE DOUBLY SURE TO FIND OUT ABOUT YOUR CHILD'S WORLD.
Ask, "How did things go today?" or "Tell me, what was your day like?" As you listen to your child, smile. Touch your child. Nod in response to your child's conversation. These are the little signs of approval that motivate children to meet parental demands and expectations, the tiny reinforcers that many parents do hundreds of times a day without even realizing it—and that many parents do not do at all. These are the ways to help break through the defensive and denial strategies budding bullies often adopt.

TEACH YOUR CHILD TO ASK FOR THINGS. EVEN LITTLE THINGS.
Aggressive children take things without asking for them, which greatly reinforces their aggressive behavior. Out of such everyday events are aggressive kids turned into irritable, explosive, and abrasive adults. Asking your child to articulate what he wants helps build language skills, which lag in aggressive kids. It teaches children when it is that they need to use language in the first place, and it helps establish the habit

of asking for things and not taking them. Of course, the child has to be rewarded positively for asking—otherwise, he quickly comes to feel that no one cares or notices and that there's no point in changing behavior.

REWARD PROSOCIAL BEHAVIOR AT EVERY TURN.
Punishment is not the only way to control behavior. Positive reinforcement for things well done, or attempts at doing things better, creates a far richer climate for success.

Praise your child when he expresses anger or frustration in nonphysical ways, when your child listens well, shares something.

A Done Deal by Age Two

Says Dr. Tremblay with bemusement, "I started out studying aggression in adult criminals. Then I found I had to look at adolescents. Now I'm looking at young children. If you had told me I was going to be studying two-year-olds, I would have said that you were crazy."

But he has come to believe that the life-style of aggression is a done deal by age two. And with that, the terrible twos just got a lot worse. "Physical aggression is normal at that age. It builds up from nine months and reaches its highest frequency at age two. And then you learn that it hurts when aggressed. Adults intervene and indicate it is the wrong behavior. Language skills increase, and physical aggression decreases. If you don't get it by age two, then you are on the pathway to being a physically aggressive child. You lose out. You haven't mastered social skills, which are mainly verbal. There's something about language." What it may be is that language is socially acquired in the caregiver-child interaction. And some kids get more of that than others. "Infants who are neglected do not learn language skills," says Dr. Tremblay, "especially if the parents are not highly skilled."

Most parents of two-year-olds are confident that their children will outgrow aggression. But some of these children will not, Dr. Tremblay observes. "A child has to learn to inhibit the impulse to

take away another child's toy when he feels the need for an object.''
A bully is a bully is a bully, but a bully is more aggressive today than
ever before, he finds. ''The problem is less control. There is a tendency not to restrain kids. Kids feel the right to express needs. We
live in an environment that has not favored that control. Among those
who have not learned how to control themselves between two and
three, the problem is getting more out of hand.''

Hey—What About the Girls?

Bullying has been studied largely in boys because they are so much
more overtly aggressive. The problem, contends psychologist Nicki
R. Crick, Ph.D., is that aggression has always been defined strictly in
terms of what boys do that's mean. Researchers have ignored the
possibility that there may be gender differences in the expression of
aggression. And that's just one more instance of male bias distorting
the way things really are. She and her colleagues now know that ''girls
are just as capable of being mean as boys are.''

Indeed, the research shows that boys engage in such physical aggression as kicking, hitting, pushing, shoving, and verbal aggression
like name-calling and making fun of kids more than girls do. The
interpretation is that boys are just a lot more aggressive than girls are.
But Dr. Crick prefers to go back to the textbook definition of aggression. ''It's 'the intent to hurt or harm,' '' she points out.

For the past five years, Dr. Crick, who is associate professor of
psychology at the University of Minnesota's Institute of Child Development, has been looking at the ways girls try to harm others.
While boys' aggression plays out in physical ways, the aggression of
girls plays out in social relationships. It involves hurting others through
damaging, manipulating, or controlling their relationships in aversive
ways like:

- spreading vicious rumors in the peer group to get even with
  someone or spreading rumors behind someone's back so that
  other people will stop liking that person
- telling others to stop liking someone in order to get even with
  him or her

- trying to control or dominate a person by using social exclusion as a form of retaliation: "You can't come to my birthday party if you don't do x, y, and z."
- threatening to withdraw friendship in order to get one's way, control another's behavior, or hurt someone: "I won't be your friend if . . ."
- giving someone the silent treatment and making sure that they know they're being excluded as a form of retaliation

It makes intuitive sense to Dr. Crick. Bullying is a way to exert control. For girls, there are sanctions against physical methods of control. So they use the relationship sphere. "If you want to hurt someone and you want it to be effective, shouldn't it be something they really value? Numerous studies have shown that women and girls really value relationships, establishing intimacy and closeness, and dyadic relations with other girls. That led us to looking at the use of relationships as the vehicle for harm, because if you take that away from a girl, you're really 'getting her.' " Similarly, boys' aggression, she says, plays into goals shown to be important to boys in the face of their peers—physical dominance and having things, or instrumentality. But it just "doesn't capture the full range of harmful or neglectful events that children sometimes experience as part of their peer interactions."

Relational aggression, however, is subtle, complex, and indirect, making it difficult to study. It doesn't hit observers in the eye. Nevertheless, Dr. Crick has been able to smoke it out by asking descriptive questions of children. For example, "Some kids tell their friends that they will stop liking them unless the friends do what they say. How often do you tell friends this?" Or "Some children when they get mad at a person ignore them or stop talking to them. How often do you do this?" In studies of children ranging from three to twelve years, she has determined that parents and teachers and kids themselves see the behaviors of relational aggression as problematic, hurtful—and common.

Both boys and girls regard kids who are relationally aggressive as mean and manipulative. "This behavior cuts across all socioeconomic groups and all age groups," says Dr. Crick. "Adults do these things, too." In fact, her studies show that the older girls get, the more normative relational aggression becomes for them when they get angry.

Particularly as girls move into adolescence, themes of social exclusion increase in frequency in girls' conflicts with their peers.

Among aggressive kids, 27 percent of them—mainly boys, like Windy—engage in *both* overt and relational aggression. But the overwhelming majority of aggressive kids—73 percent—engage in one or the other form of aggression, not both. Relational aggression is far more characteristic of girls, at least throughout the school years. Taking relational aggression into account leads to a startling conclusion: Girls (22 percent) and boys (27 percent) are aggressive in almost equal numbers. By contrast, in a number of studies, fewer than 1 percent of girls were found who engaged in overt aggression.

While most overt bullying is carried out by boys toward other boys, most relational aggression is carried out by girls—but directed toward both boys and girls. Just as in the case with physical aggression, neither relational bullies nor their victims do well either in the present or in the long haul. Exposure to relational aggression is damaging and harmful for children. Those exposed are unhappy with their social relationships. They feel emotionally upset and are at risk for social and emotional problems ahead.

Relational aggression is a dysfunctional way of expressing anger. Studies show that those who engage in it—whether girls or boys—have internalizing attributes that make them at risk for depression. They have negative perceptions of themselves and are unhappy about their social experience. They are subject to loneliness and depression. But like overt bullies, they also develop externalizing problems. They blame their peers for things not going well. They may be impulsive and defiant. It may be that their talent for creating enemies compounds the risk of later problems, as it certainly compounds their stress.

Their aggression cannot be written off as a passing phase. It is an enduring behavioral style because, like other forms of aggression in children beyond the toddler years, it reflects an underlying way of seeing and taking in information about the world and making decisions about responses. Relational bullies have deficits in understanding and processing social information. Like reactive bullies, they misread cues, misattributing hostility in ambiguous situations. Two girls are huddled together talking. They're really talking about birthday-party plans, but the relational bully thinks, "They were talking about me." As with the reactive physical bully, her misperception is constituted of equal parts egocentricity, suspicion, and paranoia. Her misattributions, however, are confined to relationship situations. But once she makes the misattribution, she is provoked by what she regards as malicious intent by her peers. And she begins spreading lies about the two girls. Her aggressive act is an angry, defensive response; she self-justifies the harm she does purely as retaliation—a means of getting even. Such girls also minimize the deviancy of their own aggressive acts by clinging to the belief that most girls would do the same nasty things to other girls; in fact, in Dr. Crick's studies, when she presents vignettes of ambiguous provocations and asks subjects what is going on, most girls do not see the situation the same way or endorse an aggressive response.

Being the social bully puts girls at increasing risk of rejection over time. Such girls may start off the school year with a bang—indeed, they have a certain amount of social authority and control—but they end it in loneliness. While overtly aggressive boys are sometimes admired by other boys for being tough, relationally aggressive girls are not liked by either male or female peers. Few people, it seems, want to be around a mean girl. Others grow increasingly tired of their behavior, weary of being manipulated. While most relationally aggressive kids are rejected by most others, a very few are "controversial"—that is, they are well liked by some kids and actively disliked by others; it is probably the case that those who dislike them have felt the sting of their exclusionary tactics. Either way, their own behavior brings them problems because it strictly limits the pool of potential friends. While studies have not yet been done on the academic performance of relational bullies, Dr. Crick, on the basis of anecdotal evidence, is "putting my money on them not doing well at school."

Kids who are the targets of relational aggression do not have problems in processing social information—at least not to start with—but being the victim brings its own array of difficulties. It leads to high levels of negative feelings and psychological distress, and further difficulties in getting along with their peers. And while relational aggression is directed at both boys and girls, it is more distressing to girls. Like those who are targets of overt aggression, victims of relational abuse experience depression, marked by problems ranging from stomachaches and headaches to sleep problems to bouts of sadness or crying.

However, unique to being on the receiving end of aggression that takes aim at relationships, victims are also subject to anxiety in social situations. They look for ways to get away from the other kids, and thus by avoidance set down their own path to loneliness. But, like a deer caught in the headlights, their own response to danger may put them more fixedly in harm's way. They may be caught in a self-perpetuating cycle of victimization in which their anxious vulnerability is sensed by others, which only invites further hostile attacks from aggressive peers. In this vicious cycle, Dr. Crick observes, mistreatment by their peers leads to emotional distress, the distress leads peers to believe that the child is an easy mark, peers' views lead to increasing levels of victimization, and the child feels increasing levels of distress.

She also thinks that being the victim of relational bullying may set up girls for cardiovascular disease later in life. If you look at long-term studies of baboons, she points out, the animals at greatest risk for cardiovascular problems are two completely different types. Among the males, it's those who are top bananas. They are the most stressed, as they are constantly engaging in fights to maintain their dominance, and they die young, of heart disease. Among the females, those at risk for cardiovascular disease are those who do not groom the others. They don't groom, says Dr. Crick, because they are socially excluded, not allowed to interact with their peers. She sees direct parallels to the effects of relational bullying.

It's bad enough that relationally aggressive children develop both externalizing and internalizing problems. But those problems are compounded among boys who engage in relational aggression. Boys who engage in relational aggression are violating the norms of behavior for their gender, and as a result are likely to be recipients of more rejection and more negative comments and sanctions from their peers, parents, and teachers. They are also particularly likely to be friendless. The violation of gender norms exacerbates the adjustment problems such children are already subject to by virtue of engaging in aggression.

Relational bullying starts young. Dr. Crick has found it in the behavioral repertoires of children as young as age three in a preschool setting. And while preschoolers are not the best informants about the extent of this behavior, because of its subtlety and indirectness, teachers are. Young children have not yet learned to inhibit their aggression when teachers are around. But even preschoolers know that relational aggression is a form of meanness.

Friendship, in general, brings many benefits, and is known to buffer even maladjusted children from some social hurts. Indeed, relationally aggressive and nonaggressive girls both report doing fun things with their friends. But being the friend of a relationally aggressive girl—and 75 percent of them have at least one friend—is no safe haven. It's more like being sucked into the vortex of a tornado. Their friendships are storms of conflict and betrayal. While there's more intimacy in their friendships—more self-disclosure, telling secrets, talking about their feelings—there's also more negativity and aggression. Relationally aggressive girls don't protect their friends from their aggressiveness; they visit it on them, too. They may threaten to divulge secrets—that Suzie likes Paul—learned through intimate exchanges. They also construct coalitions and demand exclusivity, getting jealous when a friend pays attention to or plays with anyone else. Their demands for exclusivity suggest a kind of over-involvement. "We think that intimacy is for them a medium of control," Dr. Crick says. "They want to be intimate because that is how they get information to use to control others."

Only rarely do relational bullies form a friendship with one of their own kind; they typically choose a friend who is very nonaggressive. And guess what? The relationally aggressive girl controls the friendship. Normally, friendship is a highly positive experience for people and buffers them from a host of ills. But friendship with a relational bully can be a passage to psychopathology.

If other researchers have missed such behaviors, it's because they are subtle and sophisticated, and far less visible than the black-eyed bullying of boys.

Of Peers and Cheers

So you or your kid is not a bully or a victim. Yet he or she still may be part of the bully's sphere. Even observing aggression from the sidelines is not a neutral activity.

The nature of bullying is such that even kids who aren't necessarily antisocial get drawn into it. "I no longer think of bullying as something that happens just between two people," says Toronto's Debra Pepler, even though more than 90 percent of episodes involve a single bully and a single victim. "Peers are so often present when we observe it on the playground. It's really in some sense an interaction that unfolds in a context rather than in isolation. I hesitate to say this, but there's the entertainment and the theater value of it. The other children may feel a part of that. They may feel anxious, excited, afraid—but that feeds into the interaction."

In 85 percent of the episodes of bullying, says Dr. Pepler, other children are involved in some capacity or as an audience. "If you're going to establish dominance, the only way to do it is with other children around. In the longer episodes, there's a tremendous building of excitement and arousal."

Sometimes the roles peers play in promoting bullying is less marginal. Two bullies kick a kid to the ground and bystander peers, through a process of social contagion, join in, particularly if it's a kid they dislike. The group is empowered by the numbers, their individual responsibility diluted to the vanishing point.

Take the "slam book" that circulated in one Toronto classroom. Each page bore a heading: who's the stupidest, who's the ugliest, who's the most unpopular, and so on. "Almost all the girls in the class nominated someone," says Pepler. "It had a huge negative impact on the kids being named. Most of the girls in this class were really nice kids. Eight of the ten involved would never have done it on their own. But because of the peer pressure and context, and the importance of being part of a group, they engaged in antisocial behavior that just wasn't a part of their person."

Psychologist Antonius Cillessen, Ph.D., calls group dynamics "the hidden purpose" of much bullying behavior. A developmental psychologist at the University of Connecticut, he finds that peer groups fan the flames of bullying by conferring reputations that keep bullies and victims frozen in their roles. They especially reinforce victimization.

"When children have negative expectations of another child, they act more negatively to that child. This negative behavior then seems to trigger a reciprocally negative reaction from the target child," thus creating a self-fulfilling prophecy. No matter what victims do, and even if they change their behavior, their peers filter their observations of that child through their negative expectations—and still give a negative interpretation to those kids' actions. The way peers see them, they can't do *anything* right.

Cillessen is concerned. The power of reputational factors among peers is so strong that what look like obvious remedies will not solve bullying problems. For example, teaching victims social skills—more assertive and socially competent ways of interacting—is necessary but not sufficient. Their peers' perceptions still remain the same, and they act accordingly. His studies furnish proof that bullying can be tackled only with a schoolwide program.

How They Get That Way

Most kids try aggression in the course of growing up. And most of them give it up. But some kids, says David Perry, "are encouraged by parental behaviors or by neglect" to hold on to aggressive behavior. In other words, bullies are made and not born. That is not to say there aren't inborn temperamental differences among children that predispose some of them to difficulties in parent-child interactions, or perhaps subtle differences in brain biochemistry that prompt some kids to try out aggression.

There is no big bang, no one crisis of development. It's largely in the nuances of parent-child interaction. And so unexceptional, so mundane is the process that it's taken Gerald Patterson over twenty years of observing parents and children together to nail it down. But he distills it into four words: the coercion parenting model. It gets played out in relatively trivial, but frequent, bouts of disobedience.

Parents—many parents, he says, are marginally skilled at parenting, and their numbers are increasing—come up against an active, willful, "difficult" child. The mother says something reasonable to the child: "Would you close the door, please." The child doesn't do it; he is noncompliant. "The core of aggressive behavior in children and adults is noncompliance," Patterson says.

The child goes over to the TV set and turns it on. Five minutes later, the mother asks again: "Please close the door." The kid ignores her again. Then the parent shouts and threatens, "If you don't close the door, I'm going to spank you." At some point, the kid may get up and close the door, says Patterson, but he has the mother reduced to four or five minutes of yelling. "The child is controlling the mother by his noncompliance. Then the mother gets so upset at the back talk and exasperated with the noncompliance that she strikes out and hits the child. These are not crazy parents. They get caught in a process that is controlling their behavior."

The basic problem with their parenting is that it's noncontingent. The noncompliance (say, a two-year-old hits his sister) goes unpunished—until the parent is so full of hostility she lashes out unpredictably. "Instead of being contingent, these parents natter and scold. They threaten but don't follow through and say, 'Okay, that misbehavior will cost you . . .' and name some chore. And if the child still doesn't do it, 'I'm going to lock up your bicycle'—and really do it. And start the process all over again the next day. They don't do that." The inconsistent use of ineffective punishment winds up intermittently rewarding defiance. Even a little reward goes a long way.

Given the lack of a consistent adult response, a child cannot develop trust in a caregiver, sowing the seeds for a hostile view of the world. Noncontingent parenting breeds in kids the belief that others will treat them unfairly and unpredictably. The use of physical punishment as a solution to aggression and conflict problems only teaches the child the same solution—and fosters humiliation and resentment. Their experiences may leave them overwhelmed with intense retaliatory feelings

But it isn't just the discipline. In between the bouts of inconsistent parenting there's a lack of parental monitoring of children's behavior. And that comes across as uncaring. Children of parents who use such a discipline style may become more worried about how to get their own way, meet their own needs. They don't—can't—think about other people very much.

Here's the kicker: Bullies are more aggressive as kids, so they often receive harsh punishment from their parents, which teaches them how to be even more aggressive and bullying.

"Noncontingent parenting is unable to stop deviant or aggressive behavior," Patterson emphasizes. "What goes along with it that makes it a kind of Greek tragedy is that the families that get swept up in it not only inadvertently reinforce antisocial behavior, they fail to reinforce prosocial behavior. They don't sit down with their kid, give him a nod, a hug—the kinds of things good parents normally do hundreds of times a day." They don't engage in the dance.

That dance, Patterson says, is "extremely important to foster growth. These kids get slowed in language development. The child doesn't learn to ask for things; he takes things," living on the edge of his impulses. In fact, Dr. Crick's studies show that boys and girls who engage in any kind of aggression rarely engage in any prosocial behavior; they rarely help other kids. So in addition to being unable to restrain their angry, antisocial behavior, these children lack positive interpersonal skills.

To cite parenting practices as "the primary proximal cause" for the earliest form of antisocial behavior, as Dr. Patterson does, is not to rerun blame-the-mother views of what's wrong with people. It's a meticulous analysis of the ways that children learn to join the society of others, to curb their impulses and frustrations. All that's needed, says Dr. Patterson, are nonhostile, nonthreatening, nonphysical sanctions for rule-breaking applied consistently.

Patterson freely admits that the reams of data he and others have collected show that the coercion-parenting model doesn't fit for girls unless they are extremely overtly aggressive. Relational aggression probably begins differently.

Recently, Nicki Crick has begun looking into the family relationships of relationally aggressive children. "We think that these behaviors may get modeled for kids, say Mom doesn't speak to Dad when she's mad at him, she punishes him by giving him the silent treatment, or she may withdraw love." In addition, she suspects there are family variables, such as discipline, that might increase a kid's need to control, or need to have affection.

She also thinks parents may be directly teaching kids to make hostile attributions. The way they respond to the child may help lead a child to view a peer's actions with hostile intent. "They were talking about you in the hallway. That's really terrible. How could they do that? I think you should not invite them to your party next week, then." Kids learn a world view from their parents: Is the world a nice place or a mean place?

For some children, bullying and aggression are closely related to hyperactivity and distractibility. By no means are all bullies hyperactive. But many hyperactive children are prone to aggressive behavioral tactics. Aggression and distractibility are not appealing characteristics to peers, and these children are highly unpopular with their schoolmates; their overtures to others are likely to be rebuffed. These children, however, also are frequently victimized by their peers, so they resemble reactive bullies. Observational studies show that their aggression grows out of impulsivity and frustration, rather than intentional attempts to dominate their peers.

No matter how bullies get that way, there is ultimately only one way to stop bullying. And that's to establish a climate in which aggressive behavior is not tolerated—and enforce it. As a nation, Sweden is leading the way. As of July 1994, it outlawed bullying, following a suggestion of Olweus, himself a Swede. Norway, he hopes, will soon follow suit. In 1997, Britain began an antibullying campaign in its schools.

Big Bullies

What do bullies do when they grow up? In one sense, they never grow up; they are locked in an infantile pattern of noncompliance, frozen into one way of solving problems. Lacking social skills, and especially the ability to handle conflict, their relationships are likely to be unstable and short-lived. But when they do take partners, they often become spouse abusers.

Bullying is virtually a *sine qua non* of domestic violence. Battered wives themselves commonly describe what their husbands do as bullying, reports Neil Jacobson, Ph.D., a University of Washington psychologist whose novel studies have looked at batterers both internally and externally, measuring both physiologic and behavioral characteristics. He recalled his most recent discussion with a victim of spouse abuse, a woman who had finally decided to end the relationship. "She told me she had said to her husband, 'If you're going to be a bully, get out of here.'"

Bullying and battering share a dark mission. "Battering is using violence or the threat of violence to control another's behavior," says Dr. Jacobson. "That is the essence of bullying—it's just directed to one significant other." As in, "Remember the last time my eggs weren't cooked right? Make sure you get them right this time." Last time, he turned over the table, dumping all the food off. "You only have to do that once or twice," notes Dr. Jacobson, "and the threat of that happening again hovers and exerts influence."

While no one has directly observed bullying transforming itself into battering, the evidence points to a direct convergence of bullying and battering behavior across the life cycle. Looked at in retrospect, the life histories of adult batterers parallel the course bullies' lives take as development unfolds. Batterers are likely to have been delinquent as adolescents.

There is an even more remarkable suggestion that bullying and spouse abuse are two stops along the same dead-end street. Both batterers and bullies sort themselves into distinct types that share certain peculiarities of reactivity and physiology. Dr. Jacobson observes two batterer types among adult men—calculating cobras and reactive hotheads; they fit not only those of Kraemer's motherless monkeys but the reactive and proactive bullies. Think of it as a kind of disharmonic convergence.

Like batterers, bullies tend to minimize their own aggressive actions. Reactive bullies and hothead batterers make identical cognitive distortions, attribute hostility to others where it does not exist, and strike out in an out-of-control angry way. Proactive bullies and calculating batterers alike misconstrue aggression as an effective means of getting what they want in social situations and actively decide to use force; the very submission of peers or partners reinforces their belief in its value. Either way—misinterpreting the behavior of others as having been done with hostile intent or misreading the effects of aggression on others while overvaluing the instrumental results—gives bullies and batterers alike a way to justify violence. It is the greasy gear with which they typically shift onto others blame for their own misdeeds.

But as if bullies aren't bad enough, they tend to have children who are bullies. Not only do they model aggression as a solution to conflict, but they are likely to lash out at their children, use physical means—and so hand-feed to the next generation a belief that the world is a very uncaring place, an excuse, if you will, for another go at hostility.

A Nonaggression Pact

Like wife abuse and child abuse, bullying is a conflict in which aggression is used to demonstrate power. But aggression and power are not synonymous. "I don't think we want our children to learn lessons about aggression and violence when they have power," says Debra Pepler. "Aggression is the wrong way to use power. Power does not have to be aggressive to work. There are benevolent kinds of power. There are wonderful ways to be leaders without being aggressive."

Dr. Tremblay points to what he defines as "tough leaders." These are boys who are aggressive but have prosocial skills. They don't get their way by physical aggression or verbal abuse. In new situations they quickly take over and establish their dominance—by verbal fluency. In his studies, they are the most socially successful, the best liked. And they have the highest testosterone levels of all.

Bullies wind up being very costly people for a society to have, says Gerald Patterson. "We're talking about the production of marginally skilled adults who are going to be at the margins of society even if they don't commit crimes. They cost the rest of us a lot." They have more accidents, more illnesses, shorter lives, less productive ones, pay less in taxes, and utilize welfare services. In schools they tended to get lots of services, things that were not very effective.

But the most profound case against bullying is made by Dan Olweus. He sees it as a blow to the very soul of freedom. "Bullying violates fundamental democratic principles," he argues. If two kids were merely to challenge each other, they'd fight fair, one would win and the other lose, they'd shake hands, and that would be the end of that. Like our presidential elections. "But the problem is that bullies seek out the victims and persecute them. They follow them up, wait for them in order to harass them. It is a basic democratic right for a child to have a safe school."

The tragedy of aggressive kids is not that they are unpopular, but that they appear to be clueless about it. And so neither they nor their parents take steps to correct it. Because their rejection, at least at first, is not likely to be overt, these children are not aware of being disliked and may not feel very lonely. Nevertheless, the consequences of rejection set in just as reliably. Parents who recognize the early signs of aggression can choose to intercede before the downward spiral of rejection takes hold. Chapters Eight and Nine detail what parents can do and how.

CHAPTER SIX

Picked On and Pushed Around

On December 1, 1997, fourteen-year-old Michael Carneal, a bespectacled ninth-grader who was small for his age but otherwise unremarkable, walked into Heath High School in West Paducah, Kentucky, carrying a large parcel wrapped in a quilt. "Props for a science project," he told a mildly suspicious teacher. Shortly before 8:00 A.M., the boy, the son of a respected lawyer and elder in the Lutheran church, put down his bundle and coolly inserted earplugs into his ears. Then he drew an item from his backpack and, just before the bell rang for the first class, fired twelve shots into a circle of students gathered for Christian prayer in the school lobby. Suddenly students began screaming and sobbing. Two girls lay dead. A third died a short time later. Five others were hospitalized; two were partly paralyzed. "I'm sorry," Michael calmly told the principal when another student forced him to drop his weapon and pinned him against a lobby wall. A week before, he had bragged to classmates, "Something big is going to happen on Monday at prayer meeting." Four days before, on Thanksgiving, he entered the garage of a neighbor and walked off with five guns. To a stunned community, principal Bill Bond reported that Michael Carneal's school essays and short stories revealed a recurring theme: He felt weak, powerless, and picked upon. The boy apparently "had been teased all his life" and "just struck out in anger at the world," the principal said after reviewing Carneal's writings. "This boy had a lot of hatred and he took his hatred out on the world." The Associated Press reported that those who know Carneal described him as small and emotionally immature, but a good student with no serious discipline problems. He was arrested on three counts of murder.

On November 14, 1996, thin, freckle-faced Jonathan joined forces with a much chunkier fellow high-school freshman, Jerod, outside Crittendon Middle School near Santa Clara, California. There, with three thirteen-year-old middle-schoolers, they waited for Chris to walk out the door. And when he did, the five boys immediately set to work. They "escorted" him to the home of one of the five. On the way, they made him pull down his pants and eat plant leaves. Once indoors, they handcuffed him, beat him, and kicked him. They forced him to drink from a toilet bowl. Then they dripped hot candle wax on his back, buttocks, face, and into his mouth. The torture went on for two hours, causing internal as well as external bleeding. What is perhaps most astonishing is that the victim had been *picked on for a year* before the most recent attack. He never told anyone. He was afraid to.

Meet Lauren, a tall, shy eight-year-old in third grade at a suburban Philadelphia school. When some kids have nothing else to do or are in an irritable mood at school, she is an easy target for them to pick on. "Borin' Lauren," they tease. Not only are the other kids unconcerned when this happens, they often join in the teasing and exclude her from their play. Because she feels awkward and anxious around other kids, Lauren is given to blurting out embarrassing things. That makes other children uncomfortable being around her, so they largely ignore her. Usually, she can be found playing by herself, or at home sprawled on the floor in front of the television set.

Her mother is especially concerned because Lauren has been home sick this year even more often than during her first year of school, and when Lauren misses school, Mom misses work. Her grades have taken a turn for the worse, although everyone agrees that Lauren is a very bright child. Her perplexed family is considering sending her to private school next year, though it would be a serious financial strain.

■

Among children who are rejected, about half are socially withdrawn. Where aggressive-rejected children are likely to be boys, rejected withdrawn children may be boys or girls. They shy away from other children. They do not participate in peer activities. They experience a great deal of pain in social settings. They are frequently the targets of bullying and abuse. Unlike aggressive kids, they are acutely aware of being disliked, feel lonely, and want help with friendships. This is the child who says, "I have no one to talk to in class."

Unfortunately, these are the very children whose parents are most apt to miss such a cry for help. It is extremely painful for parents to imagine that their child is disliked. So most parents of kids who wail "I have no friends at school" are especially likely to try and dredge up evidence why it's not true rather than take the complaint seriously.

Over and over again, these children are subjected to the experience of being bullied, avoided, and excluded from peer interaction.

Bullies Don't Pick On Just Anyone

It's as sturdy a finding as they come: Up to about age seven, bullies pick on anyone. According to Illinois's Gary Ladd, almost a quarter of kindergartners are victims of peer aggression. But after age seven, the field of victims shrinks. Bullies limit their attacks, singling out specific kids to prey on. And those bullied at one age tend to be bullied later on. "Whipping boys," Norway's Dr. Olweus calls them. Even the term is searing. Between ages eight and sixteen about 10 percent of children are the consistent targets of bullies, chronically abused physically and/or verbally by their peers.

And, says Dr. Ladd, bullies engage in a "shopping process" to find those peers they can control. They become increasingly selective of whom they will pick on. At the beginning of the school year, when children do not know each other well, about 22 percent of children report having a victimization experience on more than a moderate level. But by the end of the school year, only 8 to 10 percent of kids wind up being regularly singled out by bullies. About half of all kids are victimized at least once a year.

How many kids are bullied from year to year is not clear. There are transient victims, whose victimization status changes from one year to the next, which suggests that situational factors play some role in victimization.

Still, if all children get attacked at some point by their peers, why are some kids consistently targeted? Researchers now know that the younger a child, the more likely he or she is to experience physical aggression at the hands of peers. For if there's one thing bullies do, it's pick on children who are younger and smaller than they are. And weaker. Most bullies are physically strong, and they specifically seek out kids who are ill equipped to fight back.

But bullies don't pick on just any nonaggressive kid. Like a lion on the veldt, they can "smell" when they are in the presence of a bona fide victim. Perhaps differences first show up in the ways a peer responds to teasing. From preschool through preadolescence—and especially at preadolescence—the ones bullies choose are not merely physically weak, they are unpopular and unwilling or unable to assert themselves successfully or defend themselves. Perhaps most of all, bullies target those whose actions feed and reinforce their own behavior, locking themselves into an aggressive interaction style with each taunt and jab and constraining their victims as well.

Those who are consistently victimized reward and reinforce their attackers in three flamboyant ways:

- They easily acquiesce to a bully's demands, handing over their bikes and toys and other possessions. This rewards bullies materially as well as psychologically—a double whammy of reinforcement for their exploitation.
- They cry and assume defensive postures. They wince, they cringe, and generally provide elaborate displays of pain and suffering. These highly visible responses have a great signaling value to other children. The reactions of the victim publicly proclaim the bully's dominance.
- They offer no deterrent to aggressiveness; they refuse or fail to retaliate, leaving their attackers totally unpunished. They do not make any attempt to stick up for themselves, or are grossly incompetent when they do so.

Here's an irony to ponder: By doing nothing, victims are still doing something to maintain the culture of bullying.

> *When I was in first grade up to sixth grade, I have been bullied [sic]. I think it's because I'm very petite and was an easy pushover, plus I wasn't very confident. When I was in first grade, I had no friends, Bullies were after me like flies to a garbage truck. In sixth grade, I started getting bullied by my own classmates, which is REALLY embarrassing. It made me soooo angry, I just wanted to hurt them so much. But I had always been raised not to fight and such, so they just kept throwing my books around and pushing me and taking my stuff. It was awful.*
>
> *I never really did anything about it. In second grade, I told my parents about it, but they somehow elaborated it into so much that I had to tell them that it wasn't so bad, and then they assumed that I was lying about the whole thing. I didn't tell them anything more until sixth grade, but then they just told me to fight back. But I wasn't used to fighting, and I also didn't want to get into trouble, being the goody-two-shoes of the class. So when I told them that I couldn't, they just got really mad and told me that it was my problem and that they didn't want to hear about it, which simply crushed me. I had no friends in sixth grade, and I was really beginning to hate myself because everyone else hated me.*
>
> *There are many people I will never forgive, ever. But there are others that I realize were being mean because it was the ''cool'' thing to do. I feel sorry for them, knowing that they will be followers for the rest of their lives. It made me grow up fast, seeing that I had to deal with such stuff all alone with no help from my parents whatsoever. And learned that I couldn't depend on adults to help me out all the time.—Y. F.*

Neither teachers nor parents are very good at identifying victimized children. Teachers don't know because, once kids are in elementary school, they curb their aggression in front of adults. Besides, they carry out their worst bullying acts far from the putatively watchful eyes of adults—in bathrooms, in out-of-the-way or unsupervised corners of the school and schoolyard, and to a lesser extent in cafeteria lines. What's more, most teachers are loath to admit that either bullying or victimization goes on; they consider such acts an open indictment of their adequacy as supervisors.

But kids know exactly who gets singled out for abuse by their peers. Dr. Perry of Florida Atlantic University is probably the country's foremost expert on victimized kids. He has developed a no-fail way to find out who gets targeted—he taps into what kids know. "Kids know what's going on," he says. He asks kids to name one or more classmates who can be described as follows.

Kids make fun of him.
He gets beat up.
He gets called names by other kids.
Kids do mean things to him.
He gets picked on by other kids.
He gets hit and pushed by other kids.
Kids try to hurt his feelings.

POINTERS FOR PARENTS

BE ALERT TO SIGNS OF VICTIMIZATION.
Many victimized children are too ashamed to talk about their experiences to an adult. They are afraid parents or teachers will blame them—because they already blame themselves. Also, they feel that they should be able to handle situations themselves. Sometimes they don't talk for fear of reprisal by a bully, or because they feel parental pressure to cope on their own. Once victimization occurs on a regular basis, no child can be expected to handle the situation on his or her own.
   Ask if there's a bully at school if your child:
- develops a new dread of going to school or draws out morning rituals
- comes up with consistent complaints of headaches or stomachaches
- spends much more time than usual at home after school
- experiences a drop in grades
- comes home from school without possessions or with bruises or torn clothes

- asks for extra money with plausible-sounding explanations (bullying sometimes takes the form of extortion)

REMEMBER, VICTIMS THINK IT'S THEIR OWN FAULT.
They're not likely to announce they've been bullied or humiliated. They think they're doing something wrong—and are afraid they will only be reprimanded. This is especially the case where teachers and schools do not take bullying seriously, or think kids should work it out on their own.
- It's your job to ferret it out if you suspect there may be a problem.
- Be very matter-of-fact and nonblaming.
- Describe the kinds of activities that go under the rubric of bullying and harassment. "Sometimes there are children around who do and say mean things to other kids. They tease them and make fun of them. They take things from them. They do things to hurt them and even pick fights with them. They really make life hard for some kids. Are there any kids like that at your school? Does anyone ever bother you?"
- Discuss bullying when incidents arise even involving other children.
- Let your child know that being victimized stems not from being "unlikable" but from lacking social skills—and that social skills can be learned.

AVOID COMMANDING YOUR CHILD, "DON'T BE SHY."
It's a form of public humiliation to draw attention to a problem in front of others. And at any time a negative label undermines confidence, which is self-defeating. In addition, commanding your child not to be shy focuses your child's attention inward, on himself—instead of outward, on others—which is a core problem in shyness.

But, perhaps worst of all, it still doesn't help your child know what to *do*. Sensitively coach your child instead: "Why don't you tell the new kid your name and ask if he'd like to play."

SEE THAT YOUR CHILD IS ASSERTIVE.
Assertive, self-confident children do not generally become victims of bullying. Of course, talking about the value of assertiveness is dangerous for some parents, notably those who have an aggressive view of assertiveness.

- Assertiveness means being able to make overtures to other children, standing up for oneself nonaggressively, speaking up when others make demands of them, and making verbal requests of others or suggestions to others in a group. It is not a license for meanness.
- It may come as a surprise, but studies show that children who are fat, wear glasses, or are scholarly are no more likely to be bullied than others.
- Children usually are singled out because of *psychological traits* such as extreme passivity, sensitivity to criticism, anxiety, insecurity, or low self-esteem.
- And most victimization is *not* physical. Children are much more likely to have kids say mean things to them and to be "picked on" than to be actually hit or kicked.

HELP BUILD SELF-CONFIDENCE.
The real first line of defense against victimization of any kind is self-confidence. It does not come from patting your child on the back and telling her how wonderful she is. Children do need unconditional love. But they develop self-confidence a different way—through the experience of their own effectiveness in the world.

- The way to build self-esteem and self-confidence is not through vague praise.
- Make sure your child feels valued.
- Make sure your child experiences successes of her own.

- Your child needs to feel effective and to experience genuine success in *specific domains of experience*. Research suggests that by the time children are in first grade, they are already on the lookout for information about their competence in five distinct spheres of activity: social, scholastic, appearance, athletic, and conduct domains.
- Competence in any domain, and especially in the social sphere, makes a hard, irrefutable contribution to self-confidence.
- Promote achievement through working at skills.
- Encourage varied competencies. Urge your child to enroll in classes or groups that develop abilities in activities that are valued by peers. Don't push your child to join Little League. But what about body building? Karate? Musical groups?

"Nobody Likes Me"

Here is the remarkable thing about victimized kids. They are picked on by nonaggressive peers as well as by aggressive ones. By far, most kids in a classroom are not aggressive. But even *they* occasionally act up out of boredom or irritation or to take something out on someone. A situation arises where they sense they can get away with something. And when they do act up, it's likely to be against a child already made safe for victimization by a bully.

In fact, contends Dr. Perry, nonaggressive peers probably learn just which kids they can safely target by watching the highly theatrical reactions of victims under siege by aggressive peers. Attacks by known bullies probably hurt more physically, but attacks by nonaggressive peers may make children feel devastatingly humiliated, betrayed, and isolated.

Like bullies, victimized kids are rebuffed by the larger peer group. Simply, kids don't like other kids who are involved in conflagrations, period. It doesn't matter whether they're on the attacking end or the receiving end of aggressive conflict. Neither victims nor bullies are able to manage conflict constructively.

Like aggressive-rejected kids, victimized children can't take teasing. But they part company on the reasons for their lack. The submissive-rejected tend to be oversensitive. Short on humor, they mistake teasing for outright criticism. They are wounded, and implode. Aggressive-rejected kids, on the other hand, misinterpret teasing as hostility. They explode.

The lives of bullies and victims are intertwined not just because their behavior styles are so negatively complementary; they are thrust together also because they are both outcasts from the larger peer group of better-adjusted kids. Both bullying and victimization are, after all, forms of social interaction. A kind of relationship gets established; bullies and their victims come to know what to expect of each other. The actions of bullies and victims are, in a highly negative way, mutually affirming. The victim, after all, is the repository of the bully's power. At least bullies and victims pay attention to each other; the alternative is to get no attention paid to you at all. Bullies and victims tango to the tune of rejection, a tune that deepens and darkens over time.

Two Kinds of Victims

"The big question," says Ladd, "is where does victimization start? Do kids emit signals for others to test them? Or is it that bullies pick out those they see they can dominate?" He finds clues in the fact that some kids are victimized later in the school year but not early on. "Something increases their likelihood of being picked on—probably, vulnerabilities are revealed in a class environment. Maybe they don't do well in gym. Or they stumble in a reading task."

Just as there are two kinds of bullies, so are there two kinds of victims. One group is pervasively nonaggressive; they don't pick on others or do anything to invite being picked on, but when targeted for provocation do nothing to defend themselves. Theirs are acts of omission. Still, researchers observe that they behave in ways that elicit attack or at least reinforce attacks against them. They radiate fearfulness. They lack self-confidence. They lack humor, especially in response to teasing. They are ineffectual at finding ways to join their peers at play or in influencing their peers in any way. They hover when others are playing and mistime any overtures they make.

The others are much more socially active. They are highly aggressive and actively invite extreme abuse through their own provocative actions or lash out in response to abuse. They are restless and disrupt peers when they are doing other things. They create tension by irritating and teasing others, get other kids into trouble, make fun of others, hit and push, and are easily angered.

In most instances, Dr. Ladd finds, victims really may be weaker and smaller than the bully. "Thus, their fears of losing fights might be quite real." Some victimized children, however, refuse to fight on moral principles. According to Dr. Becky Kochenderfer, who has collaborated on studies with Dr. Ladd, "There is some evidence to suggest that victimized children come from very passive, nonviolent homes in which the parents do not believe in fighting (and even when 'given permission' to fight, these children do not do so)."

It is not clear exactly what percentage of victims fall into the aggressive camp in the United States. According to Dr. Ladd, only a small percentage of victims are aggressive themselves. In his ongoing Pathways Project, a long-term study of the influence of social factors on school performance, now in its fourth year of following a cohort through the elementary grades, only eight of all two hundred students are aggressive victims; by contrast, there are twenty passive victims. In David Perry's studies, victims divide more equally into both camps.

However the victim pie is sliced, both types lack prosocial skills such as friendliness and cooperativeness. They may like other children, but they don't know how to communicate it. As a result, other children do not reciprocate the liking.

Every kid learns that sticks and stone may break his bones while names can never hurt him. But that mantra is scant protection for the reality that Dr. Perry uncovers. It's not just that words harm deeply, and scar psychologically. It's that the same kids who hurl names also hurl sticks and stones. Further, children who are victimized verbally are also victimized physically. And each kind of abuse makes its own separate contribution to damage in the victim.

Being the target of extreme abuse is not limited to children of one gender or one age group. Boys and girls are equally victims of overt abuse. It happens in preschool, grade school, middle school, and high school. Children in early elementary-school grades are just as likely to be attacked physically as verbally, although throughout elementary school physical aggression tends to decrease in frequency, especially against girls. It does, however, take a leap upward among boys about to go into middle school, when dislike of victimized kids is at its zenith. Experts worry particularly about victimization in elementary school, because those are the years when a child's self-concept is forming. And while self-concept is always undergoing revision, negative ways of seeing the self that victimization brings about during those years may be particularly durable. They may play a major role in causing suicide among children.

Of Peers and Jeers

Both nonaggressive and aggressive victims have few friends. Precisely because they are devalued and rejected by the whole peer group, victims are especially important to bullies. In the first place, bullies come to *expect* tangible rewards from them. In the inverse and reciprocally negative world that bullies and victims inhabit, victims actually represent more of a danger to the bully's position than other children do. After all, losing a disputed object to a victimized child would be more of a threat to their status among peers than losing it to a popular kid. In addition, bullies expect to have the pain and suffering of victims all to themselves. Because victims are widely disliked and wear their distress on their sleeves, their suffering elicits little sympathy from *all* children. By picking on kids no one likes, bullies may be using them to win points with the larger peer group.

Some Kids Just Radiate Vulnerability . . .

Nonaggressive children who become targets bear a particular set of psychological characteristics. They are more sensitive, cautious, and quiet than other kids, Dr. Olweus finds—and they are more anxious. They seem to be suffused with apprehension. They also have a negative view of violence. It's not just that they are nonaggressive, for lots of kids are nonaggressive. These kids withdraw from confrontations of

any kind and cry when attacked. Their insecurity is palpable. They radiate what Olweus calls "an anxious vulnerability." They look anxious and depressed at home and at school, reports Florida's Dr. Perry.
They have a hovering style with the peer group. And they are physically weak. They do not engage in sports or are not good at them.

Faced with conflict of any kind—even the highly ritualized conflict of team play—they are gripped with fear. They fear being assertive or aggressive. Their fearfulness and physical weakness probably
set them up, signal to others that they will be unable to defend themselves successfully against attacks.

Submissiveness

It's one thing to be submissive when challenged, but researchers now
know that the children who become bully victims are submissive in
social encounters even *before* they're picked on. At Vanderbilt University, where he was a research associate before moving to the University of Southern California as professor, child psychologist David
Schwartz conducted a novel study of 155 children, none of whom
knew each other at the outset. He drew them from eleven different
schools, and sorted the children into thirty play groups, each consist-
ing of one popular, one neglected, two average, and two rejected
boys. Then he silently monitored and, with the use of hidden cameras,
videotaped them in a series of play sessions held on five consecutive
days. "Even in the first two sessions, before bully-victim situations
develop, these kids behaved submissively," Schwartz told me.

Quite deliberately, he chose to study boys who were in the first
and third grade, six and eight years old. "Early elementary-school
children were of particular interest because there is evidence that individual differences in aggressive tendencies stabilize during this developmental period." He wanted to see whether elementary school
might also be a period during which the tendency to be victimized
by peers crystallized, at least in some kids. The short answer is: yes.

In nonconfrontational situations the boys who later came to be
victimized showed themselves to be "pervasively nonassertive."
Schwartz catalogues the ways. They didn't make prosocial overtures
to others, didn't initiate conversation. They made no attempts to in-

fluence verbally or persuade (or dissuade!) their peers—no demands, requests, or even suggestions about how or what they should all play. They didn't ever take a leadership role with their peers, so their playmates rated them low on leadership. They were thoroughly socially incompetent and spent their time in passive play, playing parallel to and apart from their peers, rather than with them.

Even when, in the first two sessions, their peers approached them to engage in rough-and-tumble play or to interest them in doing something, children who became victims responded wildly inappropriately. They shrank from the bid, with submission, a show of pain, asking peers to stop, or just yielding their position. Their play style wasn't just passive, it was inflexibly so; no matter how they were approached, they capitulated. Rough-and-tumble play, while it mimics aggressive action, is usually prosocial in nature. It is a good indicator of social competence because it requires such complex skills as emotion regulation. Absent that, the play can quickly turn into a battle—a smile becomes a snarl, a foot lands too hard, someone misreads into the horsing-around a real intent to harm.

Being submissive in nonaggressive contexts—and particularly being submissive early in the acquaintance process with peers, when kids are more or less trying each other out—kicks off a downward spiral of events. It sets submissive children up as "easy marks." "It seems to mark these kids for later victimization," says Schwartz. "And that only made them more submissive."

When the children who became victims were the recipients of aggressive overtures early in the play sessions, they just gave in. By contrast, nonaggressive children who did not become victims responded more assertively. They didn't simply fork over the toys or yield ground; they tried to dissuade their attackers. Unfortunately, giving in to the aggressive overtures of others without a peep plays "a particularly prominent role in the development of chronic victimization," says Schwartz. It has the effect of rewarding and reinforcing such behavior in those peers. Flush with easy success in getting what they want, they are thus encouraged to home in on the submissive and selectively abuse them.

And so a special dyadic relationship is established between bully and victim. "Kids develop histories with each other," says Schwartz.

It is one of the characteristics of this relationship that the bully dislikes the victim more than the victim dislikes the bully. Victims feel bound to their bullies.

Over the course of the play sessions, victims increasingly withdrew from group interactions, played more by themselves, and their nonassertive behavior increased the likelihood they would be targeted for victimization. The attitude of the *entire* group grew more negative toward them. Others picked on them more, and more intensely, over time. If they themselves ventured a positive approach to their peers, they increasingly got in-your-face refusals.

Here's the catch: Being victimized leads to feeling bad, feeling anxious, which then increases vulnerability to *further* victimization. This is the spiral Curtis Taylor couldn't—and shouldn't have been expected to—untangle by himself.

To say that victims are socially incompetent is not to say that they are to blame for the aggressive behavior of bullies. It is simply to recognize that certain patterns of social behavior make some children vulnerable. After all, even the most passive child isn't victimized unless there's a bully in the room. The trouble is, there's almost always a bully in the room. That's why, researchers agree, the responsibility for eliminating attacks on victimized children lies both with aggressive children themselves and with adults.

. . . And Others Act as Irritants

Aggressive victims, more recently subjected to scrutiny by researchers, go by a variety of labels. Some call them reactive bullies, others provocative victims, collaborative victims, or ineffectual aggressors— terms that imply attempts to understand the nature of the behavior. Dr. Perry prefers the purely descriptive term aggressive victims. Whatever they're called by researchers, kids know them as hotheads. "They get hot under the collar," says Dr. Perry. "They cry easily. They are rated more dishonest and disruptive than other kids. They are the most disliked, the most friendless." That helps explain why they are most at risk for later problems.

They seem to be emotionally disregulated, says Dr. Perry. They experience both negative emotions of anger and fear, and live in a state of irritability. "They are easily threatened. If someone criticizes something they've done—laughed at a picture they've drawn—their self-esteem is at stake." But they not only have a low threshold for being challenged, they misread social cues, imputing hostile intentions to others.

By contrast, passive victims don't seem to misread cues. They don't have a problem processing social information. "They simply don't know how to act," says Perry. "Or, if they know how to act, they can't do it—they are so gripped with fear. Their fearfulness, combined with their lack of strength, takes over. Their problem is not cognitive. It is low self-esteem."

If an aggressive kid sees something another kid has that he likes—a Discman, say—he may demand, "Hey, can I have that?" Or he may deliberately bump the kid. A nonaggressive kid will walk away, explains Dr. Perry. "An avoidant response is adaptive in that situation."

But neither an aggressive victim nor a passive victim can walk away from conflict. Passive victims stand and cower, frozen in inaction. Aggressive victims can't disengage once provoked. "They won't walk away. They'll start sputtering. They may take a stance of bravado. And they will lose and cry."

Provocative victims are exceptionally argumentative, always having to have their own way, ready to blame others for things they don't do, persistent in attempts to play with peers who don't want them, prone to lie and steal, and likely to respond to teasing with anger. Once they get emotionally aroused, they can't stop. Sometimes, Dr. Perry finds, they pick fights with stronger aggressive kids and get beat up by them. Then they prey on nonaggressive victims.

Both aggressive victims and passive victims, like all bullies, have trouble managing conflict. Submissiveness, Dr. Perry observes, "surely must be considered a form of conflict mismanagement." Especially in the United States. And aggressive victims get stuck in emotionally heated conflicts they tend to lose.

When he first started his studies, in which he looks at victimized children through the eyes of their peers, Dr. Perry was sure that the more passive victims would be more likely than aggressive victims to provide the biggest rewards for their aggressors. After all, they quickly appease their attackers and yield whatever they have. Despite their acquiescence, that did not turn out to be the case. What matters most to their attackers is not the speed of surrender but the pageantry of pain and suffering. Unlike you and me, bullies do not feel bad when causing pain and suffering—they actually escalate their attacks in order to *magnify* the signs of pain and submission, because these broadcast to the whole peer group their success at domination and control.

In Dr. Perry's studies, hothead aggressive victims were actually perceived by their attackers to provide *more* of every kind of victim reaction—they handed over whatever goods they had; they grimaced and whimpered more. And they were least likely to punish their attackers by retaliating. "The picture one gets of the aggressive victim is that of a child who gets embroiled in conflicts but ends up losing the battles amidst exaggerated display of frustration and distress."

Hotheads are to some degree victimized just because they have difficulty inhibiting their anger and impulsivity; those who pick on them and provoke them do it because they are rewarded with a great display of emotion. They provide a kind of live fireworks of the playground.

Part bully, part victim, aggressive victims are most at risk for problems over the life course. They are subject to the internalizing problems of victims, and the externalizing problems of the aggressive. They do poorly in school and drop out. And they hang around with deviant peers, which only drives them deeper into deviant behavior. They become the most rejected kids in school. These children, Dr. Perry believes, may grow up to commit crimes as loners and become child abusers and spouse abusers.

An Absence of Allies

Passive victims have something of another advantage over aggressive victims. While neither group is well liked in general by their peers, the passive victims at least may have a friend or two. But here's the catch: Their friends tend also to be passive victims. They are similarly anxious, withdrawn, and depressed, and have the same kind of internalizing coping style. As a result of lack of friends or poor-quality relationships, neither kind of victim can be said to enjoy the big benefits of friendship. They get little emotional support. They get little in the way of active help. Perhaps more strikingly, their friendship patterns have the supreme inconvenience of marking them as fair game for victimization. They telegraph to peers that there's no one who will come to their rescue. The road is clear for exploitation.

After more than a decade of scrutinizing victim behaviors, Dr. Perry is now convinced that victimization results not simply from individual vulnerabilities and actions that reward bullies but from the social context, factors that lie outside individuals but within the peer group. Having no friends, or having friends who themselves are weak and fearful, and being widely disliked by the peer group act to *disinhibit* bullies and other children so that they can ply their brand of bad behavior, aggression. It means the aggressor has even less need to worry about retaliation, ostracism, or other forms of punishment.

Being rejected by the peer group and lacking allies in the form of friends are "social risk factors," says Perry. They are visible markers and thus known to other children in the peer group. "It's pretty clear that kids know who's friendless, left out, and disliked. I believe this state of affairs permits all kinds of abuse toward the unfortunate, because attackers know that no one will come to their rescue (perhaps even teachers)."

The converse is also true. Having a friend is good. Having a friend around who is also physically strong, Perry's studies show, is better, a valuable shield against the probability of victimization. With the lack of friends, victimized children lack more than allies. They get none of the benefits friendship has to offer. Plus they miss out on opportunities for intimacy. And of course, they are deprived of any way to acquire and practice relationship skills.

Don't Forget the Victims of Relational Aggression

Among the range of harmful behaviors that children direct toward their peers, relational aggression is remarkable for its invisibility. Typically, the aggressor does damage to a child's peer relationships by manipulating others to attack the victim or by spreading lies, or threatening to spread lies, about the victim among the peer group. Both boys and girls say that "this kind of stuff goes on all the time," but until the mid-1990s this arena of aggression and victimization remained virtually unexplored. Since then, Nicki R. Crick, first at the University of Illinois and now at the University of Minnesota, has done her best to change that.

Crick ferrets out relational victimization, as well as overt victimization, by having children respond about themselves to a Social Experience Questionnaire that she recently developed. She asks, for example: How often does another kid say they won't like you unless you do what they want you to do? How often does another kid tell rumors about you behind your back? How often do you get left out of activities because one of your friends is mad at you? How often do kids tell lies about you so that other kids won't like you anymore?

Although relational aggression is directed at both boys and girls, being a victim of it turns out to be more distressing for girls than for boys, because personal relationships are valued more by girls than by boys. Still, being the victim of both forms of aggression may be even more distressing for kids than being the target of only one. Children who are both overtly and relationally victimized are very lonely children; they have no one to talk to at school.

Although most relationally victimized children have been rejected by the entire peer group, a surprising number of them are children of average social status. Whether boy or girls, socially unpopular or average, relationally victimized children are at risk for the same developmental difficulties as overtly victimized children—school failure, criminality, loneliness, depression. But they also develop problems more specific to relational aggression: namely, social anxiety, feeling nervous about meeting new people, worrying about what other kids think of them, and social avoidance. As a result, they say they often try to get away from all the other kids and do something—anything—by themselves. They come to expect little that is good from interacting with their peers. That, of course, derails further emotional and social development.

Victimization, the experience of maltreatment by peers, is bad. But the hurtfulness stems from yet another factor—the lack of prosocial acts extended to the victimized child. Not receiving help when needed compounds the feelings of loneliness and depression and magnifies the psychological damage to children.

What Parents Don't Know

Sadly, parents offer little help to their victimized children because they are often the last to know that their children are being picked on. Bullying and victimization are generally covert activities known almost exclusively among agemates. In fact, says Dr. Ladd, most parents don't seem to know much about how their children are treated by their peers, whether good or bad.

Victimization is a humiliating experience. It is painful. It is scary; victims feel a tremendous lack of control. It is so psychologically distinctive that the memory lasts well into adulthood, usually in excruciating detail, a perverse tribute to the power of social experience. Decades after even one instance of peer abuse, the memory can still make victims wince and motivate their behavior. Children confide to researchers that victimization is one of their main worries. The puzzle is, why do kids conceal it from parents even though they may experience victimization regularly or routinely?

Still, children are unlikely to report specific episodes to adults. "Children hesitate to report victimization for a variety of reasons," observes Toronto's Debra Pepler. Victims may feel that they should be able to handle the situation themselves. Or they may view the incident as minor and deem it not worthy of reporting. But perhaps the greatest reason is that victims do not report incidents for fear of reprisal or because of social pressure to cope on their own.

Victims also don't talk to teachers and parents because they feel shame. "They feel they are doing something wrong," says Connecticut's Dr Cillessen. "They are afraid of being reprimanded."

Dr. Pepler cites another reason why students are loath to speak up. They perceive adults as uncaring or unable to provide protection. Children's lack of confidence in adults is stoked by the well-documented tendency of teachers to underestimate the prevalence and severity of bullying and to ignore it when it occurs. In a study conducted in England, 91 percent of teachers who admitted that there was bullying in their classrooms dismissed it as minor. Fully a quarter confided that it was helpful sometimes to ignore bullying. Dr. Olweus's studies of victimized children in Norway confirm that teachers seldom take action; up to 60 percent of victims reported that teachers rarely or never put a stop to bullying.

In Canada, Dr. Pepler found, only 35 percent of students reported that teachers intervened. However, 85 percent of teachers insist that they intervene nearly always or often. Her conclusion: "Children do not view adults as effective interveners, even though the adults themselves think they consistently address the problem."

When she recently trained the unblinking video camera on the school playground and captured 404 bullying episodes in fifty-two hours of playground time, she found that the school staff intervened in only 4 percent of incidents—although they were standing *right there* during 17 percent of them.

If you have no allies among peers or teachers—and they are the people who are most likely to see or hear about victimization taking place—it's easy to conclude that no one cares about your plight. And if your self-esteem is in tatters and you lack assertiveness, it's hard to press your case that an incident that lasted less than a minute had a more sinister cast than standard teasing. Who, after all, is going to take the solitary word of a child demeaned by peers, disregarded by teachers, and possibly also by parents? Especially parents who value compliance in their children?

A Blueprint for Depression

Just as certain as there will always be a bully around (at least in most countries, including the United States), victimization has many negative consequences. It can lead to a host of devastating social-psychological difficulties, as well as physical hurts. By far, most of the damage happens through a strictly internal process; it is not visible to others. It, in turn, sets up a vicious cycle that perpetuates victimization and worsens peer abuse over time.

No one likes a bully, but no one likes a victim either. Peers rate them negatively, and more negatively over time. "Negative peer relations always have a bad outcome," says Dr. Schwartz. The failure—

or inability—of victims to stick up for themselves seems to make other kids highly uncomfortable. After all, says Dr. Ladd, "part of growing up is learning how to stick up for yourself." Gradually, whipping boys—and girls—become more and more isolated from their peers. And submission and isolation become increasingly conspicuous and increasingly abnormal as children head toward adolescence.

While bullying is painful, it is the social isolation that probably is most damaging to victims. An emerging body of research shows that social isolation, to say nothing of active rejection, is a severe form of stress for humans to endure. Further, rejection deprives these children of the very opportunities they need to acquire and practice socially competent skills.

For them social rejection takes an inward path and becomes a major contributor to later psychopathology: Their social status seems to nip their self-esteem in the bud. They are at especially high risk for lifelong depression. Their entire lives may be marked for loneliness. Children blame themselves for lack of social success, and that may cause them to give up trying to establish relations with their classmates. In any case, they come to believe they are socially inept. They see their social ineptitude as an intrinsic part of their makeup, something they can't readily change, which makes them unlikely to try to improve their social situation.

The maltreatment victimized children receive at the hands of their peers gives rise to feelings of fear and anxiety. Victimized children develop a lack of trust in others. And being shunned by their peers only compounds their problems of self-image.

Victimized children are acutely aware that they are rejected. As a result, they perceive themselves as incompetent. Since self-esteem is the outgrowth of experiences of competence, their self-esteem is devastated—not only socially but academically and physically as well. The sense of incompetence spreads like a bad stain over their entire self-concept. Researchers have found that these children *know* what social competence is—they just can't do it. They just can't assert themselves during conflict. The anxiety they feel in conflict situations freezes them and makes them overly deferential and submissive. Just as their awareness of their own social ineptitude devastates self-esteem, their isolation condemns them to loneliness.

Studies of hundreds of victimized children give a whole new meaning to "vicious cycle." David Perry chronicles the damage that peer abuse can do to self-esteem in the course of a single school year—from November to May. Among victimized children in the fall, only one component of self-esteem is low: their perceptions of social competence among their peers. Visible behavioral incompetencies such as fearfulness and crying set them up for maltreatment by peers. Then victimization creates its own set of emotional difficulties. Feeling socially inept, left out, disliked, and friendless leads them to become anxious, submissive, and emotionally disregulated during conflicts with their peers. The lack of self-confidence and well-being that come from knowing they have supportive friends and classmates, their feelings of insecurity in the peer group, and the knowledge that they stand alone, along with their sense of social failure, keep these children from asserting their needs and defending themselves during any kind of dispute or confrontation.

Peers' plummeting view of the child leads to heightened levels of victimization over the course of the year. And the child faces future encounters with peers with greater levels of distress. Lowered self-esteem makes these children feel unworthy of asserting themselves. At the same time it leads them to *expect* and *accept* negative treatment. That's one of the hallmarks of victims—their expectation and acceptance of maltreatment. The self-deprecating identity they now project invites abuse. By spring, victimization has laid siege to other domains of the sense of self. The now globally devastated self-esteem is like the negative pressure at the center of a tornado, setting everything in motion about them, spinning a cyclone of increasing victimization.

Self-esteem shreds further not only through the experience of being victimized but also from the lack of positive treatment by others, the experience of ineffectual functioning, and knowledge they are treated badly in comparison to their peers. Eventually the cycle of victimization is thoroughly self-perpetuating.

"Most children are at least occasionally tested by threats from aggressive peers," says David Perry. "But children with high self-regard do not tolerate such attacks and defend themselves more assertively and effectively against them than other children do." High self-regard, he believes, is a "coping resource" that helps children deal with all kinds of stresses and threats. In fact, he says, there are children who share the same behavioral vulnerabilities as victimized kids—they are physically weak and/or temperamentally inhibited. But they will not be victimized unless they lack self-confidence and assertiveness.

By the middle of elementary school, these children are unhappy and know that their tendency to withdraw is keeping them from forming satisfying relationships. They blame themselves for their social incompetence and draw negative conclusions about themselves. Attributing social rebuke to something inside themselves rather than to circumstances or some temporary factor further inhibits their social responsiveness. As a result, these children experience increasing levels of loneliness over time—and increasing levels of *self-blame*. They travel a swift downward spiral from repeated rejection to loneliness to self-blame to depression.

For these children, loneliness is not a momentary mood state, as it is for most. It is an enduring experience. Missing out on further opportunities to acquire social skills and to learn how to function assertively, such children are likely to encounter lifelong difficulty in relating to other people.

"There are lots of kids in schools who are being victimized, who, as a result, are not living up to their potential, not getting as much out of the school experience as they could," says Dr. Ladd. "They get very negative views of themselves and their abilities. That's a waste of important human beings. And it is a serious threat to the health and wealth of the country."

Dr. Olweus, who has followed thousands of Norwegian children into adulthood, finds that by age twenty-three, some "normalization" is taking place among those children who were victimized ten years earlier, in middle school. By that age, having left school, they are at least no longer harassed. Their anxiety levels are measurably lower. They are free to choose or create their own social and physical environments. However, they are still susceptible to depression and to negative feelings about themselves. In fact, these feelings, having become internalized, now take on a life of their own.

Humiliation:
Breeding Ground for Revenge

"We know from what happens in other forms of abuse that victims of bullying come to have negative ways of seeing the world," says UCLA's Dr. Schwartz. And even if they later become successful in life, revenge for their early humiliations sometimes motivates despicable, even deadly, treatment of others.

In Dr. Crick's studies, relationally victimized children report that they can't squelch feelings of anger. Mistreatment overwhelms them with intense hostile or retaliatory feelings.

Children who are victimized by other children not only experience hostility toward others, they do not experience much sympathy for the feelings of others. Victimization makes it especially difficult for them to empathize with others' distress. It is not usual for victimized children to take their feelings out on others; characteristically, their internalizing style leads them to lash out against themselves. But in some victims, and Michael Carneal was likely one, the absence of feelings for others mixed with chronic humiliation becomes a recipe for revenge.

How They Get That Way

How does the tendency for victimization arise? In Dr. Olweus's pioneering studies, victims have close relationships with their parents and tend disproportionately to come from overprotective families. As a result, they get no practice in handling conflict, one of the basic facts of social life, and no confidence in their ability to negotiate the world on their own. Overprotection prevents them from learning the skills necessary to avoid exploitation by others outside the home.

Most observers now believe that social withdrawal in children—what they call social inhibition—results from a combination of factors. Some children are born with a **temperament** that predisposes them to shyness and withdrawal, although that by no means makes it inevitable that they grow up fearful and withdrawn. Other children seem to be headed for victimization largely as a result of assorted kinds of **parenting** practices and the nature of the **parent-child relationship** at home, which shape the child's response patterns outside the home as well. And still other children develop shyness and social withdrawal in childhood or adolescence primarily in response to their **self-perceptions** of their own social competence in stressful circumstances.

A Push from Nature

At Harvard University, where he is professor of psychology, Jerome Kagan, Ph.D., has found that about 20 percent of newborns start life with a push from nature toward inhibition. They have an inherited biochemical makeup that creates excitability of the nerve cells in the amygdala of the brain. This shows up as an overactive fear response, a high-strung hair-trigger readiness to react to stimulation, that is, to anything new or unexpected. These infants are easily aroused and temperamentally irritable. "They are biased to become shy," says Kagan. They become dispositionally shy.

The amygdala, which sits on top of the brain stem, is a central switchboard in the brain for relaying signals related to emotions and stress. Because their nervous systems do not accommodate easily to things new, infants born with this high reactivity are prone to sense danger where it does not exist, become anxious and fearful in all kinds of unfamiliar situations, and consequently avoid them.

Dr. Kagan and his colleagues have been closely monitoring the development of 462 healthy infants, all from emotionally secure homes, for more than five years. When, at four months of age, such infants were deliberately exposed to something unexpected—a tape recording of a human voice was played, they were given a whiff of a Q-tip dipped in alcohol, or a brightly colored toy was moved back and forth in front of their faces—seventy-three of them started thrashing their limbs and fretted or cried in distress, at a pitch and with the sustained tension that communicates urgency. They were classified as highly reactive.

When he tested the infants again at fourteen and twenty-one months of age in more than a dozen kinds of situations, Dr. Kagan found that two thirds of the high-reactive infants were now highly fearful toddlers, which made them appear generally subdued. They had developed an inhibited behavior style. Plunked down in a new play situation or placed with new playmates, they did not cautiously explore their surroundings or even slowly, tentatively approach their peers. Instead, they clung to their parents.

At four and a half years of age, most of those who had been high-reactive infants were still wary; they neither talked spontaneously nor smiled when tested in a social situation. Freezing of speech, Kagan points out, is the human equivalent of the immobility that animals like rabbits and deer experience in response to unfamiliar situations, similarly orchestrated by the amygdala.

All told, half of the high-reactive newborns displayed high levels of fear at both fourteen and twenty-one months and were still emotionally subdued at four and a half years old. They were essentially living in a state of high anxiety. Their neural hypersensitivity inclines such children to avoid situations that give rise to anxiety and fear—meeting new people, going to a new school, or being thrust into any new environment. At school age, they become cautious, quiet, and introverted—behaviorally inhibited. These children, other studies show, have a thoroughly internalizing coping style. They grow up shrinking from social encounters. They lack confidence around others. They see themselves as socially inept. They find it hard to join in groups of others.

Between a touchy temperament in infancy and persistence of anxiety stand two highly significant things—parents. Babies may be born with a propensity to overexcitability in response to stimulation, but it's parenting practices that determine whether such infants become fearful of unfamiliar people and events in childhood and withdraw from social interaction. While innate reactivity contributes powerfully to later anxiety, the development of anxiety is scarcely inevitable.

Parents' actions affect the probability of anxiety in the child, Kagan says. Those who overprotect their children—which he observed by conducting interviews in the home—keep their children from finding some kind of comfortable level of accommodation to the world. The children grow up anxious and shy. Those parents who do not shield their children from stressful situations, but instead are patient, let them explore on their own, but impose firm limits on their children when they are misbehaving, have children who overcome their inhibitions.

Although 40 percent of highly reactive infants became behaviorally inhibited, among those parents who allowed their children to feel out the world on their own yet imposed limits, none of the excitable infants wound up fearful at age two.

True, behaviorally inhibited kids experience stress in situations most others find unthreatening. But shielding them from stressful events is hardly the best solution.

"All the parents in our study are middle-class and loving," Dr. Kagan observes. "Among them, two philosophies are represented. One is, 'I have a sensitive child whom I must protect from stress.' So this parent, finding the child playing in the kitchen trash, tends not to set limits with a firm 'Don't do that,' but distracts the child. As a result, the child does not get the opportunity to extinguish the fear response."

The other philosophy—more authoritative, not authoritarian— views discipline as education, and requires the child to adjust to the world. This parent has few qualms about saying, "No. No trash," and lifting the toddler's hand from the trash before distracting him. It's a subtle difference—but a profound one.

Parents who allow their children to deal with life's day-to-day troubles help them develop more resiliency and better coping strategies. Overprotective parents, says Kagan, actualize the vulnerability to anxiety. Overprotectiveness brings out the worst in kids. It prevents them from becoming confident and self-assertive.

As a result of Dr. Kagan's studies, social inhibition in young children is now seen as a classic model of the interplay of nature and nurture—perhaps the clearest example that exists of the interaction between biological and familial influences.

One way to look at the job of parenting is to see it as modulating the "fit" between the young child and the environment. As every parent swiftly learns, all children are different, even within one family. And what one child needs help to achieve is not necessarily what another child needs. Some children need more support in certain areas than others. Some children, for example, seem just innately given to enjoying physical activity; others need more supportive engagement every step of the way. So it is with social development.

Parents can spare themselves and their children a great deal of pain by learning to recognize the inhibited temperament early on and preventing the development of internalizing problems. Parents can choose to intercede before the downward spiral of rejection and victimization takes hold.

A Push from Parenting

ANXIOUS ATTACHMENT

The quality of a parent's sensitivity and responsiveness to an infant's needs is like a cross-country train. It's only one locomotive, but it carries a lot of freight and covers a great deal of distance, given time. And it sets a great deal else in motion. Parental responsiveness determines the nature of the attachment between infant and caregiver. And that, in turn, gets carried directly and indirectly into the world of peers by the child. Long-term studies show that when children receive irregular or unresponsive early parenting, as opposed to reliably responsive care, they develop an insecure attachment to parents that plays out over and over again in later relationships. It becomes both a template of later relationships for the child and influences the child's orientation to and expectations of others.

Children with insecure attachments to caregivers fail to develop the autonomy and confidence to explore the worlds of objects and others. When parents respond in a way that is contingent—that is, rapid, regular, and related to the child's needs—they communicate a sense of interest and involvement, and provide children with the experience that their own actions and overtures matter, that they can have an effect, and that the world is a relatively safe and controllable place. They learn to expect others to be positively responsive.

When children receive unresponsive early parenting, they become anxious, a thoroughly inhibiting emotional state. "When these children are looked at in middle childhood," Dr. Perry observes, "they are preoccupied, clingy, and their nervous systems stay aroused when they are apart from their mother." They have trouble separating from the parent. They develop an anxious, fearful, preoccupied—in short, internalized—style of coping with the specific variety of inept parenting they have received. "Coping styles are associated with the roles of victim and aggressor. The research literature bears out that kids with preoccupied coping styles become submissive victims."

OVERPROTECTION

Even in the absence of a biological disposition toward shyness, overprotection can create the tendency for victimization. This is particularly the case among boys.

"When we ask kids to tell us what discipline their mothers use and how they cope with their mother, different patterns emerge for boys and girls," Dr. Perry reports. Among boys, only maternal overprotection leads to victimization. If children feel that their mothers are limiting their exploration and intrusively fighting their battles for them, that makes them perceived as victims. It is especially predictive of passive victimization.

But of course, not all boys with overprotective mothers become victims. What matters is how such children feel in conflicts with their mothers, which depends on the discipline strategies parents use. "Maternal overprotection predicts victimization if during conflict children feel compelled to submit—*and* are also afraid," Dr. Perry explains. "If boys internalize the negative messages about themselves that are *implied* in the inept parenting of overprotection, and come to feel that Mother's wish is their command, then the boundaries with their mother are blurred."

Dr. Ladd's research amplifies this finding. "The parental correlates for passive victims are overprotection, and an overly close and mutually emotionally intense relationship with the mother"—known in psychological parlance as an enmeshed relationship. Parents become overinvolved in their children's lives, overbearing, and overcontrolling. They are also intrusive and demanding, which leads children to become compliant and dependent, having no opportunity to practice assertiveness skills. In his observations, such parents might interrupt the child during an interaction, or override the child's initiative, or abruptly negate or change the child's topic of conversation; at the same time, they might demand that the child change a facial expression or "sit up and pay attention" or stick only to certain topics of conversation.

"What's important is that almost all other studies have used questionnaires. We went into the homes of children and observed and videotaped their interactions with their parents." Significantly, however, Dr. Ladd's Pathways Project did not gather information on the fathers' behavior at home. That doesn't mean that fathers are not a crucial link in the family system. Other studies suggest that some mothers may be forming overly close relationships with sons because their husbands are emotionally unavailable to them and to their children.

Having internalized the negative message contained in overprotection, the child virtually implodes. He is consumed with anxiety, develops a fearful and submissive stance in the world, and becomes a sitting duck for those who are given to misusing power. "Boys with this history do not develop the way normal boys do," says Dr. Perry. Most boys are encouraged to solve things on their own. Overprotection shields children from conflict and prevents them from learning skills necessary to avoid exploitation. This makes them more anxious and fearful in peer conflict. It sets them up to become victims to bullies.

At home, Dr. Ladd observes, overprotection provides a support system for the child. But exactly what is it that the child is learning from overprotective treatment? If he shows some vulnerability, such as fears, self-doubts, or anxious postures or facial expressions, he'll get support from the parent. But in the peer group of boys, being open about vulnerabilities is not valued. Bullies' radar picks them up and reads them as a sign of weakness. "What works in the home is maladaptive in the peer group," says Ladd. His studies are all the more remarkable because he looked at children at the time they were entering kindergarten, when children first establish ties in a group made up of unfamiliar age-mates.

Whether maternal overprotectiveness is a reaction to stresses in her own life, a response to inborn qualities or other vulnerabilities observed in the infant, or whether it reflects constitutional anxiety in the parent, it has the same effect. "It curtails the growth of independent autonomous functioning beyond the family," says Dr. Perry. In Dr. Olweus's retrospective studies of middle-school boys, he found that the mothers of victimized children treated their sons as younger than their age and overcontrolled their spare-time activities. Infantilization and discouragement of autonomy interfere with boys' development of ability to explore and take risks—activities highly valued by male peers.

And Some Shoves from Parenting

Maternal overprotectiveness does not seem to figure into victimization among girls at all. But that doesn't let family life off the hook. Bad parenting takes many forms. One of the most corrosive is punitive, coercive parenting marked by harsh discipline that comes across as parental hostility.

In David Perry's studies, victimized girls, distinct from other girls, reported that when they misbehaved, their mothers used a form of coercive-emotional control. They threatened to abandon them, to send them away, and to stop loving them. And the girls tended to respond to such explicit threats of rejection with anxiety and feelings of worthlessness that invite victimization. The hostility threatens their sense of connectedness in the most fundamental relationship in their life. At the same time, it undermines development of empathic and prosocial skills, which are especially valued by female peers, and leads them to feel even more incompetent and distressed and helpless in difficult peer interactions.

Yet another combination of forces shapes aggressive victims. Children who become aggressive victims may, like the infants and children Dr. Kagan studies, start with a temperament that prevents them from making an easy adjustment to change. And their parents may be overprotective. That's what sets them up for victimization. But what puts them on the path to aggression is what puts *all* children on a path to aggression: a family environment marked by hostile, coercive cycles of parenting. In the child it sets in motion feelings of hostility and a pattern of resistance that begets only more coercion from parents. It promotes the development of aggression and other externalizing styles of coping. Often these are families under the stress of financial problems, often from lower socioeconomic strata, or perhaps marital discord inhabits the house. Both parent and child start fights. Into this milieu of high conflict, a parent allows conflicts to escalate—and then unpredictably lashes out and ends the conflict.

"If during conflicts emotional arousal escalates," explains Dr. Perry, "and if, because of inconsistent parenting, a child can't predict how it will end, a child is getting no practice with the parent in getting under control; in fact, he's getting practice in being out of control. The child stays in a state of hyperarousal—he fights like heck and just keeps on fighting. This same emotional disregulation is transferred to the peer arena. It comes from an interaction of high-intensity arousal and unpredictability."

It's the special combination of both internalizing and externalizing coping styles that distinguish these kids, along with their physical weakness. Their hostile and stressful family background breeds aggression, with a strong need to exert power and control over others. But the anxiety they feel during conflict makes them emotionally disregulated.

In an important new study, Dr. David Schwartz carefully examined the early home life of boys who become aggressive victims—years before he knew whether any and which ones would later have peer problems. He and his colleagues first extensively observed and interviewed the families of 198 boys the summer before the children entered kindergarten. Each school year, they tracked the boys' social standing with peers and their behavior. After five years, when the children were in the third and fourth grades—and behavioral patterns stabilize—they classified the status of the children with regard to victimization and aggression. Of the 198 boys, 16 had become aggressive victims, 21 passive victims, 31 out-and-out aggressive, and 127 neither aggressive nor victimized.

"Boys who emerged as aggressive victims in third and fourth grade were found to have preschool histories of experience with harsh, disorganized, and potentially abusive home environments," Dr. Schwartz and his colleagues report. Mother-child interactions were marked by "hostility and restrictive and overly punitive parenting." There was lots of marital conflict.

These were parents who expressed annoyance or overt hostility to their child during hours of home observation. They would shout at their child, tell the child to behave or pay attention, even brush off physical contact from the child. Their emotional tone with the child was clearly negative. Parental hostility is particularly painful because it comes across as threatened rejection—a scary prospect indeed.

What further distinguished these children was their direct exposure to aggressive treatment. Mothers were physically aggressive with their children in conflict situations. Nearly 40 percent of the boys who became aggressive victims were judged to have been physically harmed at home. "Only the experience of violence disposes a child toward the combined problem of aggressive behavior and peer victimization," the researchers emphasize.

The early experience of victimization and harsh treatment by adults entrusted with their care disregulates the children emotionally. These children become perceptually hypervigilant for any possible sign of hostility, finding provocation in thin air, and emotionally overreactive. Deploying their angry, disregulated behavior with peers sets them up for victimization.

Peers easily recognize that these children have deficits in emotion regulation. In Dr. Perry's studies, children cite the characteristics of aggressive victims. They get emotionally upset. They show distress easily. They get angry easily. And when faced with conflict, they quickly become oppositional and stay stuck there. "There's lots of anger behind it," he says. And they are persistent. They get invested in their fights. Something is driving them. What's driving them, he believes, is a low threshold for arousal in the first place. Then, simply, they can't calm themselves down. They are unable to soothe themselves. They continue fighting long after they should have picked themselves up and walked away.

It is still not entirely clear just when parental hostility leads to victimization and when it leads to aggression. But either way the conclusion is clear: Parental hostility, like overprotection, is bad for children's development.

The Case of Shyness

Some children come to feel humiliated and rejected by their peers less as a consequence of what their peers do to them than as a result of what they do to themselves. But they wind up in the same place—socially isolated, apart from their peers. These children develop shyness and withdraw from the social community at some transition point during childhood, perhaps as a result of some negative change in family circumstances or in their social milieu. Perhaps they are thrown into a peer culture that is newly demanding in some way or alien to their values.

Their shyness is acquired through an awareness of negative evaluations from others. They trip over their own developing social self-consciousness and newfound ability to make social comparisons. Suddenly observing themselves to lack needed social skills, feeling themselves to be social failures, they are consumed with thoughts of themselves and worry especially about teasing, criticism, and saving face.

If some shyness is inherited, most shyness is made through experience. While 20 percent of children are biologically inclined toward shyness, with a high level of reactivity in the amygdala, another 20 percent are born with a very low level of reactivity. These children begin life with a minimally excitable temperament, and tend to grow up sociable. They will not become fearful or shy—unless life tosses them some curve ball of vicissitudes. But the vast majority of children—60 percent—can more easily go either way.

Somewhere between fifteen to eighteen months of age, infants develop the start of a self-concept. An infant becomes aware of being a separate entity. Between ages three and five, children develop a sense of social evaluation. They acquire an awareness that the self is being evaluated by others—and a concern for just how well that evaluation will go. Children's awareness of social evaluation normally shows up in two major ways—as the ability to be embarrassed and the ability to feel shame for certain actions. It comes from the fundamental human need for unconditional positive regard.

"The problem," says psychologist Bernard Carducci of Indiana University, "is that some children generalize the sense of evaluation from those who are important to them to other individuals and situations. We all want to be accepted, first by our primary caretaker, then by other family members, then by our peers. As our social network expands, so does the range for acceptance; for the shy, the desire for unconditional regard extends beyond a small group to the entire range of encounters."

A little shyness is not a bad thing; it breeds caution. It keeps people from making fools of themselves or hurting others. Most people have some degree of social inhibition; they think about what they are going to say or do beforehand. And they think about the possible consequences of saying or doing.

But the shy are excessively self-conscious. They are so focused on themselves, they may pay no attention to signals from others. They are overwhelmingly preoccupied with what others might think of them, and—in a kind of preemptive strike—constantly sizing themselves up negatively. Consumed by discomfort in social situations, the shy respond as if an alarm goes off in their amygdala, which then triggers the physiological symptoms of genuine distress. Through its many neural connections to other parts of the nervous system, the amygdala makes hearts pound, faces blush, pulses race, palms sweat, and butterflies swarm in the stomach. Facial expression is frozen; children can't smile. Shy children freeze up in conversation, becoming tongue-tied and stumbling over their words. Memory is impaired under the stress of shyness. Unable to think clearly around peers or adults, shy children blurt out private thoughts and feelings. Their lack of assertiveness is so thorough they are unable to make eye contact.

For some children, says psychologist Paul Pilkonis of Pittsburgh's Western Psychiatric Institute, shyness arises early, out of the emotional bond parents form with infants. Children form attachments to their caregivers from the routine experiences of care, feeding, and caressing. When caretaking is inconsistent and unreliable, children fail to develop a sense of security and their needs for affection and comfort are not met. Their bonds of attachment are insecure. But the attachment relationship is a vitally important one not just for care and feeding; as the first relationship, it becomes the blueprint for all that follow.

"The damnable part of it is that this insecure attachment seems to become self-fulfilling," observes Pilkonis. Because of a difficult relationship to their parents, children internalize a sense of themselves as having problems with all relationships. They generalize the experience, and come to expect that teachers, coaches, and peers will not like them very much. They are quick to become disappointed in relationships, quick to feel rejection, shame, and ridicule. "They are self-defeating because they interpret even neutral or sometimes even positive cues in negative ways, reinterpret successes as failures. They have negative perceptions of themselves and of themselves in relation to others that they hold on to at all costs," says Pilkonis.

For other children, shyness is acquired at times of developmental transition, when children face new challenges in their relationships with peers. Thrust into the new academic and social whirl of elementary school, some children feel awkward and inept. Other children and teachers label them as shy, and they begin to see themselves as shy and act that way.

Later in childhood and early adolescence, when the social playing fields expand greatly, the growing importance of the judgment of peers can precipitate social withdrawal as young people become aware of how they are being evaluated. According to Dr. Pilkonis, most people who become shy point to the transition to middle school as the most difficult. Becoming acutely aware of social performance can bring on anxiety, insecurity, the full flush of shyness symptoms, and a new feeling they are awkward around others. An image of themselves as shy begins to set.

The unpleasantness of their own feelings and anticipation of negative evaluation lead them to fear and avoid social interaction. But their fear helps create the outcome they are most trying to avert. By focusing inward on what they want to inhibit—being laughed at, saying something dumb—their attentional focus helps bring it about. And that only confirms their worst fears about themselves. Like bullies, the shy tend to construe a more negative, hostile world than really exists.

At the same time, being in situations that kick off their fear responses produces feelings of more general apprehension. Because of the way the brain makes associations, this generalized anxiety gets transferred to those environments where social interaction takes place. So even though they are not afraid of any particular person, the shy come to avoid parties, classes where there is group discussion, and anything that singles them out.

Whatever the pathway to shyness, the shy feel nervous and apprehensive around others, which seems to mark them for victimization. Even though they may have friends, they tend to view their friendships as inferior in quality and feel unappreciated and neglected even by their friends. Studies show that they expect their friends to call more than they do, and include them more in activities. When they are with peers, there's a lot of deferring to others' preferences.

They may slip into solitary activities—even though they would much prefer to be social. But anxiety inhibits whatever social skills they have, and they lack self-confidence. Of course, avoiding social activities virtually forecloses the possibility that they will develop self-confidence in social situations or learn the social skills that are constantly evolving among their peers.

They are on a downward slope toward teasing and rejection. They make prime targets for bullies—just because they scare easily and cry, rewarding the bully with what he or she needs most . . . a reaction. And that not only inflicts its own humiliations, it isolates them further, leading to loneliness and feelings of disconnection from others. Loneliness, through the absence of social support, makes the shy vulnerable to depression.

Rising Above Adversity

Victimization, everyone agrees, is bad for kids. But it sometimes has effects that are not entirely negative. It can prod some children into finding a way to salvage self-respect. While victimization drives many children away from school, there are those whom victimization by bullies drives deeper into the world of books and to excel in schoolwork—both activities with long-term payoffs—although it's scarcely a predictable outcome and a terribly aversive route to excellence. By means not at all clear, some kids rise above adversity.

When I was pushed around, I let them push. I was told never to fight, push, or get other people mad. Yet, when push came to shove, I learned to shove back. These bullies were my makers. Who I am today, what I will be in the future, were all, in part, due to the people who pushed me around or made fun of me, and who beat me up. Thanks to all you bullies

who knocked me down, because WE must get up, then start all over again.
—B. W.

I was the youngest of three children each about two years apart. My sister was the oldest. My brother went through a phase where he picked on me after our father died (when I was about ten). I typically was very submissive and avoided confrontation. I still do to this day, but I did become much more outgoing in college. Sports and my mother's confidence helped develop good self-worth. In high school I also avoided getting near the "tougher" kids in school. But I believe a person's personality is set to some degree at birth; some of us are more aggressive than others. On the other hand I am living proof that a shy, submissive person can develop aggressive traits, etc. I am a successful salesperson and pride myself on being able to be nice to people while getting what I want in most situations. I believe in "win-win" negotiations. It's easy to be a bully, be aggressive and get your way. It's also pathetic to let people take advantage of you. To combine kindness with assertiveness takes thought and discipline, and I am proud to say I am good at it!—P. H.

I was a major shy person my first twenty-eight years, says Peter Doskoch, now executive editor of a major magazine and in his early thirties. *I always remember acting shy. I was awkward and clueless in social situations and around new people. I grew up in a complex of apartments that was a small, self-contained community. There were four or five families with kids that played together as a group. I never got a chance, didn't need, to learn how to meet new people. Only in first grade did I discover I didn't know how to approach others. I was shocked. I suddenly felt like an outsider because I didn't know what to do.*

I remember being picked on in the second grade. I was skinny and weak, although I was taller than average. I didn't have the social skills or self-confidence to challenge the physical threats made against me. By the second grade, I was aware that I was shy and that other kids had friends and were going to parties at other kids' houses. I had a best friend from our apartment complex, although we were never in the same class from kindergarten to grade six. My parents didn't see me as shy. But I was aware I was not developing a social circle. I was feeling self-conscious about making friends and talking to classmates. I remember looking desperately for someone to sit with at lunch, or on class trips.

From the second grade on, I wished I could join Little League. I played baseball all summer with my friends in the apartment playground. But I didn't have the confidence to join Little League. I would have to meet people who were not my friends, and that was a risk. My confidence was strictly limited to academics. I was breezing through school.

I was bullied in first and second grade. I remember being nervous about the schoolyard and avoiding it. By sheer wit I managed to avoid getting hurt. I was a fast runner.

On the first day of fourth grade, the teacher mispronounced my last name. I was too embarrassed to correct her. Not until two months later, on parents' day, did she learn the right pronunciation. I couldn't bear to confront her with the truth. I became the teacher's pet and that embarrassed me tremendously. When I did something she liked, she would exclaim "Peter-Peter-Peter," and I would blush, and she would comment on my blushing.

In the fourth or fifth grade, I actually got into a situation where a fight was going to develop. A kid was probably picking on my younger sister. I didn't threaten him, but as I approached he ran away. I suddenly found myself running after him. I thought it strange and I didn't know why. Then I caught up with him and fell on top of him. I was totally bewildered about what to do—throw a punch, anything. I didn't threaten him or tell him to stop bothering my sister. I just got up and left. But I had no more problems.

My shyness wasn't totally debilitating because I was smart. Here and there I'd find ways to work around it that were interesting. My family moved when I was about to begin eighth grade. I was now in a special program for the gifted and I felt less different. One day I wrote a humor magazine all my own. It was four or five pages, a parody of the local newspaper in the little town we had moved to. I brought it into my social-studies class. Everyone loved it. Everyone started talking to me and giving me positive feedback: "You're funny." Suddenly I was sitting with other kids and going outside with them at lunch. It was the first major social step on my own. I put out the newspaper every so often. People were coming to me, and giving me a forum to pick up social skills, how to make small talk. They were encouraging. I got my first party invitation not engineered by my mother.

Even at this point I feared having to go into the cafeteria, where I'd be thrown in with the nongifted kids. My studiousness was a crutch, an avoidance measure, although it had good effects on my grades. Around tenth grade, I had some beginning friendships and interaction outside of school. Girls were not part of my social orbit; I was doing activities in mixed groups.

I remember a girl, Mary, putting a dandelion in my hair. She was, I now realize, basically saying, ''I like you.'' But I didn't know what to do. Dating wasn't even on my radar screen. I didn't know how to handle it, so the relationship died.

I didn't get the courage to ask a girl out until the end of tenth grade. I was a miserable failure. I had a crush on her. She was the smartest girl, a minister's daughter. I was the smartest boy. We were both kind of nerdy. I waited until after the end of the school year. I avoided having to face her the next day if she said no. Of course, I did it by phone. I probably scripted the conversation. I have no memory of it. I probably asked, ''Do you want to go out sometime?'' leaving it vague. She said, ''Let's just be friends.''

By the beginning of twelfth grade, I had my first successful dates. Christine was definitely the aggressor. I now realize she had it all planned. She drove me somewhere—and she started to kiss me. We went out two months. Then she went out with my best friend. That's the first time I was socially hurt.

My parents were definitely overprotective. They never encouraged me to try new things. I was never encouraged to do anything outside the small group of kids in our complex. I wasn't hovered over totally. I had free range to play on the grounds for hours at a time. But I wasn't actively encouraged into new situations. My parents may not have known how uncomfortable and shy I felt in social situations. My dad is not shy. He talks to everyone. My mom has a small circle of friends. She has shy tendencies. I don't know whether she has no interest or is nervous. I got a lot of support in academics from my teachers. That reinforced my shyness. Studying is a solitary activity.

I never felt friendless until we moved, in the eighth grade. My mother tried to throw a surprise birthday party for me. I walked into the house and there were ten kids. I remember that none were my friends or knew me well. They must have been coerced by my mom. She must have had to ask around a lot. This, the birthday party full of people I didn't know, brought home to me the reality of friendlessness. Fortunately the humor magazine started a few months later. But I spent most of the year friendless.

I remained shy all through college. I met my wife my first year at Princeton. We didn't start going together until a few months before graduation. I became a scientific researcher out of an interest in science, not avoidance of people. I knew I'd be working closely with a few people in social isolation. I became friendly with them. I felt uncomfortable making small talk with people a couple of labs over. I didn't totally direct my career path.

Eventually, my interest in writing became stronger. Journalism school *was a tremendous help in overcoming shyness. It was the first time I was forced to interact with strangers, over and over again. Eventually I began to feel comfortable. Our professor sent us out reporting each day. To cover a story, we had to talk to people on the street. Every day, my heart was pounding. I was sweating. I was literally afraid going into class each week that I'd have to talk to strangers on the street. Donning a professional identity helped: This is the writer Peter. Gradually it took less effort. In three years it has melted away.*

When I have them, I definitely want to put my own kids in situations where they can interact in nonthreatening ways. I want them to learn how to make friends—with active support behind them in how to make conversation. I never got direct guidance. I definitely will give it to my kids.

I think of the times I was afraid of joining Little League and other activities I wanted. My fears were strictly social. If I had been encouraged or pushed, I would have. If I detected hesitation in my kids, I would be alert to this.

Mine was not a family where feelings were discussed. My father was social but emotionless. I couldn't say, "I'd like to do this but I'm afraid." It's not that there was a macho atmosphere. I couldn't say, "I'm scared." There was never a forum for saying, "I'm scared talking to new kids."

Making friends is a skill. It needs to be taught. Not everyone picks it up. I wish someone had given me lessons. If I weren't as smart, how different I might have been! I got a sense of self-worth through academics. If I were an average student, I might still be hiding in a corner somewhere.

CHAPTER SEVEN

Styles of Parenting

"**I** can't make this come out right," Danny sputters with frustration, banging his fist down on the dining-room table after a long, solid stretch of concentration and effort. "I hate my math teacher this year. He doesn't explain anything."

"Mom, can you help me rehearse my lines?"

"Mommy, why can't I get Superman's cape to stay on my action figure?"

"Daddy, can you help me? I want to get this drawer to go back in."

Perfectly mundane, perfectly common scenarios, routine requests and expressions of frustration voiced over and over in every household every day. Yet for all their ordinariness—in fact, *because* of their ordinariness—how they are answered, or how an answer is approached, has a huge influence on children's social status.

What determines a child's acceptance by a peer group? Increasingly, the search for answers to this question has moved beyond the behavior patterns of children to include the nature of family experience in general and parent-child interactions specifically. Parents, it turns out, play a significant role in their children's social behavior.

Make no mistake—this is not a Freudian rehash for the 1990s; it's not about Oedipal or other unconscious conflicts fostered in the family. Rather, the evidence shows that family experience is a highly emotionally charged learning laboratory. How parents discipline their children, for example, affects their problem-solving skills and their social-reasoning abilities, which in turn play out in peer relationships. A great many social skills are learned quite inadvertently through everyday parental practices. But even more fundamentally, parental approaches to their children mold the basic disposition—positive or negative—children take toward others, a disposition that tends to be set for life.

The role parents play in molding the basic behavioral style and personality characteristics of their children is increasingly the subject of controversy. For the last several years, the idea has been ascendant that virtually all that kids do and become is a product of their genetic heritage; it's all set before they're born. While genes indeed make a contribution to behavior and personality, exactly what and how much they are responsible for, and how, has never been established. Genes, after all, produce biochemicals, and these themselves are modifiable by many factors, including the internal and external environments they're released into and experience itself. Besides, it's a long way from a biochemical to a behavior. We are not held in humoral thrall.

I like to think that the belief in the determining power of genes is a passing fad, just a byproduct of enthusiasm for genetics research and the availability of new scientific tools that enable it. At some future point, we will have a more balanced idea of how genes, the environment, children themselves, and parenting all influence each other in a child's development. And we will recognize what common sense suggests—that parents in fact count.

At the same time, awareness that genes play a role is almost a necessary and a desirable corrective to the belief, held especially by parents of the middle and upper-middle classes, that parenting practices determine *everything* in a child's development. These parents, as discussed in Chapter Two, tend to overestimate the effects they have on children, particularly with regard to their intellectual accomplishments.

And yet, ironically, they also underestimate real effects they do have. Few parents, for example, are aware that how they talk to each other has an impact on their children's social competence. As that great social observer Miss Manners says, parents often reserve their best behavior for people like headwaiters, whom they will never see again, and argue strenuously for the right to "be themselves"—by which they always mean their worst selves—at home.

This cannot be overemphasized: Life with children lies, like grass on city streets, between the cracks. In our efforts to give children the Advantages of Life, we plan big events and stage-manage Important Occasions, but the great effects of parenting lie less in observable drama than in the repetition of everyday acts. The parts of parenting that most impress themselves on children can be so cloaked in ordinariness we barely notice them at the time. There is no Big Bang.

No one event creates social competence, and, for that matter, competence at any age is not guaranteed indefinitely, because new social skills are constantly being required and elaborated over the course of development. There is significant evidence, however, that a major negative event—a family move to a very different kind of neighborhood, parental divorce—can throw a child off track by producing a disruptive amount of stress. Still, what makes forces inside the family so powerful is the repetition of the mindless little exchanges of everyday life, the day-in, day-out nature of experience, in which behavioral styles get established and reinforced. Consider the case of discipline. Conflicts between parents and young children reportedly occur from three to fifteen times an hour, even more when the children are defiant. Several studies have shown that when a child is two years old, two out of three parent-child interactions focus on prohibitions. Small wonder why the way a parent handles conflicts with a child influences so much that happens outside the house.

Through a variety of pathways, most of them indirect, parents are primary architects of their children's general sociability. Children acquire some of their social competence through:

- the quality of the parents' relationship with each other
- parental beliefs about the nature of children and childhood, and about the role of parents, among other philosophies
- parental tolerance for and understanding of emotions, especially the negative ones, namely, anger, fear, sadness, and anxiety
- parents' knowledge about kids' peer competence in general

- the quality of the parent–child relationship, including how parents discipline children

It would be a mistake to think that the only influence on children's social competence is the nature and quality of the parenting they receive. Children's sociability is affected by their own temperament, by their own peer milieu (starting, of course, with siblings), and by the myriad experiences of life. What's more, children learn from many others in their environment as well as from parents—including other children and teachers. In one study of preschoolers in a child-care program, the kids who cried the most became quick to care about and respond to the needs of others—because teachers and age-mates had comforted their distress. The teachers and schoolmates wound up as models for children to observe and imitate.

And children learn from life itself, which is very dynamic and unpredictable. Children and adults rise to new challenges all the time and transform themselves in the process. Yet gaining social competence is not like suddenly discovering mathematical logic in college after nearly flunking geometry in junior high. Math skills don't even come close to affecting the kinds of life experiences that also mold a child's core behavioral style; math skills can easily be patched onto a person. Social experience cannot be remediated. Social experience is developmental, and new social skills unfold and are practiced and perfected only in social contexts. Once missed, those experiences cannot be made up. Experiences of social neglect and isolation, to say nothing of active peer rejection, leave skid marks on the self at the time they occur, and even if they don't last forever, they disrupt the highly dynamic flow of development.

As adults, when people have more power to shape their own environments, they can make up for much they lacked before—if circumstances conspire. As I write this chapter, I am witness to a series of events demonstrating exactly how circumstances do not typically wait for those in the process of remediating the basic social skills most people master in the first decades of life.

Chris is a bright attorney who six months ago was called on to head a department at a midsize New York law firm. He had been the number-two person for a year, and was well liked despite being shy.

It was clear that he was making efforts to overcome his shyness on a number of fronts. Under the tutelage of his boss, he was increasingly speaking up at meetings, sometimes taking brave positions on issues and winning the support of others by the intellectual force of his argument. He would take the initiative in organizing smaller meetings and was growing comfortable looking people in the eye. He was never a prime participant in the office social scene, but he didn't shrink from encounters either. Everyone on his staff respected him, and so they were invariably willing to defer to him on those rare occasions when their views conflicted.

Chris was growing in leadership ability when his boss suddenly resigned from the firm to head the legal staff of a former corporate client. After much discussion among the partners, Chris was moved up from his more sheltered position to department head. There were now many new demands on assertiveness abilities. It was not just a matter of winning the support of his staff, which unhesitatingly bestowed it on him, but vying for resources and jockeying for recognition with other department heads. And they were assertive and highly verbally skilled. Unfortunately, one of them also happened to be a major bully.

Chris continued to do a good job with clients and with his staff, although some felt he could have been a bit more active in teaching them the ropes, but he was increasingly locked into battles with bullying Amy, who not only would not give an inch, but went on a campaign of humiliating him behind his back and even encouraged the managing partner to view Chris as weak. His own staff continued to support him, but they increasingly felt they were losing clout within the firm. Inside six months, Chris resigned his position—to take a number-two job in a far less prestigious firm. Although he had come up to standard on some social skills, the requirements for assertiveness in the larger world he now had to operate in were still beyond him. The job, he told me, created too much internal stress— too many demands at once on his social skills—to make the salary and status worthwhile. Chris is now forever relegated to working for second-tier firms. Opportunities do not necessarily wait for even the otherwise talented to catch up on social skills.

Believing . . . Behaving . . . Beholding

When parents believe that social competence is important, and believe that it does not just fall out of the heavens on some lucky few, then, voilà, they wind up having kids who are socially skilled. The beliefs parents hold influence their parenting practices, namely, whether they teach their children about peer interaction and take the time to observe and support them as needed in their relationships. And when parents do both, they have kids who are popular with peers. Parents who think social competence is inborn make few attempts to help a child.

How do researchers know what parents believe? Typically, they present to parents a variety of hypothetical scenarios about children in peer situations—making friends, resolving disagreements, leading peers, being sensitive to others—and ask them to make judgments about the likely causes of the children's actions. Take, for example, the one about Bob, "a child who is really good at making friends with other children." Mothers were asked to rate the likelihood of three different explanations:

- "Bob has had many opportunities to play with other children." This explanation reflects a belief that general experience builds competence.
- "Bob is naturally friendly and outgoing," an explanation reflecting belief that peer competence has an innate, and presumably unmodifiable, cause.
- "Someone showed Bob how to make friends," reflecting belief in the teachability of social skills.

Mothers' beliefs, researchers have found, generally vary as a function of the age of their children. The younger children are, the more likely parents believe social competence is innate. As children grow older, parents tend to assign more importance to experience.

But here's the interesting part: Parents may discount the importance of peer relationships and dismiss the notion that they have a role in shaping children's social competence *if* they sense that their children are having difficulty with social relations. (By the same token, mothers who judge their children socially skilled sometimes take credit for their children's success when they had no hand in it.) So what parents believe about children's social competence may reflect not so much the true needs of their children but instead the emotional needs of the parents. In other words, it's stressful for a parent to feel that her child is not doing well socially, and parents sometimes take refuge behind self-protective beliefs. They then may either de-emphasize social competence altogether or see it as a skill too difficult to cultivate deliberately in children.

When children are having demonstrable problems with either aggression or social withdrawal, parents may erect other protective beliefs, researchers have found. For example, they may express concern about such behavior, but often attribute it to a passing stage or mood, rather than see it as part of the enduring pattern it usually is.

But even if parents believe that social skills are important and can be learned, that does not guarantee that they know what to impart to their children. In one study, mothers ranged from those who provided no guidance when it was needed, such as when one child would not allow a playmate to join in a game left for both of them; to those who disrupted cooperative play, by calling a child over to look at a magazine the mother was reading; to those who helped their child and another resolve disagreements through reasoning. The purpose of every chapter of this book so far has been to help parents know exactly what skills are important and why; this chapter and the next several ones will be devoted to how they can be cultivated.

Memories and Marriage

Just how do parents come to believe what they do about children's relationships? After all, if parents believe that a friend is someone who helps you, that's what the parents are likely to teach their children, transmitting their own understanding of the social world to the next generation, applying it to their own parenting behavior, and interpreting the social ups and downs and ins and outs of their children.

The models of relationships that parents transmit to children come from at least two sources. On the one hand are memories of their own childhood relationships. In one study, the more social parents recalled themselves to be as children, the more they valued social relationships as adults. And the more socially satisfied they viewed their children to be. Parents think about their children the way they think about themselves, and their own childhood memories fuse into a map for thinking about current relationships.

On the other hand are the parents' views of their own adult relationships. When parents saw their own relationships in a positive light—and this is true of fathers as well as mothers—the more they judged their children to be satisfied in their peer relationships and the more they were likely to see the benefits in social interactions. What's particularly interesting is that the researchers didn't stop there; they asked the children, thirty first- and second-graders, to rate their actual peer relationships. The more positively parents viewed relationships as adults, the more socially satisfied their children reported being.

Quality of the Marital Relationship

Parents serve as role models of social behavior through their own social relationships. Understood. It's so obvious it hardly bears mentioning. Trouble is, given the nuclear households families live in, that makes marriage the single most influential instructor of children's social development, especially before children are regularly exposed to peers. A 50-percent divorce rate, together with firm evidence that fully half of the other 50 percent of marriages are highly conflicted and unhappy, creates a scary prospect indeed for the social competence of current and future generations of children.

While divorce is often accompanied by changes that affect children's social lives—a move to a new neighborhood, a decrease in parental involvement with and responsiveness to a child, more negativity in parent-child interactions, less consistency in discipline—those are not inevitable results. What makes divorce generally toxic to children's social competence is the hostility that exists between the parents—before the divorce and even after. Continuing hostility is bad for kids whether parents stay married or not. Divorce, as any ex-spouse knows, is no guarantee of an end to civil war.

Conflict, it should be clear by now, is not a sign of unhappy marriage or unhappy families or other relationships. In fact, family

conflict provides a child's first and firsthand lesson in conflict management, a very indelible one because it is so emotionally super-
charged. In her naturalistic in-home studies of children's exposure to
arguments between parents and siblings, Dr. Judy Dunn found that
thirty-three months of age—not quite three!—may be a critical for-
mative time for the development of conflict-management skills.

Given their own inborn sensitivity to social matters, the frequency
of conflict, and the emotional intensity of family dramas, children are
riveted by family disputes. From them they pick up how to listen,
how to argue persuasively, how to see the problem from another
person's perspective, and how to resolve the conflict. That is, if the
conflict gets resolved. If it doesn't, children learn that, too—so well
that they play out those lessons in their own peer relationships. Dr.
Dunn observed that when children were six years old, they were
enacting in conflicts with friends the very same methods their mothers
had used in disputes with older siblings more than three years earlier!

Marital conflict, it can be said, has its own Boswell. At the University of Washington, where he is professor of family psychology,
Dr. John Gottman has been chronicling every grimace and groan of
marital discord for more than a decade. So far, he has monitored and
videotaped hundreds of couples discussing hot-button issues of difference between them and measured the fallout of their dissent on
themselves and their children.

The difference between happy and unhappy couples can be
summed up in three (admittedly clumsy) words: negative-affect reciprocity. Tit for tat, spouses hurl anger, hurt, and disappointment at
each other. They are mutually hostile, contemptuous, and even
mocking toward each other, making belligerent demands to provoke
a response from the other. As each attacks the other's fundamental
beliefs, feelings, and character, each partner hooks the other in and
the negativity quotient rapidly escalates. When that happens, Dr.
Gottman finds, misery reigns and couples generally separate or divorce
within three years.

Whether or not couples have divorced, the mutual hostility has
etched itself on the children. To the degree that parents were mutually
hostile, three years later their children engage in aggressive, antisocial
behavior—judged, totally independently, by their teachers. And in

those families where the husband responded to all the hostility in the house by emotionally withdrawing in anger, their children were showing signs of anxiety and social withdrawal. They felt high levels of distress, shame, and self-blame. In short, by observational learning, the children had acquired their parents' negative patterns of negotiating conflict.

Mutual unresolved hostility is overwhelmingly upsetting to children, says Dr. Gottman. They see it as a sign that the marriage that shelters them is going up in flames. The stress of that threat takes over the child and disrupts the development of emotion regulation. Perhaps children adopt antisocial behavior as a way of acting out their fears of a potential divorce. Or maybe even to distract their parents from their feuds. Whether they internalize or externalize their feelings, the children of mutually hostile parents are aroused physiologically; they are chronically in the alarm mode.

There is an interesting gender twist to the children's social and emotional difficulties. A parent's manner of expressing hostility plays out hardest on a child of the opposite sex. To the degree that husbands act in a belligerent manner in marital disputes—contesting their wife's remarks by trying to provoke a response, perhaps with derisive humor—their daughters were rated by teachers as showing internalizing behavior three years later. And when mothers are the belligerent ones, their sons become anxious and withdrawn. Children may be most affected by the opposite-sex parent because they identify and ally themselves with the same-sex parent. Anxiety and withdrawal may be adaptive responses to the threatening nature of belligerence inside the home, says Dr. Gottman; but it gives rise to peer problems because it gets carried outside the home as well.

In her studies of relational aggression, Minnesota's Dr. Nicki Crick sees antecedents of children's behavior in the marital and general conflict styles of their parents. She thinks children may learn relational aggression by watching their parents interact with each other. If children view relationally aggressive behaviors as successful in the family context, either in controlling others (Mom wins a conflict with Dad by actively ignoring him until he gives in) or in inflicting harm on others (Dad effectively punishes them by withdrawing affection), then, she says, they may reenact these behaviors within the peer context, with the expectation that these behaviors will also be successful with age-mates. In addition, she believes that other marital-conflict styles play a role in relational aggression, namely high levels of anger conflict in the marriage, but coupled with strong inhibitions against directly expressing them.

Emotional Expressiveness and Understanding

Social competence hinges on understanding the emotions of others. To become aware of the feelings of others and read and respond to social signals, children must first become aware of their own feelings. Parents are powerful influences on children's ability to read emotion in others and express emotion effectively.

All parents have a philosophy about their own feelings and emotional expression and control—a "meta-emotion philosophy," in the words of Dr. Gottman, who has spent the last several years exploring the phenomenon and its relationship to children's well-being. Their philosophy is seldom explicitly stated. "It's strongly related to the way people have marriages," says Dr. Gottman. When he interviews couples, they may unwittingly disclose their meta-emotion philosophy in such statements as "we think anger is really bad for marriage." More often it reveals itself in the way parents react to their children's display of feelings, particularly their display of negative feelings such as anger, sadness, and fear.

- "Is Daddy's little girl unhappy? You know Daddy doesn't like to see his little princess pout. Can't I see a smile? Daddy's little girl looks so pretty when she smiles."
- "If you're going to stomp around the house you can go to your room and stay there until you've finished being angry."
- "Are you afraid when Mommy turns on the machine? Oh, honey, there's nothing to be afraid of. It's just a big noise."

In intensive studies of fifty-six families, conducted with psychologist Lynn Fainsilber Katz, Dr. Gottman found that parents differ quite consistently in their attitudes to their children's emotions. Some parents are characteristically dismissing: They treat a child's true feelings as trivial ("That's nothing to worry about") or harmful to the child. They believe that it's a parent's job to change toxic negative emotions as quickly as possible, or convey to the children a sense that they could "ride out" these negative emotions without damage. Parents say, "Seeing my child sad makes me uncomfortable," or "I think sadness is okay as long as it's under control." Or "I warn him about not developing a bad character." Or "Her shouting scares me." Typically, such parents use some kind of distraction to shut the child's emotions down ("Daddy's little girl looks so pretty when she smiles"). Strong emotions, they believe, reflect badly on them as parents.

Disapproving parents are a lot like dismissing parents, only more negative. They tend to think of their children as manipulative when they are negative. They judge, criticize, even punish the child's emotional expression ("Go to your room until you've finished being angry"). They say things like "A child's anger deserves a time out" and "Children often act sad just to get their own way." Still a third type of parent is more laissez-faire, tolerating all emotional expressions but doing little to help a child handle strong feelings.

There was also a fourth type of parent, who during long bouts of naturalistic observation and intensive interviewing showed great respect for children's negative feelings. First of all, in interviews, Drs. Gottman and Katz had found they were highly aware of their own anger and sadness and knew just what to do to get their feelings under control. They also could comfortably describe their experiences of emotion right down to the physical sensations and distorted thinking their feelings produced, easily distinguishing one feeling from another and identifying what set it off. Most of all, these parents freely helped their children with feelings of anger and sadness. They essentially saw their role as a "coach" during their children's emotional moments.

"Emotion-coaching" parents recognize their child's emotions when the intensity is still low, before it escalates. "If your five-year-old is nervous about an upcoming trip to the dentist," said Dr. Gottman in an interview, "it's better to explore that fear the day before than to wait until the child is at the dentist and throwing a full-blown temper tantrum. We found some parents, when we asked, 'What do you do when Jessica is sad?' said, 'Oh, Jessica is never sad.' They never even saw that emotion.''

When observed, emotion coaches validated their children's feelings, rather than dismissed them. And they helped children put words to their feelings: "tense," "worried," "hurt," "angry," "sad," "afraid." The labels help children transform an amorphous, scary, uncomfortable sensation into something definable, something that has boundaries and is a normal part of everyday life.

Drs. Gottman and Katz have discovered that when children can label their emotions correctly, talk about them, and feel understood, negative feelings dissipate. In their studies, the children of emotion-coaching parents were rated by their teachers as more popular with their peers and more academically competent. What emotion-coaching does is *help a child regulate the physiologic arousal of negative emotional states*. In the laboratory, the researchers can actually detect that calming processes in the brain are activated when children experience validation and approval of their feelings.

"If a child is feeling sad, for example, validation and approval leads kids to have the experience of sadness in both hemispheres of the brain," Dr. Gottman told me. "Talking about negative emotions while having them blends the negative feeling with optimism," since activation of the left frontal cortex is associated with "approach" behaviors, positive emotions, and sociability and the right frontal cortex with negative emotions and "withdraw" behaviors. "We can measure that kids then calm down more quickly and focus attention better. They have higher math and reading scores. They develop many peer competencies, and really develop social moxie, or social intelligence. These kids sail through their developmental skills."

When parents dismiss their children's emotions as unimportant or unacceptable, children stay in a state of negative emotional arousal. And that directly affects their social and academic competence; they are rated less popular and perform poorly in school. Emotion-coaching lets children pay attention to what is going on in the world around them instead of what is happening inside them; they can listen to what their playmates are saying. Children normally develop the capacity to regulate their own behavior beginning in the preschool years.

When parents disapprove of their children's emotions and apply
sanctions against them for showing anger or any other negative emotion, then those children grow up to experience excessive physiologic
arousal in situations involving negative emotions—but they tend not
to display any external signs of emotional response! (Imagine how that
can confuse a friend, a spouse, or a child.) "This is because children
who receive negative reactions to their displays of emotion gradually
learn to hide their emotions but feel anxious when in emotionally
evocative situations," says Dr. Nancy Eisenberg, a psychologist at Ar-
izona State University who studies emotion regulation. This contra-
dictory and confusing response is a result of the earlier repeated
association between punishment and emotional expressivity.

In her studies of third- and sixth-graders, those whose mothers *or*
fathers reported that they minimize or punish their children's show
of negative emotions are rated both unpopular with their peers and
unable to cope constructively when they feel distressed. They also feel
socially insecure.

The ability of children to soothe themselves physiologically, says
Dr. Gottman, underlies social competence. It arises "only out of emotional connection being important in the home."

Quality of the Parent-Child Relationship

Of the many ways that parents influence their children's social competence, they all may converge, like dancing angels, on a deceptively
small matter: Exactly how does a parent respond when a child needs
help with something?

Psychologists have long identified two important dimensions of
caregiving and parenting that relate to children's adjustment in the
short term and the long haul. Various researchers give them different
names, but they are most commonly designated *support* and *control*.
Support refers to the kind and amount of affection, responsiveness,
praise, encouragement, help, and guidance—all of which add up to
nurturance—parents provide their children. At one end of this di-
mension are parents who show warmth, and at the other are parents
who are hostile and rejecting, parents who may, just with the wave
of a hand, brush away the child who comes running in with a ques-

tion. Parental control encompasses such matters as supervision, structure, rule-making, and ways of rule enforcement when there is conflict—in other words, discipline; parents vary from the rigidly controlling to the flexibly democratic to the openly permissive.

Parents tend to deploy these two basic dimensions pretty consistently in several distinct patterns, so-called parenting styles. There are **authoritarian** parents, who engage in lots of disciplinary control but display little warmth. There are **authoritative** parents, who display moderate degrees of control along with a high degree of warmth. And there are **permissive** parents, who fall into two subgroups— both exert little control, but one is full of warmth while the other is not; these latter parents are, in other words, **neglectful**.

Each of the parenting styles creates a distinct climate of interaction that pervades a wide variety of situations. As a result, parenting styles are said to undergird the quality of the parent-child relationship.

In interactions with their children, **authoritative** parents are strong on **support**. They are warm, displaying affection and providing positive emotional support and encouragement. They are involved, responsive to their children's signals. They have consideration for the child's feelings and needs. They allow children to change their behavior by giving them reasons when a change is needed. Children are allowed to discover their own solutions—and gain a sense of their own competence.

Authoritarian parents are strong on **control**. They tend to criticize their children, then exercise their own power to force compliance. They demand that a child act independently and maturely, and they impose strict rules and put limits on their children's behavior. **Authoritarian** fathers are particularly likely to show their lack of support, to display little warmth or responsiveness in their interactions with their children, and to be highly demanding. The more restrictive fathers are, studies show, the less likely are their children to behave positively with classmates or other kids.

Permissive parents generally are very accepting of their children. ''Indulgent'' is the word most often used by others to describe them. Warm and responsive to their children, permissive parents impose relatively few limits and controls. Depending strongly on the nature of the child, the net effect may be to condone behavior that makes their children unappealing to peers. A permissive parent whose child tends to be impulsive by nature, for example, can grow up "bratty." Such children can be hard to take, and are not likely to be the most popular kids around, but they are not usually the class bullies either.

Neglectful parents show neither warmth nor control. They are indifferent and unresponsive to their children. Parental neglect produces a devastating array of psychological and developmental deficiencies in children, well beyond the scope of this book.

Authoritative and authoritarian parenting styles are polar opposites in the amount of support they offer and the type of control they exercise. And that, it turns out, makes them polar opposites in producing generally competent and confident children. A large amount of research over the past thirty years has shown that parental support leads to positive adjustment, high self-esteem, verbal assertiveness, independence, and academic achievement in children, whether in the preschool years or in adolescence. Moderate levels of control that shift in accordance with a child's development also produce happy, well-functioning children—so long as the control does not involve coercive discipline, such as hitting a child.

Psychologists have also discovered that parents' child-rearing styles also make a very specific contribution to the social competence of their children. In one of the most recent studies, at the University of Nijmegen in the Netherlands, family psychologists Maja Dekovic and Jan M. A. M. Janssens found that the two major types of parenting behavior predict whether children will be accepted or rejected by their peers. Their direct observations of children at home with both mothers and fathers show that parents of popular children are most likely to adopt an authoritative/democratic style when interacting with their children. And parents of rejected children endorse an authoritarian/restrictive style of parenting.

Their study bears describing in some detail because it throws into particularly clear relief just what social skills children pick up in the family that transfer directly to their relationships with peers. From a pool of more than one thousand children between the ages of six and eleven, the Dutch team focused on fifty-eight children who were designated popular by their peers and fifty-four who were rejected. Then, by prearrangement with the families, they sent observers into the homes of these children in the early evening, when both parents were present. In each household, they gave the target child a block of time to complete each of two puzzles. One was a wooden jigsaw cube, the other a set of geometric pieces that could be put together in different ways to form figures.

The researchers deliberately chose puzzles that were too difficult for the children to complete alone and that in fact would prove somewhat frustrating—a perfect situation for testing what measures of support parents might offer and what control they might apply to help a child stick with the challenge. The researchers instructed parents to provide whatever help they felt their child needed. Then they sat back and watched.

They monitored every smile, every nod of encouragement, every pat on the back, as well as every shake of the head, takeover of the task, or twitch of annoyance or disapproval. And they rated each parent on several key behaviors:

- warmth—the degree to which the parent displayed affection, positive regard, and provided emotional support
- responsiveness—the parent's readiness or ability to recognize, interpret, and adequately respond to the child's signals
- power assertion—the degree to which the parent exercised power to achieve compliance on the child's part
- induction—the degree to which the parent gave reasons and explanations for requiring a change in the child's behavior
- demandingness—the extent to which the parent demanded that the child act maturely and independently
- restrictiveness—the degree to which the parent imposed strict rules and prohibitions and put limits on the child's behavior

The results were striking. The parents of the popular children adopted indirect and persuasive verbal strategies such as suggestions and explanations. Every step of the way they gave more direct and nonverbal support, more encouragement, and positive reinforcement. They seemed to be sensitive to the child's signals, and more involved with their child. They made positive remarks about their child and the task. They provided lots of information.

The parents of the rejected children rarely displayed positive emotions in response to their child. They were more likely to criticize the child and his or her performance without explaining why it was wrong or indicating how it should be done. To influence their child they gave more direct commands and many more prohibitions. And they often took over the task for their children, rather than helping them find their own solution. Among this group, the fathers were especially stingy with nonverbal support, showed little warmth, responsiveness, or demandingness.

But that isn't all. The parents' child-rearing style not only was directly related to their child's social standing, it was also related to the child's spontaneous display of prosocial behavior with peers. The children of authoritative parents had been rated by their peers as most helpful and by their teachers as helpful, sharing, giving, cooperative, and responsive to the distress of others. These were children who, teachers said, "try to help someone who has been hurt," show "sympathy to someone who has made a mistake," and offer "to help other children who are having difficulty with a task in the classroom."

"Democratic child-rearing and a positive affectionate relationship," the researchers report, "seem to foster the child's prosocial development." And mothers appeared to make somewhat more of a contribution than fathers in shaping prosocial behavior in their children.

By contrast, the children of authoritarian parents were not only rejected by their peers, they were rated as less prosocial by both peers and teachers. And in the authoritarian households, fathers' negative behavior seemed to have the prevailing effect. The more restrictive the father was, the less likely the child was to behave prosocially toward peers.

How do different parenting styles affect children's popularity? One way, the Dutch study confirms, is they foster the child's concern for others. Prosocial behavior is a *sine qua non* of friendship and peer competence. Successful peer relationships flourish only when children have positive expectations of others, when they are oriented to helping other children, to sharing, cooperating, and responding to distress. What breeds prosocial behavior in children is, very simply, children's prior experience in situations where they required help. Which is to say, children's prosocial behavior grows out of supportive experiences in the home.

Authorit*ative*/democratic parenting stimulates children's prosocial behavior through several channels simultaneously:

- Warm and supportive parenting confirms in the child's mind that he or she is accepted and approved of as a person. This gives children a sense of trust of others, a sense of security in the presence of others, a psychological safety net of felt security.
- It establishes the expectation that the world in general is a benevolent place and that relationships are satisfying and reliable.
- It lays out a model of positive interaction that children imitate, not just in the context of the parent-child relationship but in other settings, such as school.
- Parents' ability to take into account the needs and interests of the child establishes the value of and sets up a model for taking another person's perspective, especially in the face of conflict or in a troublesome situation.
- The mutual give-and-take prepares a child for reciprocity, on which all peer relationships are based.

Prosocial behavior is fundamental in children's peer relationships. It is, at all ages, the quality children like most in other children. It sharply distinguishes between children who are popular and those who are rejected. It is highly valued by children because it makes relationships *safe*. Yet it is only one of the social skills molded through parent-child interaction.

Children, for their part, carry their experiences at home into the world with them as attitudes. The importance of this subtle transmutation of family experience to a child's stance in the world can not be overstated. The help and support children get at home they bring to expectations of their peers and behavior toward them. And the amount of control parents use influences their children's development of feelings of social competence and willingness to work things out.

Authorit*ative* parents are demanding but responsive. They provide structure, set reasonable standards for their children's behavior, and communicate involvement. They try to direct children in a rational, issue-oriented way by explaining the reasons for setting up the rules. They recognize a child's individuality, encourage verbal give-and-take, and involve the child in joint decision-making. They display lots of warmth and acceptance, are affectionate and engaged with their kids; they pay closer attention to their children's need for attention and help. They treat their kids more like equals and usually manage to maintain the upper hand without the stern discipline of authoritarians.

When a child asks an authorit*ative* parent for help with spelling words and then stumbles, the authorit*ative* parent might say, "Why don't you try that word again?" Or "Try sounding out the middle before you spell it." Or "Why don't we come back to that word later?" So the child can first have some experience of success. If a child asks for help with a math problem, such a parent might ask, "What about it makes it hard for you?" or suggest, "Let's read the problem together to see if we can find any clues," or specify, "Try to add the whole numbers first."

Authorit*arians*, for their part, are demanding but rigid and unresponsive. They favor conformity and obedience; they require that a child follow rules without explanation, restrict a child's autonomy, and take on most of the decision-making themselves. They also tend to be less accepting toward their children; they display a great deal of *disapproval*. There is much negativity in the air.

If a child asks for help with a math problem, an authorit*arian* parent may respond with a glower or a sigh—a powerful nonverbal signal of annoyance—and say, "Figure it out yourself" or "It's obvious the answer is ten," making the child feel incompetent. Such put-downs not only attack a child's sense of self-worth, they generate resentment. If the child still comes up blank, such a parent may even insist, "You're not trying," and take over the problem himself. These parents believe in maximum discipline, minimum help, and fear that being "too soft" on kids makes them turn out wrong. Because such parents do not believe in the value of gentle (and positive) forms of persuasion like affection, praise, and rewards, they are given to more aggressive types of conflict resolution. They are more often impatient, dictatorial, or downright disinterested.

Authorit*ative* parents, on the other hand, offer more verbal and nonverbal encouragement. They smile and say things like "You're doing well" or "It's difficult, isn't it?" or "Maybe you should try looking at it this way."

Pointers for Parents

Here is a sampling of actual ways parents of both major parenting styles respond to their children when they need help with a challenging problem. These examples are taken from the study of 112 families by Drs. Dekovic and Janssens in the Netherlands.

AUTHORITATIVE PARENTING STYLE	AUTHORITARIAN PARENTING STYLE
Verbal support	**Verbal discouragement**
Positive remarks related to tasks	*Negative remarks related to tasks*
"It's good."	"That's not good."
"That's okay."	
Positive remarks related to child's functioning	*Negative remarks related to child's functioning*
"You're doing well."	"You're not trying."
"Smart girl/boy."	"You are so clumsy."
Nonverbal support	**Nonverbal negative behavior**
nonverbal approval	physical takeover
physical affection	brief utterances indicating negative mood
smiling or laughter	annoyance
brief utterances indicating positive mood	disapproval
positive tension release (Ahhh!)	negative tension release (sighing, tapping fingers on a table)

AUTHORITATIVE PARENTING STYLE	AUTHORITARIAN PARENTING STYLE
Suggestions	**Directives**
vague, nonimperative instructions or questions that stimulate a child to think about solutions	explicit commands or orders in which the child is given no freedom of choice
"Maybe you should try to find the corners first."	"Put it down."
"What should the block at the corner look like?"	"You must do it this way." "You must take this one."
Encouragement	**Prohibitions**
offering support, active concern, sympathy, encouragement	negative commands or restrictions
"We're going to make it."	"Don't do that."
"It's difficult, isn't it?"	"Don't touch it."
"Shall I hold it for you?"	
Providing information	**No explanations**
explanations on how something works	no information on why something is wrong and how it should be done
"This is the block that comes in the middle because it has two right sides."	

Beginning in infancy, studies show, the affection and responsiveness of authoritative/democratic parenting build a child's sense of security and facilitates a secure attachment between parent and child. As a child grows, praise and encouragement contribute to a sense of self-worth, build a sense of competence, and provide internal motivation to acquire new skills. The active guidance helps children establish long-term goals. Supervising children and enforcing rules communicates to children that they are cared about, while enforcing rules by explaining the reasons for them helps children understand

and internalize the rules. Eventually, that makes it possible for a child to monitor his or her own behavior in the absence of the parent; it promotes self-regulation.

The negative and harsh discipline methods of authori*tarian*/restrictive parenting and especially the intermittent use of harsh methods, which is often combined with subtle forms of neglect, may force compliance inside the home but they are exactly backward in the larger social world. They provoke negative responses of the child. They foster feelings of mistrust and resentment and lead to resistance and defiance. They force children to develop strategies for protecting themselves and for reclaiming some power and control. Overly restrictive parenting keeps children from developing autonomy. It focuses the child's attention on the power of the parent rather than on the plight of the victim or the harmful consequences of the act that the parent opposes. As a result, it keeps children from accepting responsibility for their own actions and from regulating themselves.

Being the recipient of harsh and negative parenting also makes children especially concerned with rejection. They become hypervigilant, ever on the lookout for signs of hostility and rejection. They come to misread the intentions of others and expect rejection in social situations. They personalize everyday negative events ("Sammy didn't play with me because he doesn't like me"), and, because it is so distressing, they become emotionally disregulated when they sense rejection in the air. Sometimes they call it "dissing." Whatever name it goes by, rejection sensitivity sets up children to become bullies, victims, or, the worst of both worlds, aggressive victims.

When control is excessive and rigid, studies show, kids may engage in prosocial behavior—sharing, being kind—*only* if it is a means of avoiding punishment. Remove the risk of punishment and kids go right back to antisocial behavior. Under these conditions, prosocial behavior does not become an intrinsic expression of their values.

Typically, parents from lower socioeconomic strata are more controlling and less supportive in their child-rearing. These are parents who are likely to be preoccupied by financial, job-security, health and other stresses. But high levels of stress are not limited to poor families; big moves, job changes, and divorce all put strains on people. Wherever or whyever it occurs, family stress can be bad for children and especially for their peer relations to the degree that it distracts parents and makes them less responsive and more negative in interactions with their children.

The saddest part for rejected children is that their world is doubly negative—with parents and with peers. "The whole social network of rejected children is characterized by disagreeable and conflictual relationships," report Drs. Dekovic and Janssens. Precisely because their problems are embedded in family experience, these children are not likely to benefit from help that focuses only on remedying their social skills. It's not enough to fix rejected children; their parents have to be helped to change the nature of the parent-child interaction.

Parenting: The Medium Is (Most of) the Message

Parenting style has an effect on peer competence independent of any specific practices parents may engage in to help their children socially, such as setting up play dates or advising kids in problem situations. Simply, when it comes to parenting, the medium of social transaction *is* the message.

That's how Auburn University's Dr. Jacquelyn Mize and Gregory Pettit, Ph.D., see it. The husband-and-wife team studied more than one hundred parent-child dyads to see whether parents who made explicit attempts to help their kids with social situations gave their children a leg up in the social world. The researchers looked only at mothers, not because fathers don't have effects on their children but because mothers tend to be more involved in their young children's peer relationships. Hence they could get a purer test of the relative influence on social capability of general parental style and explicit social advice and lessons.

They put each parent-and-child duo—the children ranged in age from three to five years—into a playroom and watched them from behind a one-way mirror, then introduced another child for ten minutes of play. After a snack, they showed each parent and child a series of short video vignettes of such social situations as peer rebuff and peer provocation; in these videos, actors realistically portrayed instances where a child was told that he or she couldn't join in play, or a peer knocked over the child's tower of blocks. Parents were told to imagine that it was their child these events were happening to. The researchers listened to what comments parents made to their children. Then, toward the end of the hour of study, they also supplied a reasonably difficult puzzle for each child to solve in the presence of the mother, one that was likely to require some parental guidance.

They found that when parents are positive and responsive to their children in a way that is contingent on the child's actions, so much social information is conveyed in that basic interaction style that it alone could predict children's social skillfulness, which in their study was rated by both teachers and peers. What's more, parents' interaction style influences the very *receptivity* of the children to any specific messages parents give about getting along with peers, and children's willingness to listen to and incorporate their parents' lessons.

Particularly for the first few years, the medium of interaction style is the message. "Qualities of the parent-child *relationship* have implications for children's functioning in other relationships," report Drs. Mize and Pettit. It gives kids a general disposition toward peers. Through myriad mundane acts of competent parenting, kids learn responsiveness, sensitivity to others, and a positive orientation to others.

Kids get a bit of a social boost if their parents also coach them in response to specific problem situations, particularly if the parent-child relationship is less than ideal. Engaging children in constructive discussion of peer problems helps kids learn specific social strategies.

In their studies, social coaching proved somewhat more effective for girls than for boys, suggesting that the parent-child relationship carries most of the freight for boys. Social coaching also had a measurable effect when a child was the victim of some negative action, like being rebuffed in a bid to play. In victimization situations, the team observes, parental coaching may be of specific value in guiding children to make benign, nonhostile attributions in interpreting the actions of peers and to have optimistic attitudes about the outcome.

When it comes to coaching, the team found, it is less important that parents know exactly what to do than to stimulate the child to think about what to do—exactly the same thing a responsive and supportive parenting style accomplishes. The children who were most popular with peers had parents who framed the problem vignettes so as to focus on a resilient response ("I don't think he meant to knock over your block tower. You can build it again, right?") rather than on a negative interpretation ("He's just a mean kid") or retaliatory reaction ("Why don't you take his blocks away?"). If a prosocial orientation is the very soul of social competence, then its heart is *the ability to make positive responses to others even in the face of negativity.* This is the same characteristic that keeps marital arguments from escalating to the point of no return.

The popular children also were the ones whose parents encouraged their own problem-solving and gave nonspecific hints, such as suggesting what part of the puzzle to pay attention to or asking what the next step might be. And their parents were generally the most responsive in style; when playing with their children they had the same focus of attention, they stuck to the same topic, parent and child mirrored each other's feelings, laughing at the same time, and they responded to each other's signals. They were, in a word, synchronous. Their children were not only better accepted by peers but were judged by teachers to be more socially skilled and less aggressive.

Many facets of parenting style play a key role in children's general competence, the researchers believe. Control, for example, helps children feel secure and focus on a task. But they single out synchrony as the crucial part of a parenting style most responsible for creating social competence. Finely tuned responsiveness gives children opportunities for learning the rules of social discourse, including turn-taking, contingent communication, and reading social cues. "You look a little sad," a parent says to a child, and so a child learns what to pay attention to in relationships with peers—emotional expression.

Parenting style is also a vehicle for transmitting emotion regulation. "My baby's upset," a parent observes, and then soothes her child. Through the parent's actions the child learns patterns of calming and soothing, learns how to change bad feeling states to good ones. Parental sensitivity makes children active and attentive participants in outside social encounters.

CHAPTER EIGHT

Creating
Social Confidence

hildren move very quickly from the family to the peer culture, in which they must make their whole lives. Yet, because of the emotional hold that families have on their members, virtually every action families make inside the home helps mold children's behavior outside the home. Through their roles as caretakers, models, instructors, actors, reactors, interpreters, first causes, stimulators, discipliners, coaches, hall monitors, organizers, cheerleaders, consultants, and architects and sponsors of the social environment, parents and siblings count. But that's old news by now.

The new news is, much of the influence of families on children's social competence is accomplished quite inadvertently. Given a sentence-completion test on marital conflict, for example, few warring spouses would probably pencil in: effects on children's social standing. They are a byproduct of other intentions. Because social learning is always going on in social situations, children help create much of their own social success among peers. But it is also true that families contribute to many of children's social problems. It has been shown, for example, that bullies are commonly bullied at home, usually by parents or stepparents but sometimes by older, bigger siblings. Bullies generally come from families where parents use harsh or physical means of discipline. They may be kids reacting poorly to death or other family crises. Or they may have been given direct or indirect instruction that aggression is how you get what you want.

Whether they intend to or not, whether they are aware of it or not, parents in particular—and the workings of family life in general—help shape children's concrete social skills. Even more profoundly, they affect the psychological bedrock of social life. Children's basic orientation toward others. Their confidence in exploring their world. The ways they interpret experience and attribute causes. Their ability to regulate their own emotions, or read those of others. Their approach to problem-solving. Parents' disciplinary styles, researchers believe, affect, for example, children's expectations of others as well as their reasoning, their problem-solving skills, and their ability to regulate themselves. All of which play into the quality of peer relationships.

In general, the influences of families sort themselves into two types: direct and indirect. Indirect effects are those that are not explicitly intended to enhance children's social standing with peers but that nevertheless transpire through the sibling or parent-child relationship—by such everyday actions as the way they talk, their reactions to children's outbursts or simple questions, their discipline styles, the values enshrined in their own relationships. Parents are, above all, the most potent models a child encounters, and modeling behavior is the easiest way for a child to acquire prosocial skills.

Parents also take measures that directly influence children's social activities: through the places they choose to live, the types of toys they buy, their planning of activities. And while these actions are often undertaken with the explicit intent of affecting children's peer relationships, there are often inadvertent effects of these actions, too. Consider the parents who move from city to suburbs in the belief that their children will be able to play with more children more easily—a flawed assumption to begin with (there are more children per square inch in city neighborhoods than in the suburbs). And they move to a spacious house on a hill. But just the lay of the land on which their house is located could influence whether peers have ready access to their children at all, especially in grade school. Simply, hills are not friendly terrain.

Even if they actively decline the job title, parents have the effect of being social engineers of their children's lives. In ways that are deliberate and incidental, obvious and not so, they structure children's access to peers, the strength of their connections to them, and the activities they engage in. The only real question is whether families choose to become fully aware of the impact of their actions and construct an environment that reasonably accommodates their children's needs. This chapter is intended to draw parents' attention to ways they can positively, consciously influence the social life of children—without being overinvolved in their children's lives.

From the beginning, be sensitive to and responsive to an infant's needs.

Certain kinds of early experiences can never be made up. Early social responsiveness actually structures the infant brain. There is a neurobiology of affiliation. In ways that are not even fully understood yet, responsive parenting provides some of the biological underpinning for children's own social competence. For boys especially, a positive parent-child relationship will influence the ease or difficulty a child will have in peer relationships long before peers enter the picture or any intentional social teaching takes place.

Play with your child, starting in infancy.

The ability of both mothers and fathers to sustain bouts of play with infants is associated with children's later popularity in peer groups. Infants start acquiring social and language skills through the patterns and rhythms of adult interactions with them. It's important that parents at first lead the dance of reciprocal gazing and cooing, and that they draw out positive feelings from their children. Even these simple interactions are remarkably complex, and many things are going on: The infant is not only getting practice reading emotional cues but learning she can have an effect on others, experiencing positive feelings from the presence of others, and learning to regulate internal emotional states.

Continue playing games with your children as they develop. That especially helps children learn how to balance competitiveness with friendship and other social goals later in childhood.

Children require care and attention; do not justify neglect as encouraging independence.

Child-rearing is hard work. There are no shortcuts. Especially when young, children make great claims on parental attention, and on patience. Children learn to become independent not by parental inattention but by intensive support and active supervision.

Check your underlying beliefs.

The more you believe that social competence depends on learnable skills, the more socially skilled your children will be. What you believe affects what you will do in raising your children.

Get help for marital problems.

Marital conflict not only makes adults unhappy, it makes life miserable for children. Plus it disrupts children's social development. Children adopt the conflict-management styles their parents deploy—or fail to. And they often fear the worst and act out their anxieties about divorce. If you and your spouse are locked in combat, seek help from a family or marital therapist. You may say to your children, "Mommy and Daddy have been fighting a lot lately and we are trying to stop it. We have some problems we are working out. We both love you very much."

Allow children to witness and absorb the basic rules of social interaction.

Number one: Smile and make eye contact. According to Stanford's Dr. Zimbardo, that creates a benign social environment around you in which people are more likely to smile and make eye contact back. Number two: Introduce yourself to others. It's amazing, he says, how few people do that, especially on the telephone. "Hello, this is Zara, I'm a friend of Lisa's from school." Number three: The art of communication requires that you be not only an effective speaker but a good listener. In order to hear what others say, children (and adults) have to learn to control their own emotional states (see pages 248–249).

Borrow from *Zorba the Greek*.

Use the character as a model of sociability—think of yourself as a host at life's party. At some level, says Zimbardo, everyone has the responsibility for encouraging social skillfulness in others. Enter all social interactions thinking, "What can I do to make you feel more comfortable?" People who make others feel at ease, who lessen the anxiety many bring to social situations, are well liked by *everyone* and sought out as social partners.

Actively model and rehearse crucial communication skills in your relationship with your child.

Among the most important skills identified by researchers:

- leading, offering positive play suggestions to peers ("I have a fun idea!")
- asking questions in friendly ways ("Can I use the red pen first?" rather than "How come you never let me choose a color first?")
- supporting, making explicitly positive statements, and showing affection to peers
- commenting, making statements to peers about ongoing activities ("We're making the tower very strong, aren't we?")

Active parental assistance is usually needed for peer interaction—at least at first.

Parents need to play an active role in expanding children's world beyond the family by arranging and managing peer contacts for their children, especially in the early preschool years. Play invitations and other informal social arrangements benefit young children in many ways. Children become more socially competent, better accepted by their peers, and develop closer ties with age-mates. What's more, informal play situations give children control over their social experiences and foster learning. Typically, mothers make the arrangements and supervise toddlers' contacts with peers far more often than fathers do—82 percent of the time, in one study—but this division of labor is not preordained.

As children move into the toddler years, exposure to informal play groups on a consistent basis helps them acquire the skills they need to succeed in sustained relationships with larger numbers of children. Studies show that those who participate in regular play groups become skilled at verbal communication and make a better adjustment to school.

The more parents—and parents at the behest of children—initiate contacts with peers outside school, the better their children do in preschool classrooms in many ways. They are better liked and accepted by peers—and boys seem to benefit especially on this score; they are less aggressive. In school, children spend less time in non-constructive solitary pursuits. They spend less time "tuned out" or as passive bystanders to others' activities. And they are less anxious in the classroom.

All children expect and benefit from parental monitoring or supervision.

Monitoring of activities should reflect children's development and increasing need for self-management.

- Be involved—to a point. When children are toddlers and totally dependent on parents for setting up peer contact, it's appropriate to arrange play opportunities. Even then parents may need to jump-start and guide activities, but not engage in play-by-play direction.
- Some supervisory strategies are more helpful than others to children's social development.
- The younger the children, the more they benefit from the active presence of a parent and the more helpful parents can be by directly transmitting information about how to begin interactions. Parents can act as coaches to very young children to help them not only start but sustain interactions, offering "on-line" verbal support for engagement as situations warrant. "Say hello." "Why don't you ask them if you can play." "It would be good to tell them your name." "Maybe you could ask David if he wants to play with the fire engine." "Now it's Oliver's turn to hold the dinosaur."

- At this stage, children need parents to take an active role in teaching specific skills, such as turn-taking and cooperation, especially early in the proceedings. In one study where mothers actively coached their children to share a toy with another toddler, their children directly if inadvertently benefited. During a later play session, their sharing was reciprocated; they were offered toys by the previously bereft toddler.
- Offering specific interactive instruction on entering groups is also helpful to very young children. Parents of kids who are well liked by peers coach their children on nonintrusive strategies and encourage their children to adopt their peers' frame of reference—"Why don't you ask them if they need another helper."
- Adults may sometimes even become part of the interaction in order to directly model appropriate behavior for young children. "Why don't you throw the ball to me and then I'll throw the ball to Jake. Then he'll throw it back to you."
- Studies consistently demonstrate the value of parents supervising by sensitive, situationally responsive coaching ("Try asking Peter if you can borrow the hammer for a few minutes") rather than by issuing rigid commands ("Give that toy back right now.")
- And the more parents manage by expressing feelings positively, the more socially competent their children prove to be in interactions.
- But direct supervision outlives its usefulness very quickly.
- The older and more mobile children are, the more parents need to use indirect forms of supervision. Keeping track of kids' whereabouts and play partners is basic.
- By the time children are in elementary school, parents' involvement should be along the lines of providing advice and support, acting as an interpersonal consultant, and making the world safe for talking about peer problems.
- Even beyond toddlerhood, direct parental supervision is a form of interference that restricts kids' attempts to negotiate and manage their own social relationships.

- Remember, the goal of child-rearing is self-management. Children need to develop a sense of their own competence at social affairs.

No child is too old for parental monitoring of the nonintrusive kind.

The less monitoring parents do, the more their sons are likely to be delinquent, whether in fourth grade or tenth grade.

The failure to provide monitoring at any age is a form of neglect and is experienced as a lack of caring by children. That lesson was brought home to me in a very personal way when my older son, Danny, was fourteen.

A very curious, indefatigable, and positive child, Danny and his entire peer group slammed into adolescence early, around age twelve. Overnight everything changed. Danny had a large circle of friends, many of them since the first grade, and while they were all basically smart and sensible, a lot of them now looked pretty scary, experimenting with ways to look and be. I think that was the year Danny lived in camouflage. Camouflage shirts. Camouflage pants. Army boots.

Then the parties started. On Friday afternoons, Danny would call me at my office to negotiate his curfew for the evening. He'd constantly lobby for midnight. I always wanted to know what he was doing, with whom, and where he was going. We'd have many back-and-forth calls—sometimes he'd hang up on me if he didn't like what I was saying; then he'd call back in two minutes. Eventually, we'd reach an agreement. Then Danny would invariably call back one last time: "It's not going to be like this when I'm eighteen, is it?" I tried to suggest that he wouldn't be interested in doing the same things when he was eighteen. He was not amused.

Pretty soon, Friday afternoon was too late for the negotiations to start. Discussions began Thursday evenings. Then Wednesdays. Pretty soon, all our family time seemed focused on Danny's curfew. I felt I had no time for Gabe, then ten. How had our family life come to revolve around this one topic? One night, at a social function, I confided my dismay to a wise friend whose three children were slightly older than my two. "Why don't you do what we did? We didn't give them any curfews. We let them decide themselves.'' My husband and I were dumbstruck by the idea. It was intriguing. But frightening. Our friends lived in the suburbs; their kids were too young to drive when the issue arose. We lived in the city; there were ways to get anywhere, and Danny was very sophisticated.

We arrived home that night to find the entire house had been plastered over with little square Post-its. All they had written on them was: 12:00. They were on doorknobs, inside lampshades, in the medicine cabinets, inside the refrigerator, on the pillows. They were on mirrors and drawers, inside closets, on the toilet seats, on sheets of toilet paper. We found Post-its in funny little corners for weeks. We were amused at Danny's persistence. The next morning, we said nothing. During the day, my husband and I conferred. The suggestion still looked attractive enough to warrant a go. When Danny called my office, I told him we would speak to him at home.

When I walked in the door, Danny trailed me into my bedroom. There he parked himself on a corner of the bed, and I remember thinking how "together" he looked and sounded for someone just fourteen. I declared that we adults had an announcement to make. From now on, I said, he had no more curfew. And with those words, Danny seemed to shrivel before our eyes. From the very body that had seconds ago seemed so mature there emanated a fragile little voice: "That doesn't mean you don't love me anymore, does it?"

It doesn't get any clearer than that. One of those defining moments.

"No," I said. "Nothing's changed. I still want to know where you're going, with whom, and what you're going to do. Only, instead of us telling you, you'll tell us what time you'll be home. And if you're going to be late, you'll call and let us know what time you'll be home, so I won't be up all night composing your funeral oration."

We had a few hairy nights when Danny didn't get in or call till . . . late. And I was too ashamed to tell other parents, even though this felt right for Danny. Two other mothers and I, collectively parents of eight boys who had been friendly for years, had been meeting occasionally as a kind of reality check. Still, I dreaded the call I'd get sooner or later: "Josh says that Danny doesn't have to be home at all if he doesn't want to. I knew that couldn't possibly be true." But before long, we noticed a curious thing. We'd go out on a Friday night, say, to a local movie, and we'd be on our way home by 10:00 P.M. when we'd notice that all the lights were on. And there we'd find Danny, often just hanging out with a friend. He had learned to regulate himself very quickly. So by the time I got the call from Josh's mom saying she was getting this weird story about Danny, I could say, Uh, yes it was true. And to tell the truth, it was working. For Danny. And for us. I make no further claims. It also later worked for Gabe. But then, he and his peer group slipped into adolescence far more gradually.

Eventually we noticed an even more curious thing. Danny would tell us some plans about some classmate having a party on Friday night. The party was always being thrown by a kid outside his sizable circle of friends. There was always enough vagueness to arouse suspicion. A few other mothers and I had developed a strategy (part of the reality-checking) of making sure that, say, Joey's mother knew that Joey was planning a party. But that became unnecessary. Every time one of these not-quite-right parties appeared on the horizon, come the night of the party, Danny would always manage to pick a fight with me and storm off to his room, where he'd spend most of the evening. The next day, we'd get a flurry of calls from other parents commiserating that their kids, too, had gone to the party, which was invariably unsupervised by adults, and where fourteen-year-olds drank beer or worse. Very quickly we realized that Danny was quite consistently managing to avoid every one of these events. We were happy to be his fall guys.

Make an extra effort to monitor children during times of family stress.

Divorce and other family crises derail children's social competence and especially cripple their confidence largely because they divert the attention of parents. (That's how sensitive children are to signs of caring.) Paying special attention to children at times of adversity may not only prevent the development of children's peer problems, including aggression or withdrawal, it may be emotionally gratifying and stabilizing for parents, too.

Yes, restrict television viewing.

You've heard it a million times. It's still worth repeating. Television probably has its value, but it's a big contributor to aggression in children. Television presents far too many violent solutions to problems and legitimizes aggression—and those most susceptible to that message are those who tend to watch the most TV. Besides, kids should spend more time in active and social pursuits rather than loafing in front of the TV.

While we're on the subject, eliminate violent toys, games, and movies as much as possible. Young children often find them deeply disturbing.

Make yourself human.

If you sense that your child has a problem making friends, or being liked, remind your child that even people who look accomplished didn't start out that way. Most children harbor the strange belief that their parents in particular were born perfect. Tell your child stories about yourself growing up, making sure to recount some of the specific social difficulties you had. "You know, I used to be afraid of making new friends when I was in third grade." Or "I used to think the other kids hated me." This often gives children the motivation to improve social skills.

Be in touch with teachers.

Get teachers' perspectives. Teachers know, for example, what all third-graders are like. In addition, they are seasoned and reasonably accurate observers of classroom social life. They have a good sense of how kids act in peer groups. Besides, kids who have the hardest time relating to peers also have a difficult time relating to teachers. Teachers can be helpful in confirming whether your child has a persistent problem.

But teachers don't see everything. You may uncover a classroom social problem through talking to your own child. And then you will need the teacher's help to solve it. Not every teacher responds positively to being told by an outsider that there's a problem; some see it as an indictment of their supervisory skills. Try to make the teacher your ally in finding a solution.

If academic difficulties arise, explore the possibility they have a social cause.

Children can't learn in a sea of loneliness or hostility. School is a very aversive place when they feel their peers don't like them. The corollary is: To improve academic achievement, it is often necessary to foster social functioning.

Never humiliate your children for failing to greet or thank someone properly.

In fact, never humiliate your child by correcting him or reprimanding him in front of others, period. Instead, perform the proper greeting yourself ("Michael, thank you for letting Jake ride your new tricycle"). In private, you can explain to Michael why it's always good to greet people and thank people, and remind him how good it makes him feel when other kids are nice to him. Humiliating a child over social skills makes social experience aversive. And it creates hostility.

But do compliment your child for handling difficult situations well.

The more specific your praise, the more effective it will be. And reserve your praise for truly challenging situations. Otherwise it will be meaningless ("Jenny, that was really generous of you to let Alice play with your new doll").

Factor your child's social experience into decisions on family moves.

You may think of it as finally getting the chance to live in the kind of house you've always dreamed of, but children view a family move differently. They rate moves as highly disruptive of their young lives. It's like getting a sudden, unasked-for divorce from supportive peers.

Whenever possible, make family moves after the end of the school year.

Not everything you need to know about choosing the "right" neighborhood comes from real-estate brokers. Since children gain the most social confidence when they can play a role in structuring their own social activities, pay attention to neighborhoods that provide many of the resources for social development.

- Number one on any list is the presence—active and visible— of other children.
- Don't discount myriad other factors. Like sidewalks. Sidewalks enable children to get around safely on their own to play with others.
- Proximity to playgrounds is also important. Playgrounds are gathering places for children, places where they not only play freely but can mix with and learn to relate to many kinds of peers. The more accessible a playground is, the more likely caretakers will escort children there when young, and the more likely children will gather there on their own when a little older.
- Unless a child has had considerable prior exposure to the values and play styles of new neighbors, moves to neighborhoods that involve a major change in life circumstances—whether up or down the scale—can make social adjustment particularly stressful.
- In general, children have more social mobility, more opportunity for peer contact, more spontaneous peer interaction, and larger networks of friends when they live in neighborhoods that are geographically flat, where the houses are closer together and have few barriers between them, and where there are sidewalks and playgrounds.

Because there is a greater density of children, those living in urban neighborhoods tend to have more friends than those in suburban settings. What's more, kids who live in diverse urban neighborhoods usually have more places to meet and interact than children in isolated rural settings. Children themselves prefer neighborhoods with commercial areas, since they believe they have more spots—shopping areas, schoolyards, and parks—for kids to gather in.

In areas of lesser child density, play arrangements tend to be more formal and children are at the mercy of parents for making arrangements and getting them to and from involvement with peers. As much as that is a burden on parents, it robs children of privacy, autonomy, and spontaneity in social relationships.

One friendship is worth a thousand nerds.
Children who are generally rejected by their age-mates may be protected from the ravages of peer dislike if they have even one good friendship. Support a child's efforts at making and keeping friends. Especially for children who have few friends, friends are not replaceable nor are they interchangeable.

Help your child understand his or her effect on others.
It's important for children to know what to do. But social competence requires accurate information-gathering about how others are doing and how they themselves are doing. Children need to be in touch, to know what other kids think of them. About half of all rejected children do not even know they are rejected.

Teach your child to take in feedback while interacting with peers. The simplest form of feedback is to look at the other person to notice how she or he is reacting. Negative reactions—and one of the functions of emotions is to act as social signals—should be interpreted as a signal to change one's performance accordingly.

Help your child regulate emotional arousal.
Intense negative feelings create body tension that hijacks attention, makes children overly responsive to the negative feelings of others, or leads them to withdraw. In other words, it prevents children from managing difficult social situations (to say nothing about what it does to the ability to focus on schoolwork). Teach your children strategies for calming themselves. Try simple breathing exercises that involve inhaling deeply and slowly through the nose and exhaling slowly

through pursed lips. Taking time out is another. Reaching for a favorite blanket is fine for young children.

Encouraging children to shift attention to the positive aspects of distressing situations is a coping skill that will help them modulate their own negative emotions. It's a generally useful coping technique for adults, too.

Be an "emotion coach" to your child.

You can directly assist your child in regulating negative feelings such as fear, sadness, and anger by your own reaction to a child's emotional outbursts. When a child is upset, do not derogate his or her feelings or punish your child for them; respect and actively validate the feelings instead. The aim is not to banish emotions; you want to help your children find appropriate ways they can be used as guides for living. Help your child label his or her emotions. And then talk about the situation and the emotion while the child is upset. That's the time to talk about strategies for dealing with the emotion. Not only does such talk have a physiologic effect in soothing your child, it's the exact moment the child can assimilate information about additional ways of managing feelings.

Consider preschool a great investment in social and intellectual competence—whether or not both parents work.

Peer competence and life competence grow through exposure to peers. The evidence is in: Kids who attend preschool programs not only have more opportunities for social interaction, they become more sociable and more involved with peers. They develop more sophisticated forms of play, and they have fewer problems getting along with others. Even during preschool, children form emotionally supportive relationships, and these are sometimes remarkably enduring.

The effects of these early friendships survive preschool. One piece of evidence: Children make the adjustment to kindergarten much more easily if they have a friend from preschool in their class. They are less anxious about school and they then make more friends in school. Further, the focus of kindergarten has shifted from social to academic activities, putting on preschools more of the responsibility for preparing children socially for school. The consistent access to peers that preschool provides is an advantage to children no matter whether their parents send them expressly for the social exposure or as a form of custodial care.

The value of preschool in later social and school adjustment makes a good case for selecting a high-quality program. Relationships can endure only when there is a stable population of children.

Respect the importance—and difficulty—of some common experiences.

Some social experiences are extremely challenging for all children and make maximum demands on social intelligence and skills. Generally they involve ability to cope with certain visible problems, rather than avoiding them. As a result, they are very sensitive indicators of a child's overall ability to adapt now and in the future.

One such experience is initiating social contact by joining other children at play.

It is a task that is absolutely essential for further social interaction and calls upon all your child knows socially at the same time that, very realistically, it ignites all your child's fears of rejection. To top it off, your child feels highly visible, standing outside the group, and must swiftly acquire an understanding of the group and its context. Small wonder that half of all attempts to join others in play are rejected or ignored.

Teach your children appropriate social strategies and pointers for success.

- Let your child know that *all* kids have trouble with these tasks sometimes.
- Encourage your child *not* to take rejection personally; it often has to do with the situation and not the child.
- Kids who succeed in joining others do not make demands of their peers. They instead position themselves in relation to the group's needs. As if jumping aboard a train that's leaving the station, they orient themselves to the ongoing activity and take

action in keeping with the focus of that activity, rather than calling attention to themselves or changing the direction of play.

- It is not the fact of rejection that distinguishes popular from unpopular children. It is how they deal with rejection.

Help your child generate alternative responses.

This applies either to situations that did not go well or to difficult situations that lie ahead. The more ways of responding kids can come up with, the better liked they become. "What are some other things you can say the next time that happens?"

Another critical social experience, particularly for children age eight and over, is managing conflict with friends.

When Sarah and Beth go to the movies each week but this week can't decide which movie to see, it's not trivial. Don't take it at face value. What they're really struggling with is a way of balancing the needs of the friend with their own needs. Who gets to choose; on what basis did they decide last week; how will they decide this week? They're struggling to find a way to maintain reciprocity, or equality of spirit, in the relationship.

Regard disputes as opportunities for providing guidance.

Instead of rushing your child into peacemaking, give your child strategic help in managing conflict. Make sure your child knows how to make a positive offer to play to another child. Coach your child to understand the other child's perspective. "Why do you think Keri is so angry?" "Why do you think Matthew pushed you? Do you think it was because he wasn't having any fun while you worked the game?" "Why do you think Lisa told Alex your secret?"

And help children find solutions to their problems. "How could you use that game so that you both have fun?" "There's only one red pen. What's a good way for two people to get to share it?" "If Heather rides the tricycle first, what could you be doing?" "Peter, you've had the truck to yourself ever since Kevin got here. The more you ride it alone, the more Kevin wants to ride it, too. Don't you think he deserves a turn? You can ride it all you want after he goes home."

Encourage both children to express their reasons for disagreeing. By itself that is received by each child as a conciliatory move and suggests a workable solution.

Consider intervening in intense sibling conflict.

But do it only to coach your children in conflict-resolution strategies. Don't send them to their rooms, even if that is easiest in the short term. And don't brand one as "the good child," because the other one is then cornered into living up to an impossible reputation. When the hostilities are only escalating, help them find a better solution than they were headed for on their own. Start by showing there is more than one perspective. "Timmy, why is Ally crying?" "Ally, do you agree with Timmy's story?"

Be sure they know how to make a specific offer to play to the other. How to take turns listening to each other. And to explain their reasons for disagreeing. Also, coach them in constructive ways to end a bout of play. "I'm getting tired of playing this game. Let's take two more turns and whoever is ahead wins."

Categorically, it is never enough to tell children "*Don't* do that." You have to point out to children what you want them to *do*. Handling the situation positively also models a way of problem-solving.

Be available to advise your children on peer relationships.

Beyond the toddler years, children benefit from informed discussions and advice *outside* the context of peer interaction.

Coach your child to solve social problems.

When a child describes a troublesome situation, ask questions that prompt him or her to diagnose and solve the problem. Why does he think Jesse is bothering him? How does he think Jesse feels? What are some ways to get Jesse to back off without hurting him? And some other ways? And what other things can he do to get Jesse to stop bothering him?

It is not necessary for parents to have the answers; in fact, it's better if they don't. The goal is to encourage creative solutions. The more alternative solutions children can generate, the more socially skilled they become. "If you get your feelings hurt, how can you make yourself feel better? What else can you do to join in?"

How to split a box of Cracker Jack, which has only one toy? Ask your child to come up with solutions.

Coaching extends to helping your child interpret experience in a constructive way. "Oh, boy, that kid knocked you down. I don't think he meant to do that" is more likely to lead a child back into the swing of things without engaging in aggression than "He's a mean kid." Or instead of making a hostile attribution—"Maybe he doesn't like you"—opt for a more neutral and constructive one: "Maybe he doesn't want to play that, but there might be something else he thinks is fun." Such reframing of experience—or positive cognitive restructuring, as it's called in the psych biz—helps children become resilient.

Also, encourage your child to gather information about a peer's intentions before deciding how to react. Aggressive-rejected children especially tend to read hostile intentions into peers' behavior, and that allows them to justify aggressive acts as retaliation.

Auburn's Dr. Mize witnessed the following exchange:

MOM: Hmm, gosh, what if he grabs your truck again, what do you think you'll do?

CHILD: I'd probably just whap him upside the head.

MOM: You would? What'd he do, do you think, if you whapped him?

CHILD: He'd give it back and never take it again.

MOM: You think so? You don't think he'd just whap you back, and ya'll'd get in a big ol' fight and then he wouldn't want to play with you again?

CHILD: Oh, yeah.

MOM: What else could you try?

CHILD: Say "please"?

MOM: That'd be a nice thing to try. Do you think it would work?

CHILD: No.

MOM: Well, maybe not. It might, but it might not, huh?

CHILD: I could say, "I'll come get you when I'm done."

MOM: Hey, that's an idea. That works sometimes with your sister, doesn't it?

Prepare your child for problematic peer encounters.

Discuss past events that were troublesome. "How could it be better?"
Help your child prepare for similar events in the future. "What if
someone tries to take your bike away again. What do you think you
should do?"

"You didn't get invited to Benja's birthday party. What are you
going to say to her when you see her tomorrow?" "And what will
she say when you tell her that?"

Let your child describe her social fears, whether it's speaking up
in show-and-tell or asking someone to dance at a party. Then role-
play with your child. Take the role of a peer. Let your child direct
you to act out anxiety-provoking scenarios.

If your child is young, use hand puppets or stuffed animals or dolls
to enact the roles. The younger children are, the more they learn
from concrete depictions than from verbal instruction.

Help your child come up with ways to improve the outcome.
Rehearse the strategies and solutions so your child feels comfortable
with and natural in them.

Teach your child to handle provocations.

The temptation is great, but it is extremely unwise for children (or
adults) to respond to a deliberately hostile remark or action by reciprocating the negativity. If the aggressor is a known bully or an unknown quantity, the best response may be just to look the aggressor
in the eye, say, "Leave me alone" in an assertive voice, and walk
away. Assertiveness of body language is as important as verbal assertiveness.

If there is a bully in the neighborhood, work with your child to
develop multiple strategies. It is important for your child to have
multiple options so that he or she doesn't feel trapped.

**Fortify children who are smaller than average, physically
immature, or who have handicaps or disabilities.**

Such children are particularly likely to be bullied. Not much works
against bullies, but humor is most likely to be effective. Help your
child come up with a set of clever verbal comebacks to be used in
the event of victimization by verbally abusive peers.

Dr. Wallace Goddard of Auburn University in Alabama tells the story of a high school where the bigger students had the distressing habit of tossing the smaller students into the garbage cans in the hallways. One day one of the biggest students menacingly approached one of the smallest. But the little guy stood pat. He put his hands on his hips, looked up at his antagonist, and declared, "If you're going to do that, I'm going to have to hurt you." Everyone, including the bully, broke up laughing.

Help your child come up with constructively assertive ways to deal with the curiosity of others.

In their book *Teaching Social Skills to Children and Youth* (Allyn & Bacon, 1995), Drs. Gwendolyn Cartledge and JoAnne Fellows Milburn of Ohio State University recount the story of Phillip, a nine-year-old fourth-grader born with a congenital malformation. A very short arm grew out of his right shoulder and ended in a single digit above what would have been his elbow. He refused to wear a prosthesis or long-sleeved shirts because he felt they got in the way of his activities. His exposed arm provoked much curiosity in new acquaintances, and some, especially younger children, often asked what happened to his arm. Over the years, his reaction evolved from quietly looking away or hiding behind his parents to being snappy ("A shark bit it off!") and outright aggressive ("What happened to your head?").

Recognizing that her son would always be confronted with public reactions, his mother decided he needed to learn more constructive ways of dealing with the situation, giving a truthful, positive, and assertive response to questions about his disability. She asked him whether he reacted the way he did because he thought others were cruel or merely curious, or if he found the questions simply intrusive. Phillip said he thought others were curious, not mean, and that his responses were just "joking."

Phillip and his mom identified the ingredients of an appropriate response. When he was approached about his arm, they decided, he would just smile, look at the person asking the question, answer the question truthfully, and use a normal tone of voice. For example, "I was born that way. It may look different, but it doesn't cause any problems at all." Phillip and his mother role-played his response according to various possible situations. His mom devised assorted scenarios. "When you are on vacation, a little girl who is eight years old comes up and asks, 'How'd you break your hand?' Here is what you say: . . ."

Then his mother tested him. Phillip "missed" only one of seven responses. He refrained from making a positive statement telling what he "could" do, as in "I can do anything any other person can do." When questioned, Phillip said that he didn't feel he had to prove anything to strangers. "He had a good point," said the authors; "it was in his best interest to be assertive rather than passive or aggressive, but he was not obliged to ingratiate himself to others."

Make yourself aware of bully/victim problems.

Experts on bullying behavior indicate that teachers and parents alike often seem unaware of bullying and victimization. They therefore do less than they can to stop bullies or to help children cope with being bullied. Here are things parents can do:

- Pay attention to your child's reports of school or neighborhood violence.
- Watch for signs that a child is being victimized, such as torn clothing, unexplained bruises, moodiness, withdrawn behavior, a drop in grades, lack of friends, loss of appetite, coming home to use the bathroom, or low self-esteem.
- Be suspicious if your child needs extra school supplies or lunch money. A bully may be extorting things your child claims he or she loses.
- Take an active role in the school to keep up on potential problems.
- Record bullying incidents.
- Report all incidents to school authorities and insist that they ensure your child's safety—and the safety of all children.
- Bullying is a school problem. That's where it flourishes, whether teachers see it or not. Encourage your child's school

to develop a bully policy. Bullying can dealt with effectively only on a school level.

Teach your child about bully/victim problems.

The best way is to open the discussion on the heels of an actual bullying incident children experienced, witnessed, or heard about from peers. Then any information is not hypothetical.

Research shows bullying is most frequent in grades two through six, most serious in grades seven through nine, and tapers off after that. About 10 to 15 percent of children are regular victims of bullies, and about 10 percent of school-age children are bullies. Boys are somewhat more likely than girls to be the victims of bullying and are considerably more likely to be overt physical bullies. Interestingly, 30 to 40 percent of the bullying of girls and 15 to 20 percent of the bullying of boys is done by girls.

Do not teach a child to fight back. Fighting back is the worst defense. In most instances, kids who are picked on are actually smaller and weaker than the bully—thus their fears of losing these fights are quite real. Besides, not all bullying takes the form of physical aggression. Counteraggression to any form of bullying actually increases the likelihood of continued victimization.

What is more, advising children to strike back tells the child that the only way to fight violence is by using more violence. It also makes the child feel that he or she needs to solve the problem alone and that parents and teachers don't care enough to help.

Especially if your child is small, be sure your child knows that some kids get picked on just because they're there—bullies are usually bigger and older. You don't want to create anxiety. You just want your child to know the facts of life.

A wise line of defense is avoidance. Advise children that it is thoroughly adaptive behavior to avoid a bully. Being picked on is not character-building.

Teach your children that bullying is not acceptable behavior and people are harmed by witnessing it as well as participating in it.

Do not expect children to work out bullying problems on their own. Bullying is not just a problem of individuals. Given the influence of peer groups and reputational factors in maintaining the behavior of bullies and victims, it is extremely unrealistic to expect children to alter the dynamics of bullying by themselves. Therefore, they should always get a teacher or other adult involved in stopping bullying incidents.

Always intervene in bullying incidents.

Anytime adults do not intervene, they are training others to solve problems through aggression. Declare emphatically, "This is not acceptable behavior. You cannot do this here."

It takes more than behavioral transformation for rejected kids to be accepted by their peers.

Even if rejected children change their behavior, the negative reputations others hold of them will keep them from being seen as socially competent. It can take a long time for reputations to change. What's more, because they embody negative expectations, negative reputations exert a powerful pressure against the deployment of newly acquired social skills.

Avoid physical punishment as a solution to conflict situations.

All it does is legitimize the use of force. In addition, physical punishment overwhelms children with intense retaliatory feelings. Instead, apply nonhostile, nonthreatening, nonphysical sanctions for rule-breaking. Harsh and punitive discipline styles are associated with children's peer difficulties; at the very least, they overfocus children's attention on getting their own way with others in order to feel powerful. The most effective punishment is moderate, swift, and used in conjunction with positive reinforcement for good behavior. Children who are competent with their peers come from homes where parents more often use positive discipline—praising and reinforcing children for accomplishments.

Be active in community efforts to build and maintain safe playgrounds.

Of all the things that parents can do for their children, one of the most important is to provide safe places for them to play together, by themselves, watched from a safe distance but not hovered over. Kids need a place where all types of children can gather and move in and out of loosely formed groups, where the play and the groupings are fluid.

Often that means making sure there are safe playgrounds in neighborhoods, for all children as well as your own children. Here is where children learn to be welcoming, really test their entry skills, experience the many rhythms of social life, and get to practice what they know. The playground is the breeding ground of civil society.

CHAPTER NINE

Helping the Aggressive Child

ggressive behavior has defied many attempts at cure. That is
probably because it is part of a more general antisocial attitude
and rule-breaking stance and is embedded in a constellation of
problems. Typically parents are themselves stressed out by circumstances or depression, need skills in child-rearing, and tend to deal in
coercive, even violent, but ineffective discipline methods.

Yet some experts have made a dent. Yale University psychologist
Alan E. Kazdin, for example, has found that educating both parents
and children could make improvements that were still detectable in
the children's behavior a year later. The combined approach produced
greater and longer-lasting results than treating either parents or children alone.

Children were taught problem-solving skills. They learned how
to generate options for interpreting the behavior of others and dealing
with specific problems. They learned responses that were nonviolent,
and they rehearsed them. Separately, parents were trained in the same
skills. They also learned to reward their children's efforts, and to discipline consistently, without resorting to physical means.

This chapter makes explicit what should be obvious by now: The
best route to helping an aggressive child to be less disliked by peers is
not to "fix" the kid by disciplining more, but to "fix" the parenting
while exposing the child to an array of behavioral skills. Parents unwittingly contribute to a child's aggressiveness by paying most of their

attention to aggressive behavior; sometimes the only attention they pay is to beat the heck out of their kid for such behavior.

What should a parent do when a child needs help building blocks, or getting dressed, or tying shoelaces? What should a parent say when a child reports, "No one picked me to play in the soccer game"? Or when a child asks for help with homework? What happens when a child decides it's too disappointing to ask for help? How does a parent handle misbehavior that took place outside the house? The response children get inside the home is crucial in molding their behavior outside the home.

Windy's father, for example, could have begun to offset the effects of years of rigidity by deliberately creating a situation where his son would need help—and then supplying it, as Windy had long since stopped asking for it or expecting it. He could have brought home some brain-teaser puzzles and given them to his son. He could have looked in on Windy after a few minutes of puzzle-working and offered, sympathetically, "Tough, aren't they?" And he might have helpfully suggested, "What happens when you turn the page upside down?" Or together they might have sat down and worked one out jointly, each offering suggestions for solutions.

Made or Born? Does It Matter?

A great deal of evidence suggests that genetic factors give some children a jump-start on aggression. But though it is fashionable to believe so, that doesn't relieve parents of the responsibility to socialize their children; children still have to learn the general rules for behavior that their own culture subscribes to and the complex dance of social interaction. In virtually every society, families are the first, and the key, socializing system for children.

Biology is never destiny. Biology or genes typically decree the stages of development, but the process does not unfold automatically. Whether biological or psychological, development proceeds only in the presence of a *supportive environment*.

What's more, genes work indirectly, by the way they shape environments. A child with a difficult or highly spirited temperament contributes to the possibility that a parent will resort to harsh, coercive disciplinary strategies, which give rise to aggressive behavior in a child. Still, however much the child might evoke the unfavorable treatment from the adult, the child is only one element contributing to that possibility; there are many other factors driving parents' neglect or use of ineffective methods—family stresses such as illness, divorce, or economic problems; maternal depression; lack of knowledge about children's development. Indeed, the extent to which a family is exposed to such negative life events puts a stress on the family's capability to act as socializers.

Many such negative elements, unfortunately, are present in poor families living in poor neighborhoods, which is why aggressive behavior is more common in children of such families. However, all of these elements are, sadly, in rich supply across the socioeconomic spectrum.

A genetic push toward impulsive or aggressive behavior may make lively demands on parents' need to monitor their children. Parenting practices—particularly their discipline, monitoring, and problem-solving approaches—are still, says psychologist Gerald Patterson, "the primary proximal cause" of the very early forms of coercive and antisocial behavior. No matter how you look at it, "the training for aggression begins during the preschool years." Nor is Patterson being coy about the idea of "training."

Socialization is the process, tucked into routine, everyday exchanges, by which all of us are trained, as children, to restrain certain impulses so that we can live more or less together in society. "No, Eric, you cannot hit Lisa because she took your tape. Ask her to give it back—please." "No, Courtney, you cannot pull the cat's tail. It hurts the cat and annoys him; you're lucky he doesn't scratch you. Pat the kitty instead."

These conversations contain a great deal of information. It is explained what not to do—and, better, what *to* do, and, better still, just why. The effects of the action are spelled out, so children come to realize that their actions have consequences. A child is given a way to understand that others have feelings, too, and that to live in a world of others, you have to take into account their feelings—see the world from their perspective as well as your own. It is a day-in, day-out process, both for children and their caretakers. When responsible adults pay attention to children, they are motivating them to curb their impulses in exchange for approval and membership in society at large.

Under ideal circumstances, socialization is a years-long process. The corollary is, when it has gone off track, even at an early age, you can expect that it will take years to correct.

Findings on the Fast Track

In 1991, the National Institute of Mental Health began a massive study—fourteen thousand children, four hundred classrooms, four cities—to test current theories about aggressive behavior, implement a program of prevention built on years of research, and evaluate the long-term effects of the intervention. In first and second grade, three successive waves of children, all attending schools in violence-ridden neighborhoods, are taught a package of specific behavioral skills identified with social and academic success, known as PATHS, for Promoting Alternative Thinking Strategies.

Additionally, those children considered likely to develop antisocial behavior—spotted by their behavior in *kindergarten*—attend weekly groups that focus on social skill training and self-control. Their parents participate in training groups to decrease negative parenting and coercive discipline, and boost knowledge of child development and communication with school and with child. The leading edge of children is now in the seventh grade, and all children will be tracked through high school. Batteries of researchers monitor the progress of the children each year.

One of the prime observations guiding Fast Track, as the study is called, is that aggression solidifies so quickly and has such pervasive effects on development that any attempt to derail it must start early, run long, target a variety of behaviors, and reach into all the environments a child routinely inhabits: the classroom, the family, and peers. In other words, forget the one-cause/one-effect model of disorder when it comes to aggressive behavior. As with heart disease, there are multiple risk factors that add up and accumulate. These include parenting factors like discipline and warmth, and child factors such as emotion recognition and reading comprehension.

The Fast Track study is now demonstrating that the eventual outcome of serious antisocial behavior is by no means a predetermined certainty. But it takes both concentrated parent-focused and child-focused strategies to have an effect. And the time to make headway against aggressive behavior is *during the early elementary-school years*. If not sooner.

The advice that makes up the rest of this chapter represents the wisdom of hundreds of researchers, including many of those contributing to Fast Track.

It takes more than love.

Love is not enough to be an effective parent. It's necessary—but not sufficient.

Seek treatment if you are depressed.

Parental, and especially maternal, depression has a devastating effect on children. It essentially removes a parent. It destroys a parent's ability to respond positively to a child. Maternal depression is such a powerful negative force in the life of children that all by itself it creates externalizing problems in kids.

Depression not only curtails the availability and responsivity of parents to children. It increases parental irritability, and leads to the use of coercive parenting tactics.

Talk to your child about bullying.

Conversations between parent and child—even about negative subjects—communicate parental interest and represent a foot in the door for influencing behavior positively.

Discuss bullying when incidents arise, even involving other children. Let your child know that bullying stems not from being "bad" but from lacking social skills, and that social skills can be learned. And tell your child that bullying is, in the long run, bad for bullies; they don't do well in life. It is a bad way to use power.

Show your child that no one likes a bully.

Bullies overfocus on getting what they want. They are unmoved by the suffering of victims. They do not understand how other children feel about them, and they do not accurately perceive that they are being rejected.

Tell them how other children feel about them. And why. "It doesn't feel good to be picked on." "It hurts." Help your child understand what it feels like to be bullied. "Pretend I'm Derek. Show me what you did with Derek." Role-play the hurt and pain; demonstrate what it feels like to be attacked by another child.

And then sympathetically explain to the bully why he doesn't know how other kids really feel about him. "Maybe the other children don't tell you because they're afraid. They're scared you'll pick on them and hurt them, too." "Maybe other kids tell you by their expressions or by what they do, but you don't notice." "Maybe that's why you don't have a lot of friends." "Maybe that's why you don't get invited to other kids' houses after school."

Make it clear that you take bullying seriously.

If you don't think aggressive behavior is a problem, neither will your child.

Don't look the other way. Aggressive behavior is not likely to go away on its own. Children do not grow out of it. Rather, they only grow into it—deeper and deeper until, by adolescence, it infects their entire style of being and is difficult to give up.

Aggression is not a passing phase. About 50 percent of children who are aggressive in elementary school remain aggressive into adolescence. The danger then is that they will fall into the powerful sway of peer groups that only marginalize them further and make them harder to reach.

Make it clear that you will not tolerate aggressive behavior in the future.

Spell out to your child exactly the behavior that's acceptable and what's unacceptable. Remember, a bully sees aggression as justified by someone else's "failure" or act of aggression. So if you say "no bullying," your child may still not understand what he or she is doing wrong. Define physical aggression as name-calling or threats of meanness, declare it inappropriate under all circumstances—no matter what the child feels.

Turn off the TV—or throw it away.

The stream of murderous bloodletting that courses through the television tube leaves no viewer unaffected. But a long-term study that gives a whole new meaning to "vicious cycle" reveals that TV violence has a disproportionate effect on aggressive children.

Not only does it make children more aggressive, but those who are more aggressive turn to TV more. The TV-watching, in turn, becomes a justification for aggressive behavior. "Television violence affects youngsters of all ages, both genders, and all socioeconomic levels and levels of intelligence," says Dr. Leonard Eron, based on his study of 875 boys and girls tracked since they were in the third grade in 1960. The study started as a way of observing the effects of different child-rearing practices. But Dr. Eron made an unexpected finding: For the boys, there was a direct relationship between the violence of the programs they selected and aggressiveness at school.

Watching violence on television, says Dr. Eron, leads to heightened aggressiveness, which in turn leads to more violence-viewing. "Children who behave aggressively are less popular—and perhaps because their relations with their peers tend to be unsatisfying, less popular children watch more television and therefore view more violence."

From TV they learn new techniques of aggression, which makes them even *less* popular with their peers—and drives them back to the TV set. And such a steady diet of brutality may lead aggressive children to the "mean-world syndrome"—believing that they themselves are likely to become a victim of violence, furthering their inclination to misinterpret the intentions of others.

Poor academic performance also drives them deeper into TV violence. Those who fail in school watch more TV, which isolates them from their peers and gives them less time to work for academic success. The cycle of aggression, academic failure, social failure, and violence-viewing is so tightly bound that, sadly, it perpetuates itself.

The link between TV violence viewed at age eight and violent behavior was even stronger ten years later. Those boys who had low levels of aggressive behavior during the original study but watched large amounts of violent television were now significantly more aggressive—even more so than those boys who were originally highly aggressive but did *not* watch violent programs.

When the original 875 were thirty years old and had children of their own, Dr. Eron looked at them yet again—along with their arrest records. Those who had more frequently viewed violent programs as boys had gone on to be convicted of more serious crimes and were more aggressive under the influence of alcohol. Most striking, they more often used violence to punish their children. And, to take it full cycle, the children more often preferred violent programming.

"What one learns from the television screen seems to be transmitted even to the next generation," Dr. Eron concludes. The steady viewing of violent programs by the men as youngsters taught them ways of solving interpersonal problems that stuck over the years.

Boys aren't the only ones influenced by violence on TV. Whether girls or boys, more aggressive kids watch more violent programs, identify more with TV characters, and see violence as appearing to be *more like real life* than do less aggressive kids.

Turning off the TV set *alone* will not solve the problem of aggression. But it will help. Heavy TV-watching is really filling a void; something else is missing. It is a good indicator there is lack of parental interest. A steady diet of TV-watching is "an across-the-board marker of bad conditions at home," says Anita Werner, head of the Mass Media Institute at the University of Oslo in Norway. "When no one cares what children watch, children are in danger for other reasons; there's a lack of caretaking. When kids prefer media, it reflects a lack of other opportunities."

Spend time doing things with your child.
Have positive experiences together. Be together in warm and loving ways. Go to a basketball game together. Spend time doing something your child wants to do, and get into the spirit of it. You will gain a better understanding of your child. Together, over time, you will be

building a more trusting relationship. Out of that improved relationship a child is more willing to listen to and be influenced by a parent.

Work on many fronts at the same time.
The Fast Track and many other studies provide overwhelming evidence that to affect aggression, you have to strike at a number of problems. These are the Big Eleven:

1. **APPROPRIATE DISCIPLINE**
Once a child is past infancy and socialization starts in earnest, parents must be engaged and apply approval and disapproval *contingently*—swiftly in response to the child's action, not at the mercy of your moods. "When the child does something appropriate," says Patterson, "the parent's facial and vocal affect plus perhaps the content of what the parent says or does, all communicate parental pleasure." But rule-breaking—and *all* children do it—cannot slip by unnoticed. When it occurs, parents similarly communicate displeasure in their voice, facial expression, and word. "If this is not effective in changing the behavior, then some nonphysical punishment may be used, such as time out or loss of privileges."

The odd thing, Patterson finds, after observing children in hundreds of homes, is that parents who get swept up in discipline struggles with their children also *fail to contingently applaud prosocial behavior.* They threaten and scold their kids a lot—and everyone gets very angry—but they don't follow through on their threats. Occasionally, in exasperation or anger, they physically assault their children. Both by the inconsistent use of ineffective punishment and the failure to notice or reward prosocial behavior, parents are in fact engaging in a form of neglect. When approval or disapproval is noncontingent, children come to feel that their environment is not responsive to them, and that deters them from making efforts to try harder. You can't change negative behavior to positive behavior in a thicket of negativity.

Parental neglect is the *real* cause of antisocial behavior, Patterson insists. The children end up both socially unskilled and coercive, resorting to temper tantrums and hitting to get their way, instead of on social skills.

Avoid highly punitive forms of discipline and physical punishment of any kind, namely:

- slapping or beating a child
- shouting at your child
- threatening not to love your child
- threatening to abandon or leave your child ("If you don't stop that we're going to send you away.")
- telling your child he or she causes you distress or aggravation, or is going to make you sick
- calling your child names ("You're an idiot.")
- assaulting your child's character ("You're a liar.")
- using sarcasm ("Well, aren't you Mr. Know-It-All")

The punishment of choice is calling a time-out. Assigning family chores and taking away privileges for specific periods of time are also workable. But discipline is not just a matter of meting out punishment. You have to follow up to ensure compliance. How often does your child get away with things that really should have been punished? Does your child ignore your punishment? Shout at you? Hit you?

Be sure to give your child direct, concise, and reasonable commands. The more immediate the better ("Please turn off the television now. We agreed, only one hour of TV a day.") Praise your child if he or she complies within five seconds. If not, call a time-out for three minutes.

Following through means saying, "Okay, this is the second day in a row I've asked where your homework is and you said you don't have any. I know that's not the case. That's going to cost you. I want you to clean up the cat box and change the litter." Specify some chore.

You can't be on your child's case all the time. Overlook minor provocations—after all, that's something you're trying to train your aggressive child to do. Model the behavior yourself.

Positively reinforce your child when she does something she is told ("I like the way you put your clothes in the hamper"), when your child spontaneously shares something or takes a turn, when your child seeks affection, when he gets good or even improved grades or actively tries harder. This is not a sometime activity. This should be happening many times a day, every day. You have to actively, positively reward behavior you want to see more of.

2. PARENTAL WARMTH

To what degree do you display affection and positive regard and provide advice, especially when your child is facing a frustrating experience? Do you pay attention to your child when he or she is talking to you? Spend time listening to your child without issuing questions, commands, or criticism. Actively supporting your child helps her regulate her own emotion and provides her with a more positive internal working model of close relationships, which she will then apply to her own relationships—eventually.

Speak to your child in positive tones. Annoyance, irritation, and impatience are corrosive to all relationships.

What do you do when your child asks for help with homework? "We're supposed to answer all these questions about this story, but I don't even understand it. It's a dumb story." Your child, by vocalizing a problem, is really making an implicit request for help. If you say something like "Figure it out yourself" or "It's obvious what the story's about" or "You're just not concentrating" or "Here, give me that and I'll tell you," you're not only being dismissive of your child's vulnerability, you make the child feel incompetent. Resist the temptation to respond with a glower or a sigh, which communicates annoyance.

Offer your child encouragement, both verbal and nonverbal. Say, in a sympathetic tone, "Sometimes these things are difficult, aren't they?" Or "Maybe you could read me the story and tell me what confuses you." Then make suggestions that stimulate your child to think about an answer: "Why do you think the old man said that to the boy?" "Do you think the old man was saying he had a good life or a bad life?" Such an approach also boosts your child's reading comprehension and ability to stay focused, or "on task."

Don't be intimidated by your child's anger or other strong negative feelings. Help your child find ways to calm down when he's feeling angry, upset, frustrated. Then provide encouragement for solving the problem.

3. HIGH-QUALITY PARENTING

Be involved. Your job as a parent is to monitor your children (without hovering or being overinvolved in their activities). Monitoring is knowing where your children are when they go out. Knowing whom they are spending time with outside the house. Monitoring communicates caring—and is a deterrent to antisocial behavior, particularly for boys.

Sit down with your child and talk about something your child is interested in. There are no right or wrong answers; just have a positive conversation.

Spend time playing with your child. And be sure to let your child direct the play sometimes. Encourage make-believe play: "How about if you be the grown-up and I'm the child. Tell me what to do." Let your child make up any scenario, and go along with it.

When you come across something funny in your day—a picture in the newspaper, a funny story, a joke—share it with your child. Laugh together.

Do something special with your child from time to time. "Special" is not dragging your child around shopping with you, it's something you can both enjoy away from everyday demands. Discuss and make a date for a future activity.

If your child asks you to play or to help with something and you are too tired or worn out or have something else you must do, decline the invitation—but only by offering another time instead. "Mommy is too busy this afternoon, but why don't we plan to do that tomorrow. I'm going to make a big note reminding me and pin it up on the refrigerator." You are not only making a declaration of positive interest in your child but modeling a great social skill, too: how to turn a refusal into a new invitation.

Observe your child's play with other children at home. If conflicts escalate to the point of aggression, intervene. Afterward, when the other child has gone home, don't punish your child. Offer support. "Would you like to have handled that better?" Sit down with your child and go through the steps of problem-solving (see page 278).

Tell your child about your own experiences as a child, especially struggles with problems. One night in our house, when my husband and I were paying too much attention to my older son, Danny, we noticed that Gabe was awfully quiet. I slipped out of the living room and found Gabe in his brother's room—mashing oil paints into the brand-new carpet. I scolded. Harsh words were scarcely out of my mouth when I realized I was just compounding the damage. Too late. Gabe was sobbing inconsolably at the injustice, of being yelled at after having been ignored. We marshaled forces for the cleanup. Gabe was still inconsolable (the stains lasted until the carpet was torn out, years later).

Just when I began to feel horrible guilt for creating the double crisis, my husband proffered a tale of his own misdeeds. How, as a child, he had lobbed shingles, with a curse word scrawled on them, into an unpleasant neighbor's yard, and the neighbor paid a visit to his father insisting he punish his son— now! Soon the sobs stopped. And so began The Mischief Stories, a series of tales about my husband's misbehavior that tickled my sons for years. Their very favorite was how, to the horror and shame of his parents, he went into the barn behind his house and chopped up the brand-new wagon his grandfather had just lugged all the way from Boston as a birthday gift.

4. **POSITIVE ATTITUDE TOWARD CHILD**

How often do you smile at your child?

Treat your child with respect. Use the same manners with your child that you expect him to display with others. Even for transgressions, don't put your child down.

Ask your child's opinion about things (no one says you have to agree with it). "What did you think about that new show?"

Demonstrate that you value your child's input. "Mommy wants to get a new dog. Can you come down to the pound with me and help me pick one out?"

Share things with your child.

5. ENCOURAGEMENT OF EDUCATION

- Children absorb their parents' attitudes toward schooling. Parents' involvement with their kids' teachers expresses their belief in the value of education and discourages antisocial activity.

- Do you make contact with the teacher only when your child is getting into trouble? If so, that may subvert any feelings of comfort in talking with teachers and make it too unpleasant an activity for you.

- Instead, seek out your child's teacher periodically for information. Teachers are good sources of information about what is normal behavior for children at different ages. They also can tell you how your child behaves in school and how other children treat him or her. They can tell you which children you might want to help your child cultivate supportive friendships with. And they can suggest what specific areas of performance your child needs help with. Teachers generally respond very positively to parents' demonstration of interest in their work and their powers of observation—and that response may be channeled into extra classroom support for your child.

- What other academic stimulation do you provide your child? Do you make sure your child sets aside regular TV-free time every evening for homework? Do you praise your child for doing assigned homework?

- You can offer to test your child on spelling words (you don't have to know how to spell them yourself—just read the list) or math multiplication tables or names of the states and their capitals. (Don't scold your child for making a mistake; just say, "Let's go back to that later.")

- Do you find positive things to say about your child's school, even if there are some things you don't like (lack of safety, overcrowding, perhaps even the principal)?
- Encourage your child's involvement in school activities: acting in plays, singing in groups, joining class projects. Choral groups, in which everyone contributes to one sound, are the very model of cooperative participation you want to promote.

6. EMOTION RECOGNITION

The ability to recognize emotions accurately allows children to know what other children are feeling, understand how and why others might act in any situation—and gauge how to behave.

Start with the basics: how to recognize internal and external cues of affect, and the appropriate terms for those feelings. Ask your child to label the facial expressions of characters in books when you read together. "What do you suppose the little boy is feeling?"

Help your child recognize the physiologic cues of anger. "What happens when you get angry/sad/worried? How do you know that you are angry? What does it feel like? Where do you feel it?"

Sit down quietly with your child, saying that you'd like to talk about different kinds of feelings that children have.

Ask, "What kinds of things make you feel happy?" If your child doesn't answer, give a prompt: "Can you think of a time when someone felt happy?"

Then ask, "When you are feeling happy, what kinds of things do you do?"

Then ask your child about negative feelings.

Question number one: "What kinds of things make you feel sad?"

Question number two: "When you are feeling sad, what kinds of things do you do?"

Question number three: "If you saw another kid in your class looking sad, what would you do?"

Then ask each of the three questions about "feeling angry" and about "feeling worried or nervous."

7. EMOTION COPING

Fast Track makes use of a control-signals poster—essentially a large picture of a stoplight with red, yellow, and green lights—as a set of graphic cues to emotional control. It integrates many behavioral skills, but it was specifically designed to foster children's ability to cope with upsetting emotions.

The poster is prominently placed in the classroom, but you could make your own, or collaboratively paint one with your child, and hang it in the kitchen or your child's room at home. Encourage your child to turn to the signals in a situation that's upsetting, frustrating, or distressing, like a peer conflict or difficult work situation.

The first step in effective problem-solving is for a child to decide if his feelings are upset and then go to the red light to stop and think before acting. Teach your child to perform calming actions at the red light, and practice them.

- First take a long, deep breath (or count to ten, or think about something positive).
- State the problem. ("Kevin took the ball when it was my turn.")
- And how he feels. ("That makes me angry.")
   Once a child has identified the problem, it's time to move to the yellow light, where the child makes a plan.
- Help your child generate options for action.
   "I could take the ball back."
   "Hmm, what else could you do?"
   "I could make him miss his turn."
   "I could ask him to please give me the ball."
   "I could tell him to give me the ball and then he will have his turn again."
   "I could tell him I won't be his friend."
   "I could tell the teacher to make him give me the ball."

"We could see if there's another ball for him to play with."

"I could ask him to trade me something for an extra turn."

- Help your child weigh the pros and cons of each option.
- Evaluate the likely effect and outcome of each option.

Move to the green light. Allow your child to select the action with the best likely outcome, and do it.

Have your child evaluate the real-life effectiveness of the chosen plan, afterward. And if the plan proves ineffective, suggest a recycling through the steps.

Go over ways of self-talk that help reduce anger arousal. What can you say to yourself to help you calm down and then decide what to do? Tell your child some things you might say. "I'm not going to let them get me mad."

Discuss with your child ways that he can express anger and frustration without getting physical or mean. Come up with a list. Emphasize talking out the issue rather than hitting.

8. COUNTERING HOSTILE ATTRIBUTIONAL BIASES

One reason children are aggressive is that they think differently from other kids in social situations. They are not good at figuring out why people do what they do. They pay much more attention to hostile cues and they misinterpret the intentions of others as hostile when they're not, or when they're ambiguous. They jump to premature conclusions about others' behavior. A child who perceives social cues more accurately feels less compelled to "get even."

Make a game out of training your child to pay attention to cues that are not compatible with hostile intent. Learn from the "detective game" developed by experts.

Your child becomes a detective searching for clues to why people do what they do. You present scenarios and ask your child to decide why the character acted as he did.

Make up two big flash cards and give them to your child. One says "on purpose to be mean," the other "by accident."

Present a scenario, followed by a set of clues, and ask your child to turn over one of the cards whenever she is sure about why the character did something. Your child can listen to as many or as few of the clues as she wants, but once a card is turned over, the child can't change her mind.

Here's a sample scenario: Imagine that you painted a special picture in art class today. You wanted to take it home, but it was wet, so you left it on a table in the back of the classroom to dry while you went out to P.E. After you got back from P.E., you noticed that your picture had been destroyed. All the paint had run together and your picture was ruined. Chris stayed in the classroom during recess, and now you have to decide if he ruined your picture on purpose or whether it was an accident.

Then read the following clues, in order, with generous pauses between them:

- Chris sometimes does mean things so that other kids will think he's cool.
- Chris and you got into an argument this morning because you both wanted to use the earphones in the listening center, and the teacher let you use them first.
- Chris has paint on his fingers.
- You heard Chris say something mean about you to another kid.
- Chris stayed in at P.E. because he needed to finish his painting for art class.
- When Chris saw you notice your ruined picture, he said, "Gee, that's too bad."
- The teacher tells you she asked Chris to move your picture because she needed the table.
- Another child tells you that your teacher told him he had to move his picture, too. When he tried to pick it up, the paint ran and ruined your picture.
- Chris likes to try to help other kids. Yesterday he offered to help you with some math problems that were really hard.

Fast Track presents grade-school children with drawings depicting scenarios covering other social situations: such as where some ambiguous, but minor, harm is done (being bumped, hit with a ball) and where a child is unsuccessful at joining others at play (explicitly told he cannot join a group he approached, ignored by the children). For example:

"Pretend that you are walking to school and you're wearing brand-new sneakers. You really like your new sneakers and this is the first day you have worn them. Suddenly, you are bumped from behind by a kid named John/Lisa. You stumble into a mud puddle and your new sneakers get muddy.

"Why do you think John/Lisa bumped you?" This is a direct question about intentions.

Example of a nonhostile attribution: Your child's explanation for why kids didn't answer when he said hello is that they didn't hear him. If your child explains that the offender did what he did on purpose, or to be mean, provide more practice in making nonhostile attributions.

9. SOCIAL PROBLEM-SOLVING

Teach your child that there are other ways to join with peers or resolve conflicts without physical force or meanness.

Talk to your child about her own experiences. Start with "Tell me what your day was like" rather than "Did you get into trouble today?" It's fine to express disappointment verbally if your child was involved in an incident. "It really bothers me that you hit her back. How do you think she must have felt when you did that?" Whatever else you do, don't spank the child. Open a discussion about other ways such a difficult situation might have been handled.

"Why did she hit you?"

"Why did you take the game from her?"

"Didn't she want to finish playing with it?"

"What's a friendlier thing to do when you want a turn with something?"

"If you gave her the puzzle, do you think she would have given you the game?"

"What else could you have said or done?"

If your child mentions incidents about other children, use those as opportunities to discuss alternate strategies for solving social problems. "What could Jesse have done to make it better?" "Can you think of another thing Jesse could have done?" Praise your child for each positive suggestion. "That's a really good idea. Good going!"

Effective problem-solving always involves the following steps:

- identifying the problem
- identifying feelings—one's own, and those of others
- considering the point of view of peers
- generating more than one solution
- considering the possible consequences of each ("What might happen if you do that?")
- prioritizing solutions based on anticipated consequences
- deciding which solution to choose
- following up and later evaluating the outcome of the chosen course of action

Extensive role-playing and enacting of solutions can help your child understand social skills in action, including the responses of others. The younger the child, the more concrete the experience needs to be. Use dolls, puppets, or toy animals to model social skills. Make up stories with a character who gets teased and other characters who help. Brainstorming possible solutions *without censoring them* isn't just a way to solve social problems, it's the way to solve all problems—and the key to the creative process.

If your child is older, role-play each of the hypothetical situations with your child. "Okay. You be Kelly. Show me what she did. Then tell me what you think I should do." Or "I'll be the teacher. Show me exactly what you did. Then let's figure out ways you could handle that."

Fast Track incorporates test scenarios that reflect typical experiences in the life of children. (In each problem scenario, choose a name so that the peer's gender corresponds to your own child's.)

"James/Jean was playing a Nintendo game on his/her TV when you walked in. You ask if you can play, too. James/Jean says no."

Then ask your child two sets of questions about the effectiveness of assertive and aggressive responses in that situation.

Assertive-response questions:

"Let's say you said to James/Jean, 'How about if we both play?' "

"Would James/Jean let you play?"

"Would James/Jean still want to be your friend?"

Aggressive-response questions:

"Let's say you grabbed the Nintendo controls away from James/Jean and said, 'You can't stop me from playing.' "

"Would James/Jean let you play?"

"Would James/Jean still want to be your friend?"

"Would other kids like you if you did that?"

"What's more important to you: to play the game or to have other kids like you?"

Another way: Drew simple stick-figure scenarios (no artistic talent required!). Show your child simple drawings that depict two different types of troublesome social situations.

First, peer entry. Show your child a picture in which several kids are playing on a jungle gym (or playing a game of tag) while one child stands apart, looking at those playing. Begin with "Pretend that this is you," and point to the solitary child, "and that this is Colleen/Josh," and point to a child on the jungle gym (playing tag). "Colleen/Josh and some other kids are playing on the jungle gym at school. You would like to play with Colleen/Josh and the other kids, but they haven't asked you. What could you say or do to get to play with Colleen/Josh and the other kids?"

Let your child come up with a response. Then prompt your child for another response. "What's another thing you could say or do so that you could get to play with Colleen/Josh and the other kids?" And then one more. "Can you think of anything else you could do or say that you could get to play with Colleen/Josh and the other kids?''

If the response is vague, such as ''I'd be nice'' or ''I'd be mad,'' gently probe for clarification. ''What would you say or do to show that you are nice/mad?''

Draw another set of situations involving a child who is being teased or frustrated by another. The other child won't share a swing, or the other child pushes the child out of a line. Here the child's task is to resolve a social conflict.

Coming up with good solutions is necessary—but more is needed. Your child has to put them into practice in real life. ''Okay, I'll be Trevor. Show me what you're going to do the next time he bumps you.'' Rehearse, rehearse, and rehearse solutions to common problems. Your child has to feel natural doing them. And provide ample feedback. Correct errors in perception. ''Do you think Trevor did it to be mean, or did he maybe not realize you hadn't gone yet?''

10. READING COMPREHENSION

How often do you read to your child or ask your child to read a favorite tale to you? How often do you take your child to the library?

Reading to children does so much for them (and parents, too) it's difficult to catalogue all its benefits. It is a demonstration of parental caring and interest. It improves parents' views of themselves as parents and their efficacy as parents, and improves their attitudes toward their children—all crucial to motivating involvement in the hard job of parenting and a supportive approach to children. It increases a child's interpersonal trust. It serves the child (and parent) as a model for a soothing activity. It fosters language development. It encourages parents and children to value education. It helps children learn to focus attention. It's a source of information. Directly and indirectly, every one of these has a separate effect on a child's social skills.

And of course, it improves reading comprehension. Start even before your child can talk. Begin with short, simple stories. Ask your child questions about the story. ''Wasn't that silly of the cat to do?'' ''What's another word that rhymes with cat and hat?" "How many people went to the party?" "Why do you suppose the king got so angry?"

11. SOCIAL SKILLS

Aggressive children often don't even know any other way to be around peers—they don't know what to do to be friendly. The cultivation of prosocial attitudes, then, is at least as important as helping your child stop aggressive behavior.

Encourage your child to:

- approach peers in a friendly way and make an introduction: "Hi. My name is Kyle. Do you want to play?"
- look others in the eye
- smile
- make positive play suggestions ("I have a ball we can catch.")
- join others at play, tune in to what *they* are doing and adopt their behavior
- ask for things in friendly or neutral ways ("Can I have the red one?")
- take turns
- share things
- help others ("Can I help you load up the wagon?")
- listen to others
- express his or her viewpoint matter-of-factly
- express feelings in words
- pay attention to the emotions of others and adjust behavior accordingly
- offer support
- give compliments ("Hey, you really are good at that.")
- use manners
- accept occasional rebuffs as a fact of social life
- make play arrangements with other children

At home, role-play and rehearse even simple social strategies, over and over. Practice making conversation and sustaining it, and give your child positive feedback (a pat

on the back, a wink, a hug, a word of praise) on his performance as often as possible. And, most important, model
the behaviors yourself. Children enact strategies they have
used before or seen others use.

Be sure to play games with your child, to provide experience taking turns and cooperating. And enlist your
child in collaborative (as opposed to competitive) ventures
to achieve some tangible goal—trimming a Christmas tree,
making cookies, planting a garden (even a tiny patch).

Discuss strategies for making friends. Tell your child
you want to make more friends. Ask him for advice. Ask
about what *not* to do, too. Provide feedback on the appro-
priateness of suggestions.

Teach caring. Tune your child in to the hurt of others
in daily life—including the hurt your child may cause.

Build confidence in your parenting ability.
It increases your willingness to recognize and tackle problem behavior
in your children. It lowers your stress level and makes you more
available for responding to your children. And it maximizes the likelihood of your involvement with teachers and school—all of which
feed your child's social competence. Besides, lack of confidence in
parenting ability by itself encourages disruptive behavior in a child.

So do everything you can to learn about parenting and child development. Talk to other parents. Read. There's lots of good information available—but misguided and ill-informed advice abounds,
too. One of the best sources of information is the Clearinghouse on
Elementary and Early Childhood Education, known as ERIC. It
maintains a Web site where parents can ask questions and get fast
feedback: askeric@askeric.org. The Oregon Social Learning Center,
(503) 343-4433, might be the single best source of information about
aggressive children.

You might benefit from a boost in parenting self-competence if
you feel that:

• parenting leaves you drained and exhausted
• parenting makes you tense and anxious

- parenting makes you so busy that you never get anything done
- something is troubling your child, and you cannot figure out what it is
- it's really difficult to decide how to parent your child

Help your child build a positive worldview.

Aggressive children are not filled with psychic conflict. They are not riddled with guilt or angst. They have a negative worldview. They believe (mistakenly) that others are out to get them. They build a belief system in which aggression is justified. They believe that aggression is a legitimate response, that others do not suffer as a consequence of their aggressive actions. As a result, they evaluate aggressive solutions more positively, underestimating the negative responses of their peers. And they are less bothered by them.

Not only is their thinking distorted, their reality is somewhat askew, too. In fact, Dr. Patterson finds they are blindsided five times more often than other children. They get attacked and blamed even when they are doing nothing, for things others are doing wrong—by teachers, by parents, and by siblings. So their belief that others are out to get them, which justifies their aggression, is partly grounded in reality. "It is an unhappy description of their environment," Patterson says. "Yes, the bully helped create that environment. He is a victim and architect of his own environment."

So in order to change behavior, it is essential to change the environment. Discourage family members from pointing to the aggressive child whenever *anything* goes wrong. Instead, point to the aggressive child whenever *something* he or she does goes right. Look for opportunities to deliver praise and appreciation when the child follows a rule, displays consideration of someone else's needs or feelings. Feeling appreciated (for actual accomplishments) makes it much easier for a child (or an adult!) to give up undesirable behavior.

Let your child help make the family rules.

Every household needs rules. Aggressive children especially need to know what the boundaries of acceptable behavior are. Invite your child to help you make up at list of general do rules and don't rules for everyday behavior.

Discuss sanctions with your child.

If your child is in elementary school, he's old enough for you to have a conversation with about what sanctions are appropriate when rules are broken. "What should the consequences be when you mess up?" The sanctions should be easy to apply—but not make life comfortable for the child. Participating in such discussions clarifies rules, helps rebuild trust in others, gives the child a sense of control—all of which help to motivate more acceptable behavior.

Whatever sanctions are agreed to, of course, must be applied immediately after infractions. And they must be consistently applied.

Whenever negative consequences are set in motion, make it clear that they are applied not against the child's being, but against the behavior. "You hit Petey, and that is not acceptable ever," not "You can't even keep your word. I told you not to hit your brother."

Excessive compliance is not the goal.

One-hundred-percent compliance with adult demands gives children no room to assert their own needs. To function competently as self-regulating human beings, children need to learn how to bargain and negotiate with parents, and learn how to refuse requests without direct defiance. In other words, there is such a thing as "skillful noncompliance." Given a spirited child, demands for total compliance, even at age two, can create a negative child-rearing atmosphere. Be reasonable.

Counter a bad reputation.

Rejected kids have negative reputations. Once an aggressive child acquires more social skills, it's necessary to change the view of peers, to permit the child to be more effective. A child can't alter the opinions of others on his own. Provide opportunities for peers to play with your child, so they can see changes in behavior as they occur.

If he damages someone's property, hold your child responsible for restitution.

Help your child connect his behavior with consequences. Hold a discussion with your child so that he can suggest ways to repair what was damaged. Of course, you can act as a wise coach. "You broke

Ally's bike and she can't use it till it's fixed. It costs money to get it fixed and we have to pay for it. What can you do to pay back the money? Do you think that doing the dishes for ten days is fair? Can you let her have your bike while hers is being fixed?"

Teach your child to apologize.

But never humiliate your child by correcting his behavior in front of others. If an apology is warranted and your child doesn't speak up, model the necessary behavior yourself—"Oh, Timmy, I'm really sorry that Alan hurt you. He knows it was wrong and he shouldn't have done it"—and then privately explain to your child why and how to apologize. Everyone says or does things he regrets.

It's hard to be good in a bad neighborhood.

Tough neighborhoods and bad schools provide a heavy environmental push for children to display the kinds of posing and threatening behavior that lead to antisocial activity. They make it harder for both parents and teachers to work effectively with children.

Be satisfied with small changes.

Fast Track has found that kids make small improvements but not enough in one year to change categorical judgments of parents, teachers, or peers. That's no cause for disappointment.

Progress is incremental. Family processes don't work in one direction only; parents certainly have effects on children, but children also have effects on parents. A pattern of increased support and positive involvement of parent with child gets reciprocated in the child's behavior toward the parent. That, in turn, translates into a growing sense of competence as a parent, which in turn is reflected in increasing levels of positive parental involvement. And a child responds to that.

A child's aggression didn't spring up overnight. It won't disappear overnight.

CHAPTER TEN

Helping the Submissive Child

The opposite of submissive is not aggressive. It is assertive.

Children with a fearful temperament can grow up to be anxious, shy, and socially withdrawn, set up for loneliness in childhood and adulthood. That is the case unless they receive sensitive, helpful, but not overprotective, parenting. When such children have parents who gently insist on their participation—while taking care not to overwhelm them—they eventually develop normal social competence and acceptance among peers.

Children need to make their own adjustment to the world and to grow up able to manage their own affairs. The ability doesn't spring full-blown overnight. It develops gradually, incrementally, through repeated practice in informal everyday situations in which children are allowed to cope with conflict, rebuffs, new challenges, and new people, all on their own, albeit with the encouragement and support of their parents. The confidence even innately fearful children acquire through this almost imperceptible process of baby-step accomplishment allows them to risk new experiences, sometimes fail in their goals, dust themselves off, and try again.

Parents of the shy, the anxious, and the victimized tend to be overprotective of their children. Whether the overprotection is cause of the anxiety or response to it matters little; it has the same effect. It keeps a child from having to make a full adaptation to the world, from finding a comfortable level of accommodation to it. And it cripples performance with peers, especially that all-important ability to meet new people. Those who can't make their way among peers are sub-jected to repeated rejection, isolation, and loneliness.

Parents may believe it is their God-given duty to shield their fearful children from hurt, but to do so is to compound the damage. The longer children go without free participation in the world of peers, the more social skills they lack, and the harder it becomes for them to catch up to or feel comfortable with peers.

Small, Safe Challenges Needed

Parents should not take over even the littlest tasks for their children—say, asking for a drink of water in a neighbor's house; that is exactly the kind of relatively safe challenge where children start building con-fidence in their capabilities. But parents can—and should—help chil-dren find their own solution to problems.

The key to social competence in submissive children, as in all children, is in a positive parent-child relationship. Overprotection is not an act of support, which encourages independence and compe-tence, but an act of annexation, which fosters dependence. It does not respect the boundaries of the individual child. It is not a form of finely tuned, sensitive responsiveness contingent to a child's ever-changing needs. It is not a vote of confidence in a child's budding abilities. It communicates core disapproval. It robs motivation. When parents solve their children's problems for them, children conclude that they are incapable of handling things themselves. Overprotection focuses the child's attention on the power of the parent, rather than on his own possible powers.

Withdrawn kids don't just engage in negative behavior, they do not know how to be cooperative. They do not know how to com-municate liking to other kids. They do not smile; instead, they radiate apprehension in social situations. They focus inward, trying to will themselves into not being humiliated and rejected anew—rather than thinking about or even listening to others. Small wonder their re-sponses are often inappropriate to or out of synch with the situation! They can't take being teased, can't take a joke, and display little sense of humor. For all their social stumbling, it is, above all, their lack of a sense of humor that most does them in.

You can help your child develop a more rewarding behavioral style. A child needs not only to make different responses to a bully but to learn and deploy positive social skills with all peers. Otherwise, a child is set up for future victimization experiences and lifelong adjustment difficulties. Victimized children behave in ways that make them widely disliked by all age-mates.

They are also painfully aware that they are socially inept. They are generally very lonely. Tell your child that there are ways to become better liked, it will take some work, but it will make life a lot more interesting and fun. And reduce a great deal of stress.

First things first: how to handle a bully.
Take immediate measures to end victimization by bullies. Your child can't learn if he's worried about being beaten up or made fun of. Teach your child how to handle a bully.

Do not handle the problem directly with the bully.
It may be tempting to take the situation into your own hands, but don't. Children are picked on because they do not stand up for themselves; your direct intervention only confirms that both to the bully and, more important, to your child. When you fight your children's battles, they not only come to believe they are inept but to blame themselves for everything that goes wrong.

Do not encourage a child to hit back.
Hitting back legitimizes aggression. And it doesn't work. In fact, fighting back is the *worst* defense. In most instances, victimized children really are weaker (and smaller) than the bully—thus their fears of losing these fights may be quite real. Besides, not all bullying takes the form of physical aggression. Children are much more likely to have kids say mean things about them and to be picked on, rather than kicked or hit. Counteraggression to any form of bullying—a tactic often encouraged for boys—actually *increases* the likelihood of continued victimization. It simply locks bully and victim into an ongoing dance.

A wise defense is avoidance.
Teach your child that there are some situations from which it is smart to walk away. It is thoroughly adaptive behavior—and not at all cowardly—to avoid a bully. Being picked on is not character-building. Brushing aside provocations, such as name-calling, is a great social skill.

Advocate humor.
It is possible to defuse a bully who may be about to attack. Humor works best when it makes the situation look ridiculous, not the people: "Look, Johnny, lay off. I don't want you to get your hands dirty." Help your child come up with a set of clever verbal comebacks to be used in the event of victimization by verbally abusive peers.

Encourage an assertive response.
It is possible to resist an attack and stand up to an aggressor in an effective, nonviolent way. A child can tell a bully, "Hey, no hitting me!" or "Get a life. Leave me alone." And then walk away. This may be the best defense for girls because they are less likely to be physically attacked. It is necessary for the child to look the aggressor in the eye and speak in an assertive voice before walking away. Assertiveness of posture and manner speaks as loudly as verbal assertiveness.

Assertive responses can't just be pulled out of a hat. They have to be practiced first. Rehearse a variety of possible responses with your child—especially if there is a bully around who is a problem for your child.

Have your child recruit a friend.
One of the many benefits of friendship is that it provides tangible help and assistance. The corollary is, the lack of a friend acts as an invitation to bullying. Isolation encourages attack from bullies. It also sends a signal to bullies that there's no one to retaliate.

Observers find that having a friend on the playground is one of the most powerful protectives against bullying, especially for boys. But not just any friend will do. Studies show that friends who are socially competent and assertive—it helps if they're physically strong, too—actually serve as a *deterrent* to bullying.

In general, shy children should seek out the friendly children in the class and work at building friendships with them. It's not enough to teach victimized children how to form any kind of friendship, say Drs. Becky Kochenderfer and Gary Ladd, "but rather these children may need to make friends with those with whom they can ally for protection."

Assure your child that he or she has your support and protection.

Comfort your child, but don't make your child feel like a wimp. Your child needs to feel safe—safe at school, safe in disclosing victimization experiences. Let your child know that bullying is unacceptable behavior, that every child has the right to a safe environment, and that you will do everything you can to bring it about. (But don't let your compassion fool you into believing that the victim's behavior is socially adequate.)

Encourage your child to report bullying incidents.

It is the responsibility of teachers and the school to provide a milieu conducive to learning. Most bullying incidents escape the notice of teachers. When a child reports bullying incidents to teachers, then teachers can take measures to curtail the abuse and to help victimized children develop friendships with more socially skilled kids in the class.

Get the school involved.

Your child may beg you to keep silent about bullying experiences. That's how strong fear of retaliation is. But that is not the best approach in the long run.

If administrators do not seem to take bullying very seriously, they need to be made aware of the magnitude of bullying problems and the adjustment difficulties victimized children face. Use the information in this book.

- Ask that the school declare bullying off-limits. The incidence of bullying varies remarkably from school to school, and it positively flourishes in schools where teachers and administration look the other way or insist it does not exist. Bullying stops when adults announce they will not tolerate bullying behavior and when they step up playground supervision.

- Talk to your child's teachers to find out what the class atmosphere is like. In some classrooms children are excluded from peer interactions not because they lack skills but because they are outsiders to relatively fixed cliques of children. Other classrooms may have a more fluid social structure.

- Talk to other parents; where there's one victimized child there may be others. Get parents to join together and insist that your school develop an antibullying program.

- Schoolwide antibullying programs have the major virtue of reaching children who are not bullies but who play a major role in supporting bullying—bystanders. Children can be trained to recognize a potentially harmful situation and say, simply, "That's not fair." Antibullying programs that teach all children to take a stand for what is right can be very effective.

- Schools that have adopted antibullying programs have seen a dramatic drop in victimization. If your child's school does not have an antibullying policy, provide a model plan. Buy or borrow from the library a copy of *Bullying at School: What We Know and What We Can Do* by Dr. Dan Olweus (Blackwell Publishers, Cambridge, Mass.). Present it to the school principal.

- If all else fails, go to the school administration and demand that the bullies be transferred to other classes or other schools.

- If even that doesn't happen, see that your child is transferred to another school. The same child may thrive in a different school with a differing group of children having different values.

Allow your child increasing control over his own life.
Parents help create passive victims by overcontrolling their children's lives. In Dr. Ladd's direct observations of family life, he finds that such parents interrupt a child during an interaction, override a child's initiative, or abruptly negate or change a child's topic of conversation; at the same time, they might demand that the child change a facial expression or "sit up and pay attention" or stick only to certain topics of conversation.

Allow your child to make choices in small everyday matters as soon as possible. Just by holding up two articles of clothing to a toddler and asking, "Do you want to wear the red shirt or the blue one?" you are on your way to creating an autonomous human being.

At all ages, allow your child to control spare-time activities. Do not overschedule; being busy is not the same as having friends or being accepted by peers.

And don't treat your children as younger than they are. Infantilization makes children feel dependent, which fosters feelings of inadequacy. Stanford's Dr. Philip Zimbardo tells of a mother who, without thinking, cut up the meat on her son's dinner plate; the boy was in his teens.

Respect the boundaries between parent and child.

Some parents form an overly close and mutually emotionally intense relationship with a child, which breeds overdependence. Don't confide your innermost thoughts to your child. Your child is not your emotional pillow. In the end, it leaves your child unable to assert himself. No matter how unsatisfying your own adult relationships may be, overcloseness with your child will not solve your problem and cripples your child's ability to function in the universe of peers.

Be supportive, not overprotective.

There's only one way to overcome shyness and anxiety: by desensitization, that is, gradual exposure to feared situations. Encourage your child to take chances and try new things—while providing information, support, and praise for even tiny accomplishments. If you are afraid of your child getting sick or hurt, keep your fears under control and to yourself. Your expectation that things will work out well is important in helping your child subdue his own fears. Regardless of the outcome, taking a risk is, by itself, a kind of accomplishment.

Even children born fearful can be introduced to unfamiliar places and peers by age two. Provide support at this age by staying close by, serving as a safe haven for the child to return to as he or she sallies forth ever so tentatively into the unknown. Don't rush to your child's side at every whimper. Gently force your child to experience moderate degrees of anxiety and discomfort—while remaining visibly available in case the child feels overwhelmed. Parents can also speak soothing words of encouragement. This kind of support helps children tame their own internal arousal.

Providing support and teaching the basic rules of social interaction are crucial—otherwise, any exhortations to join others will be met with failure and disappointment. Social excursions become painfully self-defeating in the absence of skills and support.

All children need support. Children who are inhibited have, when young, a need for *extra* reassurance and nurturing before confronting new or challenging situations. As they get older, they need more explanation, more cognitive preparation, and more rehearsal to face new situations. Otherwise, they are at risk of developing lifelong anxiety and depression.

Make an agreement with your child about behavior in public.

In the presence of others, shy and withdrawn children are often clingy. Once your child is about three, you can make an agreement as to what behavior is acceptable around others. "You can talk to me in private, but it is not all right to whisper to me when we're with other people. You can whisper only when you have to tell me something really private, like you have to go to the bathroom. If there's something else you want—a glass of water, something to play with—you must ask for it. I will see that you get it, but you must ask for it first. Of course, if there's an emergency, it's okay to say, 'Excuse me, Mom, I need your help.' "

Prepare your child for new experiences.

You can help reduce anxiety by providing information about and introducing your child beforehand to new environments. Visiting a new school before classes start is often wise.

My older son, Dan, was never a shy child, but he occasionally had little spells of fearfulness facing the new. The approach of fourth grade was one such time. He wasn't even beginning a new school, just moving up to the next division, a higher floor, and new class-to-class movement in his accustomed school. Anxiety began building about two weeks before school began. No verbal reassurance that he'd manage just fine helped. So I called up the school about a week before classes and asked if we could take a look around. Danny calmed down immediately.

I was less successful on another front. Such was the school's arts program that the entire fourth grade had a weekly class in improvisation taught by a nationally known theater director. Dan was a natural, and the descriptive reports sent home periodically were positively hilarious and glowing. Toward the end of the year, the teacher called and announced, "I'm planning *A Midsummer Night's Dream* for the spring production next year. I think Danny would make a perfect Bottom. I've broached the idea and he refuses. But we have time. Do what you can to encourage him over the summer, and let's both work on it next year. I'll hold the part for him."

I never could figure out what it was, despite what I deemed great subtlety on my part. Danny was just not ready to take the big risk of performing on a stage, and I knew it would be counterproductive to pressure him; after all, he was functioning just fine. Still, a parent likes to see a child make use of talents. The next school year Danny's teacher kept in touch. We held out hope until the last minute, but the show had to be cast—and Danny wouldn't consider it, even though he didn't have to audition. I was disappointed. I tried not to let on.

When the play opened, I thought it would be a good idea if we all went to see it. I clearly remember sitting there next to Danny and being aware of him taking in Bottom. At the end of the performance, he turned to me and said, "I could have been a much better Bottom." "Then," I said, "do it." And so, in sixth grade, Danny made his debut as an Oompa Loompa in *Willie Wonka and the Chocolate Factory*. Many roles followed.

Set clear behavioral limits.

Many parents simply fail to let their children know what is acceptable behavior and what is not. Even a child who is born with an overly reactive nervous system needs to be told an emphatic no sometimes. No child is too sensitive to be shielded from all stress. Parents who can exert reasonable control while maintaining warmth set themselves up as a model of positive social behavior that children can carry outside the house.

Never threaten to withdraw love.

Children become overcompliant through inappropriate methods of punishment. It is the positive bond with responsive parents that creates the climate in which parental admonitions and prohibitions can be effective. Threatening to withdraw love is a hostile, rejecting act.

Children need parents to be available—even when they do something wrong. Threatening to abandon a child or to send a child away or to stop loving a child for misbehavior creates an intolerable amount of insecurity in the child. The child dwells in a state of physiological arousal. The threat hangs over a child's life and suffuses it with uncertainty. A child becomes preoccupied with searching out signs of rejection, and finds criticism and rejection even where they do not exist. This is believed to be a major source of the anxious vulnerability that both marks withdrawn children for victimization and keeps them from functioning comfortably among their peers.

Threats to withdraw love also make children feel worthless. They breed a sense of helplessness. And they undermine prosocial feelings such as empathy.

Don't overvalue compliance.

Yes, it's necessary, in general. But expecting total compliance with every adult demand discourages children from asserting their own needs. Leave room for your children to bargain and negotiate with you on some issues. Be open to discussion. And allow them occasionally to refuse requests—without having to get angry or upset—by stating their case in a logical and persuasive way. Ask questions that encourage your children to defend their point of view.

Teach general assertiveness.

The goal of child-rearing is to produce a child who can function on her own in the world. Value autonomy and assertiveness over total obedience and dependence.

Assertiveness is the first and best defense against abuse of any kind.

Children need to learn to stick up for themselves. Unless they come to feel that they have needs that deserve to be considered, they put up no defense in even mild disputes and confrontations.

Encourage your child to ask for things.

Submissive children do not speak up for themselves. They defer to the needs and interests of others. Ask your child to speak up for what he wants before granting even small requests. Children also learn that their own needs have a legitimate place in their world and the adult world. Of course, the child has to be positively rewarded for asking—otherwise, he quickly comes to feel that no one cares and that there's no point in changing behavior.

Solicit your child's opinion about things.

Encourage your child to think for herself. Ask your child's opinion of things. "What did you think about that new show?" Indicate that you have nothing you want to do more than listen. And allow your child to answer without interruption. Ask questions of your child in response to her statements. "What was the funniest thing about it?" Ask your child to explain her reasoning: "What makes you think that?"

Demonstrate that your child's input has value. Follow through with her suggestions and choices.

Solicit your child's input during family discussions, even during conflicts over bad behavior. Allow your child to speak up if she feels she's being unfairly punished. Don't be afraid to admit you've made a mistake; it doesn't weaken a child's view of a parent—it strengthens it.

Do not deliver messages to others for your child.

Encourage your child to make a request or deliver information directly to the person for whom it is intended.

Let your child have an impact on family functioning.

Help cultivate your child's ability to influence others. Ask your child for suggestions about family activities, games, plans, family vacations, even favorite meals. And follow the suggestions at least sometimes.

Be sure to give your child a say in making the family rules and in deciding on suitable punishments for rule infractions.

Engage your child in conversation often.

Anything is fair game. Ask open-ended questions, those that can't be answered in a simple yes or no or okay. Instead of "Would you like to go to the zoo?" ask, "I was thinking about going to the zoo or visiting the children's museum. Which would you rather do and what would you like to see there?" Give your child ample positive feedback (a pat on the back, a wink, a hug, a word of praise) on his performance as often as possible.

Some aspects of conversational ability you want to encourage include:

- paying attention and obviously listening to the person speaking. One problem withdrawn children have is that they are so focused on what they want to say they fail to listen to others, and so miss out on a lot of good information that could help them be in step with other children. Encourage your child to give some feedback signals to the speaker that indicate she's listening closely—make eye contact, nod appropriately.
- talking at a speed that others can understand. Nervousness sometimes makes shy children blurt things out quickly, to avoid being tongue-tied. The result is that their words fall into a jumble and are often not understood or are misheard by their peers.
- talking in a tone of voice suitable for the situation. Speaking up is important in most situations; so is not speaking too loud.
- waiting for natural pauses in the conversation before speaking

Develop conversational skills through play.

Help your child develop conversational ability through games; they make learning just plain fun. By giving children the experience of success, games can motivate children to apply their growing skills in real-life situations with peers.

Here's one idea. Think up others. Take turns with your child pretending to be a television interviewer, and interview each other about life experiences. "Ladies and gentlemen, here we are in Augusta, Georgia, talking to Tony Jones. We understand Mr. Jones is about to turn six years old next week. Mr. Jones, could you give our audience some highlights of your first six years. How, for example, did you get to have so many toys?" Keep it fun, but find questions that draw out your child. When you hit on a question that sparks conversation, go back and ask more questions around the topic. Then let your child interview you. You'll both be learning how to listen for important cues to build conversation.

Or use puppets for the purpose. "Benny is a TV interviewer who would like to talk to you. Maybe you can tell him about some fun things you like to do. And you can tell him how you got to be such a big boy." Let the puppet say and do silly things to draw out your child.

Encourage your child to give you conversational feedback.
One reason withdrawn children find difficulty in social situations is they create considerable confusion in others by failing to give appropriate signals. They don't smile at others; in fact, they generally don't give feedback of any kind. They do not nod when others are speaking to them or utter the little uh-hmms and yeahs that really function as social glue, a way of letting others know they are being heard and understood.

Provide clear and frequent feedback when your child talks to you. Explain to your child that you need her to give you some signals that you are being heard—a nod, a smile, an uh-hmm. Ask her to choose the signals she prefers. And smile when your child uses them—as a way of both modeling the delivery of feedback and acknowledging her good performance.

Develop conversational staying power.
Even during the preschool years, children must be able to connect conversationally. It underlies skill at playing together and therefore at making friends. It's what allows children to coordinate their play activity and generate fun together—and that, researchers find, is the main social task of kids between the ages of three and seven. Con-

necting conversationally involves making statements that are logically related to those of another child, responding in a related way, and continuing for a number of turns.

This skill can be cultivated. Make a game of it. Create a stack of cards listing on each a topic or category that relates positively to your child's everyday experience. "What I did in school today." "Who I like to talk to." "Fun places I'd like to visit." "My favorite day." And so on, as many as you can think of. Place the cards facedown. Each draw a card out of the deck. Take turns making a statement to the other that is related to the subject. See who can keep conversation going the longest. Whoever drops the conversational ball has to do something the other asks.

Sing out loud.

No kidding. Singing aloud to favorite records or tapes is a form of verbal expressiveness. Do it—and encourage your child to do it, too. There are many wonderful children's records; you'll have no trouble finding something your child likes. And it is fun. In the process, your child gains an appreciation of music. When your child goes to school, he can be encouraged to join a choral group. Singing in a choral group is an extremely positive social experience and develops many social skills, especially cooperation.

Promote physical assertiveness, too.

Assertiveness is as much a way of physically being as verbally doing. Bullies pick on kids who *cower*, who *shrink* from conflicts. Body language speaks loudly to those who would abuse. But you don't have to demand the impossible of your child. The goal is not to turn a ninety-nine pound weakling into a jock. Even kids who don't love sports may like karate, tae kwan do, and similar activities. Most martial arts actually train people *not* to fight and instill a philosophy of physical self-confidence.

Nip problems early.

The responses of victimized children become engraved through neural and hormonal as well as behavioral processes. Unless their style of responding is interrupted early, they biologically learn ways of turning inward and develop a lifelong tendency to depression.

Children who are victimized develop a distinctive thinking style and blame themselves. They are extremely sensitive about their own social performance, rate it particularly negatively, and the negative feelings about their social selves gradually contaminates their view of themselves in all domains until it is globally negative.

Pay attention to early shyness. Make extra efforts to encourage social behavior in your child by modeling effective behavior yourself, teaching social skills, and gently exposing your child to situations of gradually increasing social difficulty that she must master herself.

Curb TV.

Too much television programming reinforces the idea that aggression is the only way to deal with trouble. Every time TV displays violence, it also shows, and legitimizes, victimization.

In addition, easy access to TV allows children to wall themselves off in a ready-made social world rather than help construct the one they need. TV-viewing also reinforces the tendency of submissive children to be passive onlookers to events rather than active participants in them.

Spend time playing with your child.

Let your child direct the play sometimes. Encourage make-believe play: "How about if you be the grown-up and I'm the child. Tell me what to do." Let your child make up any scenario, and go along with it. Play just for the fun of it. Submissive children need to experience the fun of social interaction and to relax in social activities.

Help your child learn emotion-coping skills.

Children withdraw because they are extremely anxious in situations of confrontation or conflict. The negative arousal makes them physically uncomfortable. It ties their tongue and constrains their brain; it keeps them overfocused on themselves. As a result, they are in danger of blurting out exactly what they don't want to say—confirming their worst fears about themselves in social situations. Rather than master their anxiety, press their own case, or assert their own needs, they avoid social interactions entirely, while their cautiousness beckons the bullies.

Children need ways of calming their anxiety in social situations so that they can listen to other children and figure out appropriate responses that are more satisfying all around.

The control-signals poster used by Fast Track is designed to help children cope with any situation that gives rise to upsetting emotions. See pages 275–276.

Help your child understand the thoughts and feelings of others.

Most shy children are overly self-conscious. They anticipate evaluation, overly worry that other people won't like them or that they themselves will do dumb things in social situations. They overestimate the visibility of their inner discomfort, and mistakenly believe that everyone else knows how awkward they feel. It's the anxiety that impairs their performance.

"Every shy person is very egocentric," says Dr. Zimbardo. "All of their attention is on themselves, on their weaknesses, on their inadequacies. They're looking inward only."

Help your child pay attention to social cues. Among the most important are emotional expressions in others. Children even as young as toddlers need to be able to read each other well in order to play together and become friends. That underlies the ability to connect conversationally with another child and coordinate their play activity. Help your child learn to "tune in" to the thoughts and desires of playmates.

Read picture books together and ask your child to pick out characters who are sad, who are happy, who are upset, who are angry. Ask your child to tell you what the story characters are feeling and how he figured that out. "How does the little bear look? What kinds of things make people sad? What kinds of things can you say to someone who's sad?"

Draw attention to expressions of emotions in real life, too.

Develop social problem-solving strategies.

Teach your child that there are ways to handle difficult situations without automatically giving in, deferring to others, or crying. Outline the steps of problem-solving:

- defining the problem
- coming up with alternate responses
- figuring out possible effects
- deciding on an appropriate solution
- enacting solutions

Start with a child's own experiences. Build them into "What if" scenarios.

"What if the other kids cut in front of you again in the cafeteria line? How will you handle it?" Role-play a solution. "Let's say I cut in front of you, like this. What are you going to say?"

"What if you make a mistake while reading out loud again? What are you going to say if some other kids start laughing at you?" "How will you say it?" "Do you think the kids in back of you will hear it if you say it like that? Can you try it again, exactly the way you want to do in class?" "Okay, let's do this. Let's say you're reading this book and you stop when you get to a word you don't know. Let's say I'm Jake and I start laughing at you. Let me hear what you are going to say."

"What if someone takes your paintbrush? What will you do? Do you know how to ask for it back? What can you say? How will the other child react?"

"What if someone calls you a crybaby? What can you say?"

Teach children to turn negatives around. "What if you want to play a game with other children and they say 'No, because you don't know how'? How can you handle that?" "Could you say, 'Well, you're pretty good at it, maybe you can show me'?"

You can adapt a simple board game like Candyland to include "What if" scenarios among the moves. Designate numerous spaces on the path to Candyland as special "What if" spots. Put a colorful removable sticker on those spots. Then draw up a series of "What if" cards, writing on each a situation that represents a problem your child has faced or worries about: "What if the teacher calls on you and you don't know the answer?" "What if you ask someone to play with you and he says no?" Whoever lands on a "What if" spot has to pick a "What if" card and describe positive ways of handling the situation. Generating one positive response advances the player one space, two positive responses two paces, up to a maximum of three spaces.

It's not possible to overestimate the value of having your child come up with and consider behavioral options. You're not just solving a one-time problem; you're helping your child develop a more constructive way of thinking and coping in general. And responses that kids think up themselves, in their own words, are likely to be remembered and deployed when needed.

Pay special attention to group-entry skills.

One of the most valuable skills your child needs is the ability to join a game or activity already under way. Entering a group of peers at play is hard for all children, and especially difficult for submissive children. They tend to hover longingly at the fringes of activities their peers are enjoying. They have particular trouble in taking the first step in being with others.

Help your child come up with constructive strategies, reward your child for workable ideas, while providing plenty of reassurance that even popular children get rebuffed, too.

There are four components to this skill:

1. Listen to peers and tuning in to what they are doing.
2. Adopt their frame of reference.
3. Time an overture so that it is in step with peers' activities.
4. Suggest a role for yourself congruent with what they're doing. If they're playing house, don't just ask if you can play, ask if you can be the child, a neighbor, or some other role not already taken but in keeping with the thrust of the activity. "Can I play? I can be the other child."

Adapt learning methods proven to work in the Fast Track study. See pages 279–281.

Parents can also teach friendly social strategies by engaging in role-play. "I have an idea. You be one of the other girls jumping rope and I'll be you," a parent could start, and demonstrate some ways to make an overture to another child; then child and parent could switch parts.

Or a parent could furnish two hand puppets, one a shy girl named Kari and the other her classmate named Kate, and ask a young child to give instructions to Kari about making friends with Kate. The parent could lead the child by offering useful suggestions as needed: "What do you suppose Kari is thinking? What does Kari want to do? Does Kari know what to say? What if she said . . . ?" And so on through all the steps identified as important in initiating peer inter-action.

Rehearsal is crucial to success.

To enact new solutions to problems, your child has to role-play and rehearse them first.

The younger children are, the more spontaneous their responses are in social and other situations; they are apt to do what they have done before or seen others do. So for children to put new social strategies into practice, they have to see them modeled and practice them themselves until the new routines become second nature.

Role-play and rehearse, rehearse, rehearse until your child is comfortable with the new strategies. This is as true for toddlers as for teens. Of course, reward your child with smiles and pats on the back for role-played successes.

Counter self-defeating self-talk.

It's not just the behavior of withdrawn children that sets them up for social failure, it's their thinking style. Their own self-talk going on inside their heads is resolutely negative, and sounds something like this: "God, I'm going to make a mistake. I going to look like a total jerk. Nobody likes me." They need to alter thinking styles, reflected in the statements they make to themselves. These, in turn tend to rest on inaccurate, irrational beliefs about themselves

Children, for example, may think, "If I make a mistake I must be stupid, therefore it is hopeless for me to try to make friends." They don't simply blame themselves for everything that goes wrong—they attribute rejection to causes internal to them, that extend to their entire being, and that are unchangeable. Instead, they need to say to themselves, "If I make a mistake I may feel bad but it's not the end of the world; I can correct it and do better next time." When children know that problems reside in *situations* or have causes that can be fixed, they are motivated to try harder.

Some correct beliefs that can help children gain social competence include:

- For all children, some things come easy and some things are harder.
- No one is born knowing how to make friends; it rests on a set of skills that all children have to learn.
- Everyone makes mistakes.
- Some children get upset more easily than others, but there are ways to learn to calm down.
- If you make a mistake, it doesn't mean you're stupid, it means you have to learn what is the right way.
- If someone teases you or calls you names, it doesn't mean that you're bad or stupid or incompetent.

Positive self-talk is a strategy children can be taught to use at times of anxiety and upset. Ask your child, "What can you say to yourself to help you calm down and decide what to do?" Then discuss together some constructive things your child might say. "I'm not going to let them get me mad." "I can stop and think about all the things I did right today."

Share with your child stories of your own struggles as a child. It is highly shameful to be rebuffed by peers. Children need to know it's possible to survive and even handle such experiences. Tell your child things that happened to you and how you felt as a kid. "Did I ever tell you about the time a bunch of kids spread a nasty rumor about me? They told all my friends at school that I talked about everyone behind their back. For days, no one would talk to me, and I felt so hurt and lonely."

In addition, every child needs to hear made-up stories in which she stars. Making your child the protagonist in a difficult social situation shows her a way out.

Cultivate basic social skills.
Victimized children often don't even know any other way to be around peers—they don't know what to do to be friendly. "Lots of things that parents used to take time to teach are not being learned any longer," observes Dr. Zimbardo. Make a point of teaching your child the basic rules of social interaction.

Model all of these behaviors yourself. And encourage your child to:

- approach peers in a friendly way and make an introduction ("Hi. My name is Kyle. Do you want to play?")
- look others in the eye
- smile ("In America, once you smile and make eye contact," says Dr. Zimbardo, "you create a benign social environment around you, in which people make contact back. If you frown, you create a negative force around you.")
- start a conversation
- ask open-ended questions ("How do you do that?" "Why . . . ?")
- make positive play suggestions ("I have a ball we can catch.")
- speak clearly
- take turns ("You can bounce the ball, then I can get to bounce it.")
- give and accept compliments ("That was such a cool way you answered that question.") Compliments are a great social glue, and they are the verbal expression of what we are already thinking. That's why it's important to speak them.

Shy children do not get compliments because they don't give them. And if you give compliments, you must acknowledge them, otherwise the giver gets confused, increasing the likelihood of another failed social interaction. Dr. Zimbardo advises that "Thank you" is the bare essential. The next step is to accept the compliment and expand it. "Thank you. Coming from you, that's a real compliment." At a more advanced stage, a compliment can be used as a wedge to open an interaction. "I always wondered how you seem to have all the answers."

Act as a social engineer . . .

Increase the social opportunities of all kids, but especially victimized ones. They need to experience more and more positive social interaction. It has benefits for all aspects of their lives.

Withdrawn children avoid interaction because they anticipate negative consequences; hence they need experiences of social success. Help your child take the first step in as safe a situation as possible. Arrange interactions that have a high probability of success. Ask your child to tell you about classmates she likes—or ask the teacher for the name of friendly children in the class that your child seems to like. Invite them over to play, so that your child has the security of familiar surroundings, but stack the odds for success. Invite one child over at a time, starting with a ninety-minute play date—long enough for two children to warm up to each other but not so long that interest wanes or that they run out of fun things to do together. Eventually encourage your child to invite a friend for a sleepover.

Let the children decide how they want to spend their time together, but provide play equipment and opportunities for constructive play. Bullying and victimization occur when children have little else to do.

Your child has probably spent much time playing by himself with his own toys. He may need help figuring out ways his cherished possessions can be shared and contribute to fun in playing with other kids. Before another child comes over, ask your child to think about ways two children can have fun playing together with the same toys. "Okay, pretend I'm Roger and I see that truck and I want to spend some time riding it. What are some ways we can both get to play with it?" "What can you do when Roger wants to ride the truck? Can you be a traffic cop?"

. . . but also encourage playground playing.

Playing one-on-one helps children develop close relationships. But children also have to successfully negotiate the general world of peers.

Playing in playgrounds exposes children to a diverse array of possible playmates. Moreover, the activity is likely to be created and directed by children. Playground playing encourages children to develop strategies for playing with different types of children and to solve their own disputes.

Although playground playing makes greater demands on social skills, it also provides greater rewards. Children generally prefer playing outdoors, and outdoor sites are especially conducive to imaginative play.

Gradually accustom your child to playground playing. Start by going early in the day, when the commotion is minimal. Work up to going when the place is in full swing.

Expect change to take time.
Even if victimized children change the way they are with peers, they will not become more popular overnight. It takes time to change their negative reputation among peers. Promote one-on-one play dates as a way of helping other kids change their perceptions of your child. And, while recognizing the difficulty of the task, encourage your child to keep deploying newly acquired social skills even in the face of continuing teasing. Eventually, your child *will* become better liked.